Refusing to Accept the Unacceptable

The Trials, Tribulations and Triumphs of Workplace Bullying and Harassment

Denise Koster, B.A.A., P.H.Ec., WVTS, CTM

Koster Consulting & Associates

Ospreay Press

Denise Koster: Refusing to Accept the Unacceptable
ISBN 978-1-7770795-0-5
Ospreay Press

Denise Koster
Koster Consulting and Associates
www.kosterconsultingassociates.com

Editor: Heather Gardiner
Cover design by Obee Design Studio
Artist: Alfred G. Villeneuve
Page layout and print production by Beth Crane, WeMakeBooks.ca

Disclaimer: *The content of this book is advisory in nature and intended to help indviduals establish healthy and productive personal and professional environments. All legal matters and legislation should be referred to the appropriate jurisdiction or legal counsel. Any usage of this book and/or its material is the responsibility of the reader, employer and/or their duty counsel.*

Printed and bound in Canada

Dedications

To my dad

Who taught me that nothing is impossible, especially if you are a girl.

To my mom

A fierce woman who fought cancer and survived the loss of my father. She continued to dance and laugh every day despite the rain.

To Kameron

My amazing, funny and big-hearted boy who for years endured my crazy schedule, late hours and absence from parent's night in order to try to make the world a better place.

To Ely

Who through her love, caring and support allowed me to do what I needed to do while securing my son, home and pets. I am forever grateful for her.

To Pierre

Who saw my passion, encouraged me to start my company and made me believe that I had something unique to offer the world.

To Carolyn

Who taught me what it means to be a strong and game-changing woman. Who, despite being faced with male dominance and community challenges, kicked butt and took names later.

To Patricia

Who gave me the courage to pursue my dream of writing this book and believed in me even when I didn't believe in myself.

To Heather

Who, through an abundance of patience, endured months of edits, additions and deletions while demonstrating kindness, humour and gentle persuasion to help make my dream a reality.

Contents

How It All Began

I also dedicate this book to Norma, who didn't live long enough to know that she made one of the biggest impacts on my professional life.

In the mid-1980s, I was working in the seniors' department of a small inner-city community centre. Fresh out of school with limited experience outside my middle-class suburban world, I was unfamiliar with the classism, racism, sexism and inequalities that existed in the world.

When I began my career working with low-income seniors, it never dawned on me that the following experience would shape my life. Going into people's homes and assessing them for health and social services, I was exposed to countless individuals who were not only victims of society, but often further victimized by others. I was faced with individuals reaching out to me for assistance in dealing with the abuse they were facing not only by strangers but by people in positions of trust: family members, friends and neighbours. I was shocked and horrified by their stories. One woman in her 70s was paying her son $500 a month to see her grandchildren. Another woman who was 89 years old was raped by her son-in-law. A malnourished 75-year-old man's apartment had been taken over by a group of drug dealers and prostitutes.

However, nobody touched me as deeply as Norma, a woman in her 70s living in poverty. Homebound with no telephone, her only link to the outside world was her abusive husband of more than 50 years. Norma was a meek and frightened woman when I met her to arrange a shopping service. The moment I walked into her apartment, I sensed her fear and uneasiness. We chatted briefly about the shopping service. Doing my due diligence, I explained to her how I assisted people with a variety of problems; from filling out government documents, to arranging a volunteer visitor, to providing support and intervention. I further explained how I supported and advocated for older adults who were being mistreated physically, sexually, psychologically and financially. Norma quietly listened to my every word, never letting her guard down or verbally making any disclosure of abuse. However, her eyes told me more than her words ever could. I left Norma's apartment with a heavy heart, not expecting to have any further interactions with her.

Back at my office, I made the necessary arrangements for Norma to have a weekly volunteer pick up her shopping list, shop and return with her groceries. Months went by and I had no further interaction with Norma. Although she only had a grade four education, Norma was a very resourceful woman.

One day, the volunteer shopper gave me a note that Norma secretly passed to her when her groceries were delivered. The note simply said, "Help me." Upon receiving the note, I raced through the community to Norma's apartment. With the door unlocked and slightly ajar, I knocked and quietly entered her one-bedroom apartment. Norma was on the couch in the living room, which I soon discovered to be the place where she slept and spent the majority of her time. Upon seeing me, Norma quickly put her finger to her lips signalling me to keep quiet. With her other hand, she pointed to the bedroom wall. I determined that her husband was behind the wall listening to our every word. Once I indicated to her that I understood her need for me to remain silent, Norma pushed aside her blouse to reveal grip marks and bruises on her upper arms. Gesturing to Norma, I asked if she wanted me to call the police or have a doctor or nurse visit her. She shook her head, disagreeing with both options.

Shortly after this second visit, I began receiving weekly notes from Norma. It got to the point where I began to check on her on a daily basis. Ninety percent of the time I would visit her, she had either been sexually assaulted or beaten by her husband within the last 24 hours. I was so horrified by what I was witnessing that several times after seeing Norma I went to the police station to get assistance, but was told I could not file a report on behalf of someone else and that Norma would have to come forward on her own. When I spoke to Norma about getting out of the situation, calling the police or going to a safehouse like a shelter, she would simply tell me, "I was raped and beaten as a young child. I was raped and beaten as a young woman. I am raped and beaten as an old lady. This is my life."

Over the four years I worked with Norma, she always seemed relieved and grateful that I cared enough to visit her and showed concern for her well-being. Towards the end of the third year, Norma was diagnosed with terminal cancer. Despite her diagnosis, Norma was still subject to daily beatings and neglect. One day, I was informed by a local hospital that Norma had been admitted with a broken arm from an apparent fall. I went to see Norma at the hospital and she told me that her husband had pushed her. Out of all the times I had visited Norma, this was the first time we were able to speak freely without her husband standing in the next room. Norma was getting tired and I could see through the same eyes that silently spoke to me three years prior that she was giving up on life. Upon being discharged from the hospital, Norma returned to her apartment.

A month later, I received another call from the same hospital informing me that Norma had been admitted following another alleged fall. Upon my arrival, Norma told me that her husband broke her arm by beating her with her walker. Due to the cancer, her health was declining, but this time our visit was different. Norma's eyes, rather than looking defeated, had a spark in them I had never witnessed before. In a strong voice, Norma told me that she had finally had enough of being ill-treated and wanted her husband to be made accountable for years of abuse and torment. In that moment,

Norma decided to leave her husband and move to a long-term care facility. Although it took more than 70 years, Norma finally came to the conclusion that she deserved to live her final days in peace.

Norma asked me to call the police and stay with her while she reported her concerns. A male officer and a female officer whom I had requested came to the hospital and Norma, I believe for the first time, openly described years of physical abuse, sexual abuse and neglect. Norma was articulate, strong and determined to have her story heard.

Later that evening, Norma's husband was arrested and charged with assault. Upon being released from police custody, Norma's husband immediately went to the hospital, apologized to Norma and begged her to come home to him. He convinced Norma that things would be different this time and change for the better. Norma called me from the hospital and told me about her change of heart.

I went to see Norma the next day and although it wasn't necessarily the most professional thing to do, I practically pleaded with Norma not to go home. Once again, her eyes reflected her defeated heart. Norma had made a decision and I had to respect it. I asked Norma if she would grant me permission to visit her husband before her discharge so that I could arrange resources and services prior to her going home. I wanted to ensure that her time at home was as comfortable and safe as possible. She agreed to let me contact her husband.

That was the last time I saw Norma.

Later that day, I met with Norma's husband at their apartment for the first and last time. For the safety of all of those involved, I brought my boss with me for the visit. From his perspective, Norma's husband explained that he and Norma had a stormy relationship fuelled by alcohol and constant fighting over money and lack of a stable living situation. He further explained that he took on the "male role" in the relationship, which primarily focused on obtaining money and finding a place for them to sleep. When they did have a place to live over the years, Norma took on the "female role" of cooking, cleaning and doing the laundry. As Norma's health began to decline due to a number of factors, she quit drinking and was eventually unable to fulfil her designated duties. Norma's husband resentfully took on those tasks, resulting in an increase in his alcohol consumption and anger. Although he admitted to verbally abusing Norma, he only admitted to becoming physically abusive the last time Norma was sent to the hospital and subsequently called the police. Following his verbal account of the events, Norma's husband was completely compliant and agreed to all of my recommendations, including getting a hospital bed and landline telephone, allowing nursing and medical professionals to visit Norma on a weekly basis, and having an environmental home assessment conducted by an occupational therapist.

Later that day, Norma was discharged from the hospital and went home. The next day, I was contacted by the police to identify her body. Norma's husband had beaten her to death when she returned home from the hospital.

The information I received regarding her death was that when Norma arrived home that day, her husband was drunk and angry. Shortly thereafter, a registered health professional arrived at the apartment to complete an assessment of Norma's living environment. Upon entering the apartment, it was obvious that there had been a physical altercation in the unit. Food was thrown from the open-concept kitchen into the living room, furniture was in disarray and Norma was crying. As opposed to doing their due diligence, addressing the immediate situation and ensuring Norma's safety, the health professional left the apartment. The individual did not alert the police, community housing or me about the situation, but rather arrived the following day with a supervisor as Norma's body was being removed from the apartment in a body bag. It should be noted that I had given the health professional full disclosure of Norma's situation and police involvement prior to the scheduled visit. To add insult to injury, Norma's husband's initial charge of second-degree murder was later downgraded to aggravated assault.

In the end, Norma had died at the hands of her abuser. To give Norma some dignity in death that she did not get in life, I decided to dedicate my career to ensuring people knew Norma's story with the desired outcome of raising awareness to protect older vulnerable adults from being abused.

From there, my career evolved from a frontline unionized worker and executive member, to a manager and director, to an independent consultant. Over the past 30 years, I have met hundreds of young, middle-aged and older adults who have experienced bullying or abuse first-hand either at home or in the workplace.

This book was inspired by all of the people I have met through my work who have openly and honestly shared their stories with me. In many cases, I only heard one side of the story, with the exception of the times I was involved in investigating a complaint or conducting a mediation, but I know that what I heard was the individual's "truth." Many of these individuals were survivors and fought for their right to live and work in a dignified manner. Others, like Norma, were not as fortunate.

It is my hope that this book sheds light on the topic of bullying that is generally associated with children but is potentially even more dangerous when it makes its way into the adult world and workplace. From my perspective, civility and kindness should not be based on policies and procedures, codes of conducts or professional regulations; there should be a moral and ethical compass that is passed on through generations. Individuals need to take responsibility for their actions and words. We can all attribute an error in judgment on the existence of a bad childhood, addiction problem or not thinking before acting, but ultimately the choice of right or wrong is determined by one's self.

We need to stop the cycle of violence before it begins. We need to stop bullying in the playground so those children do not grow up and end up in our homes or workplaces, continuing to destroy the lives around them.

I hope now that you are resting in peace Norma, you so deserve it.

The world is a dangerous place, not because of those who do evil,
but because of those who look on and do nothing.
~ Albert Einstein ~

Purpose

If you have no capacity for violence then you are a healthy productive citizen: a sheep. If you have a capacity for violence and no empathy for your fellow citizens, then you have defined an aggressive sociopath—a wolf. But what if you have a capacity for violence, and a deep love for your fellow citizens? Then you are a sheepdog, a warrior, someone who is walking the hero's path. Someone who can walk into the heart of darkness, into the universal human phobia, and walk out unscathed.

~ Lt.-Col. Dave Grossman ~

For years I have been contemplating writing a book about my work experiences that involved abuse, discrimination, harassment, bullying and incivility. I started the process a number of times over the years only to become distracted or consumed with everyday life of being a single mother and business owner. Somehow now the time felt right, a time that crept up on me—the 25th anniversary of my company. It has also come at a time when my son is 23 years old and nervously trying to find himself and determine where he wants his education to lead him. Part of him is desperately trying to grow up and the other part is still a little boy with big dreams.

I write this book with two frames of mind: one being overjoyed about the possibility of being a published author and the other saddened by the fact that this book is a product of the pain and heartache that others have suffered from living or working in a toxic environment.

I have always believed in the greater good of humanity and that is what has kept me committed to the work I have embarked on despite the difficulty that comes with it. I believe most people come to work with the intent of goodwill, to do a good job, be acknowledged for a job well done and ultimately be able to make an adequate living to support their family and chosen lifestyle. Unfortunately, some of the people I have met through the course of my life have not been fortunate enough to fulfil those expectations; not because of a lack of commitment or laziness but because others have made a conscious attempt to hamper their happiness.

My teachers over the years, in formal and informal settings, have helped me gain insight into behaviours and challenge my own beliefs. However, the clients I have served have taught me more than any book. Real life experiences and the strength to stand up and fight for their right to live and work in a healthy environment has lit a fire inside of me to work towards civility and harmony.

The scenarios presented in this book are true stories, however, the names of individuals and some general details have been changed to protect their identities. I must also state that the stories presented may be difficult to read. My intent is not to shock or sensationalize the issue of workplace violence or harassment, but rather compel people to act before it is too late. Paraphrasing Gavin de Becker, author of *The Gift of Fear*, listen to the voice when it is still a whisper.

Primarily, it is my hope that the information in this book will be meaningful, relatable and helpful to those who are struggling in their professional or personal lives. Whether they are presently being bullied or know someone who is being bullied, my goal is that this book helps them understand the issue in all its complexity in order to make it stop.

We can all point fingers and blame others for causing us misfortune, however, I challenge people in my work and through my teachings to not only be aware of others, but to use the information presented as an opportunity to reflect on their own behaviour.

Secondly, this book is intended to be a valuable resource for workplace leaders and external consultants to understand the complexity and concepts related to workplace violence, harassment and bullying. It highlights important aspects to be considered when taking and assessing complaints, facilitating a conflict resolution process and dealing with the intricacies of conducting a thorough and comprehensive workplace investigation. In addition, best practices regarding the principles of natural justice, preliminary case examinations, interview preparation and techniques, notetaking and report writing will follow a step-by-step process to ensure accountability and avoid confirmation bias when conducting investigations. Supplemental draft templates, worksheets and checklists will assist in maintaining consistent and unbiased procedures.

Lastly, the questions for consideration will allow individuals and groups to explore and debate their own thoughts and ideas pertaining to a number of cases and practices discussed in the book.

Remember, be a sheepdog.

#MyTruth

At the time of writing this book, the #MeToo movement had been gaining momentum for well over a year. As with all other inappropriate actions and behaviours, sexual harassment in the workplace is not a new phenomenon. It appears that nearly every woman and a significant percentage of men have been subjected to sexual harassment or assault.

We all have a story, a truth. Although it may be disputed or perceived differently by others, we own it. In the book *Daring Greatly: How the Courage to Be Vulnerable Transforms the Way We Live, Love, Parent, and Lead* by Brené Brown, vulnerability is defined as "uncertainty, risk and emotional exposure."

For me, being vulnerable is not easy. Looking back on my life, I was very fortunate to be raised in a middle-class home with two loving parents. I had all of the childhood joys and some misfortunate experiences, however, I have no regrets. As with meeting Norma and how my world was shaped by that encounter, I believe our individual history shapes us into who we are.

My first memory of inappropriate sexual behaviour occurred when I was 12 years old. My second paying job (after first having a paper route) was as a babysitter to the younger children in the neighbourhood. I took great pride in the role and the fact that the children liked me and the parents trusted me. Back in the 1970s, there was no such thing as a babysitting course, but I was a trusty Girl Guide so I guess that served a purpose and showed my maturity. My parents were also well-respected in the community.

My babysitting experiences were pretty routine with the exception of one encounter. I regularly babysat for a family down the street whose father was a business executive and whose mother stayed at home with the three children. In those days, working mothers were rare. I was hired to babysit the children one Friday night when the mother was away visiting her family and the father was attending a business dinner. The father returned home around 11 p.m. As I gathered up my things to leave, he stood in front of the front door and in a slurred voice asked me to stay and have a drink with him. I was 12 years old! It was obvious that he was drunk and not going to take no for an answer. I knew that I had to quickly get out of the situation as he was becoming more aggressive and physical with me. I needed to get him away from the door so I told him I would have a drink with him. As he relaxed and moved away from the door to walk into the kitchen, I bolted towards the door, opened it and ran all the way home. When I got home, I realized that I did not have my shoes on. I looked back and saw the father standing on the sidewalk shirtless. I didn't tell my parents what happened until I was 20 years old. Needless to say, I did not babysit for that family ever again.

Starting in my high school years, I had the same job after school until my third year of university. From nearly the beginning, I experienced some uncomfortable situations with one of my male colleagues; from inappropriate sexual comments to a few physical encounters when he would walk past me and brush his body against mine. I had to be hyperaware of my surroundings when he was around. Thankfully he was only in my workspace a few times a week for short periods of time. It got to the point where if I knew he was coming in or I would see him enter the building, I would surround myself with other colleagues or lock myself in the bathroom until he was gone.

When confronted by one of my female bosses about why I was spending so much time out of my work area or in the bathroom, I finally told her what was happening. I was very uncomfortable with the conversation, but she believed me because she had a similar situation with the same man and knew about other women working there over the years who also had the same experience. I was surprised and suggested that we notify the boss about what was happening. She laughed at me, saying I was naive and should quickly learn that those who have the power can do whatever they please, while others with the least power must learn to be quiet. This response shocked me as I saw this woman as a strong, competent female role model who never backed down from anything or anyone. I knew that what she said was probably true, but also terribly unfair. I wondered why things were that complicated; I was taught by my parents to do the right thing. As she was my boss, I remained quiet for the rest of my time at that workplace, however, I still avoided any situations that would compromise my physical or emotional safety.

As a university student, I enjoyed the comradery of my peers and group work always created an interesting dynamic. In one of my classes in fourth year, students were required to pair up for an assignment and a male classmate whom I didn't know asked me to partner with him. I agreed and we worked long hours to complete the task, communicating both in person and on the telephone. He was an extremely quiet man and our conversations never became personal or went beyond the scope of our schoolwork. Once our assignment was completed, there was no need to have any further interaction with each other.

Within a few weeks, he began to randomly show up outside my classroom, my workplace and my bus or subway stop. Every time he would appear, he would simply say hello and nothing else. Each time I tried to engage him in a conversation about what he wanted and why he seemed to be everywhere I was, but he wouldn't answer me. On many occasions, he would bring me gifts such as flowers or chocolates. In the beginning it felt harmless, however, as his appearances became more frequent, the more uncomfortable I felt. Then he started wearing army fatigues. My family and friends became increasingly concerned about the situation. Much to my dismay, my mother called his mother to ask her son to stop contacting me. This conversation only seemed to intensify the situation; he was now everywhere I looked.

In the mid-1980s, there were no cellphones, Facebook or other media platforms that allowed you to find someone with the simple click of a button. So how did he know where I was other than by following me? A turning point in the situation came when he approached me one day and handed me a religious book accompanied by a handwritten card telling me that he wanted to "take me away." At that point I had no choice but to call the police.

The stalking continued even after the police went to his home to inform him that if he did not leave me alone, he would be served with a restraining order. Although the physical contact eventually stopped, in my mind he was still around every corner. For several years I was looking over my shoulder and still, more than 30 years later, I sometimes think about what could have happened if the police intervention failed.

Later, as a frontline worker, I had a few negative encounters with my colleagues. Some were simple disagreements or personality clashes, but others were more troublesome. As a union steward, I was proud to take on that role, however, also greatly disturbed that in some cases I had to represent individuals who, in my opinion, did not deserve representation. Coming into work high on drugs or drinking on the job was not something I felt I could support, regardless of my union title and responsibility. I had a difficult time in the role as I was vocal about my concerns on both a local and national level, quickly making some enemies among the frontline ranks.

Moving to a manager position from the frontlines is always an adjustment. Working alongside others for years and suddenly becoming their boss is not always an easy transition. Early in my career, I thought I could be both a friend and a boss, however, I realized that to be an effective leader, you have to decide to be one or the other. I made the professional choice, but not without some regret of losing people with whom I had developed a personal friendship. I truly enjoyed my job and all of the responsibility that came with it. I had the best executive director I could have ever asked for; she was supportive, brilliant and my greatest teacher. I also had some personal challenges that I had not experienced in the workplace before. In some situations, my competency and credentials were disrespected in addition to the authority that came with my position. Being younger than the majority of my direct reports certainly did not help. I had a number of situations for nearly a decade that required intervention from other senior leaders. Some work relationships remained intact and others were forever strained. Throughout those years, I doubted my own skill level and began to question my abilities. Whenever I felt like giving up, my boss supported and guided me to the realization that I was a good manager. It was only years later when I got involved in workplace bullying that I realized in some cases I had been a target.

During the time I was a manager, I also had a life-changing experience. Interestingly, although I have always been known as a storyteller, I never really told this story before. I believe that stories allow individuals to see the vulnerabilities of others and give them the feeling that they are not alone.

This part of my truth happened when I was 28 years old. I was married and living in the outskirts of Toronto. On Sunday, April 5, 1992, I went to a walk-in clinic due to a recurring neck problem resulting in intense pain. I arrived at the clinic and was seen by one of the doctors. After explaining to him the history of my neck problem (stemming from an accident in the 1970s), he conducted a routine examination that included checking my temperature and blood pressure. Without providing any graphic details, following this I was sexually assaulted by the doctor. When I came out of the doctor's office, my husband greeted me and immediately knew that something was wrong. I broke down and told him what happened. We later called the police. A few days later, the doctor was arrested and charged with sexual assault.

From that day forward, my life would never be the same. I was thrown into a legal system that I had only previously experienced vicariously through my elderly clients. It was a system and process that no one took the time to explain to me. I had very little support other than the detective assigned to the case and I was given bad advice. Since it was an assault that occurred in a doctor's office, I was asked to give my permission to release my medical records. At the time I thought this meant only the records pertaining to the day in question, but what I actually signed granted access, not only to the Crown attorney but also to the defence, to all of my medical records from the day I was born. I didn't realize the impact of this until nearly two and a half years later when I was testifying in court before a judge-only trial.

I spent hours on the witness stand being questioned about extremely private health and medical information pertaining to every trip to the doctor from the time I was a teenager until the day of the assault. I never had more than 20 minutes of preparation with the Crown attorney. I was simply told to answer the questions that were asked. It was a very confusing situation being asked about things that had no apparent relevance to the case. Being brought up as an assertive woman, I felt myself being attacked on all levels and became extremely defensive. When I look back to that time on the stand, I surely appeared to be an angry, confused woman. Before answering a question, I asked for the specific date of the doctor's appointment and after I answered the question I would ask, "What has that got to do with the assault?" I kept trying to get the defence lawyer to get back to the issue. The detective and Crown attorney told me during breaks to "calm down" and "stop being argumentative."

It felt like I was asked 1,000 questions with only 10 percent pertaining to the day of the assault. The legal system appeared to me to be all mixed up; I was the victim but was being treated like the criminal. The Crown attorney told me that I did not need a lawyer, however, the perpetrator doctor had one of the largest and most powerful law firms representing him. One tactic used by the defence was to try to subpoena my husband to testify against me. The defence also tried to contact my husband's ex-wife to get "dirt" on me. As a result of the traumatic situation and pending court case, my husband and I put our house up for sale. I was later told that allegedly some people on the defence team posed as buyers, came into my home and were given "a tour," further violating not only me, but my husband too.

To this day, I believe the legal process is sometimes worse than the actual crime. It was terrible. I cried every day during and after the trial. Unsurprisingly, the doctor was found not guilty and I was presented as a hysterical woman who made up a story.

One positive thing that came out of my case was that when the police arrested the doctor, his name and clinic were printed in the newspaper. As a result, two other victims came forward who were teenage girls. Their cases were heard after mine. To my knowledge, a not-guilty verdict was determined in both cases. Years later, I was approached by the other victims to join them in a civil class action lawsuit against the doctor. I declined involvement due to the stress of the criminal proceeding in addition to potentially receiving what I thought would be "dirty money." In retrospect, I wish I had the strength at the time to join the other victims in their quest for justice.

Following the trial, and due to the perpetrator's profession, in 1995 I filed a complaint with the regulatory body. I submitted my version of events. I was visited on two occasions by a representative from The College of Physicians and Surgeons of Ontario who reviewed my case, however, I was not contacted by the college to attend the hearing.

After the internal proceedings were complete, I was given an outcome letter that stated a number of factors apparently relevant to the findings:

- Patient was in a state of excruciating pain and acute anxiety during her appointment with the doctor *(I certainly was, which was the reason I opted to go to a walk-in clinic on a Sunday rather than waiting until Monday to see my family doctor).*

- Patient could not recall if she told the receptionist that she hurt her neck the previous day. However, the receptionist was called as a witness and testified that she did tell her this and that she charted it *(I am not sure how this is relevant to the sexual assault).*
- Patient testified that she was "absolutely sure" that she had arrived at the clinic at 1:30 p.m. and left at 1:50 p.m. as she had checked her watch. She was "subsequently proven wrong" by the receptionist who had charted that she had arrived at 2:07 p.m. *(I am not sure how this is relevant to the sexual assault).*
- Each version of the alleged incident the patient told was inconsistent with the others *(such as if my temperature was taken before or after my blood pressure).*

It was detailed in the document that a Crown Expert Physician stated that after reviewing my medical history, he was of the opinion that this history made it more likely that I was recalling or recounting the incident "incorrectly or inaccurately". In addition, he believed that the following existing conditions increased the likelihood of my alleged "misunderstanding and misperception":

- The patient and doctor did not know each other
- It was a walk-in setting
- The patient was in blinding and excruciating pain and in a state of anxiety
- The patient did not understand why the doctor was "conducting the examination" *(which was the actual sexual assault)*

The expert also stated that "it is appropriate in some instances for a physician to 'assist' a patient in removing articles of clothing and to turn his back rather than leaving the room to provide privacy."

The conclusion of the report dated November 20, 1995 stated: "What is obvious from the events which have followed Ms. Koster's visit to the Urgent Care on April 5, 1992 is that a fundamental misunderstanding arose between Dr. X and Ms. Koster. Dr. X feels responsible, at least in part, for this misunderstanding. In hindsight, he feels he did not communicate as clearly as he might have with the patient, and is now more careful to communicate clearly with patients. Dr. X wishes Ms. Koster to know that he sincerely regrets the misunderstanding that occurred between them and any stress or anxiety that it has caused to her. Since these events, Dr. X has modified his practice in several ways. Whenever he does an examination of a patient he now has a third person present. Further, patients are provided with a gown and privacy to undress and to redress whenever any part of their clothing has to be removed for an examination. Dr. X does not anymore assist patients with removing any piece of clothing."

After "considering the complaint", the committee rendered its decision after a review of all information gathered during the investigation: "Direction: No action will be taken with respect to this matter except as follows: Dr. X is hereby cautioned as to the need to establish and maintain sensitive and clear communication with patients at all times, to provide adequate privacy and covering for his patients, to provide explanation for examinations, to have female patients undress themselves, or where they are unable to, to have a female assistant help them, or, where that is impracticable, to obtain consent before assisting them to undress, and obtain consent for all examinations."

At the time of writing this book, the offender still operates a family practice. I will leave it to the reader to contemplate the meaning behind the respondent's response and changes in practice methods.

Fast-forward to when I became a consultant. I have always been very clear about my professional boundaries, careful not to mix my business with my personal life. With one particular client, I was placed in a vulnerable situation. I had an ongoing work relationship with a man who worked for an organization. I thought there was a great deal of mutual respect between us. After working with this individual for a few years, he made a sexual advance towards me. I feared that if I did not give in to the advance, I may lose the contract. After a short time of avoiding him, I let my moral and ethical compass guide me and refused his advance. Following my refusal, our casual and friendly professional work relationship dramatically changed to something that was stressed and filled with tension. Unfortunately, my fear became a reality as I was never requested to work for that organization again. A new female consultant was hired and I can only hope she was not put in a similar situation.

In 2018, 26 years after my sexual assault, in Lansing, Michigan, Judge Rosemarie Aquilina sentenced sexual predator and ex-USA Gymnastics doctor Larry Nassar to 40 to 175 years in prison for preying on young female athletes. She gave a voice to the more than 150 girls and women who claimed Mr. Nassar sexually abused them.

During Mr. Nassar's sentencing, Judge Aquilina stated: "[A]s much as it was my honour and privilege to hear the sister survivors, it is my honour and privilege to sentence you, because sir you do not deserve to walk outside of a prison ever again. You have done nothing to control those urges and anywhere you walk, destruction will occur to those most vulnerable. … I'm giving you 175 years, which is 2,100 months. I just signed your death warrant."

In such times of darkness of the #MeToo movement, Judge Aquilina has restored my faith in what can happen when the criminal justice system stands up and shouts, "Time is up!"

It wasn't built to be a viral campaign or a hashtag that is here today and forgotten tomorrow. It was a catchphrase to be used from survivor to survivor to let folks know that they were not alone and that a movement for radical healing was happening and possible.

~ Tarana Burke ~

Workplace Violence: The Ultimate Cost

Workplace violence is not a new phenomenon. In recent times, we have been hearing more news reports of current or former employees entering the workplace and taking the lives of others, and in the majority of cases, their own lives too. Employers are faced with the reality that anyone could potentially be violent, which includes not only customers, clients and the general public, but also their own employees. Even through the lens of a threat assessment, we cannot predict future violence, but we are best able to prevent it by listening and recognizing the pre-incident signs that are often ignored or rationalized. Employers must strike a balance between creating a safe workplace and making their clientele feel comfortable in a welcoming environment.

When discussing safety measures with employers along with the critical need to conduct a formal threat assessment when an internal or external threat is received, I am often faced with resistance because the employer does not believe that violence is likely, does not want to be viewed as "paranoid," or does not want to send a message to employees or the community that a person is somehow unsavoury or dangerous. The truth is people can be dangerous and violence can occur when one is faced with a situation or person they perceive as a threat.

In group settings, I often ask participants if they believe they have the ability to physically harm another individual. Most people shake their head in disagreement with a shocked look on their face and only a few reluctantly raise their hands. I raise my hand without hesitation. I explain to the group that I am a mother, and although it is not at all in my nature, if I was in a situation where someone was attempting or threatening to harm my child, I would in all likelihood become physically aggressive towards that individual. After exposing my mindset in this example, the majority of participants who did not raise their hands initially suddenly come to realize that they too, under certain circumstances, could become violent.

When my clients deny the possibility of violence or choose to take the mindset classified as willful blindness or deliberate ignorance, I challenge their thought process by asking them the following question, "What would be more difficult to do: telling employees that a new security system is being implemented and the public and employees could no longer walk freely into the workspace through a number of non-secured doors, or telling an employee's family that they have been injured or killed by an intruder or a peer?"

In October 2019, Deborah Onwu, a case worker for a non-profit mental health centre, was murdered by a client. Ms. Onwu, 47, got into a verbal and physical argument with a male teenager who stabbed her to death. CUPE, the union representing Ms. Onwu's workplace, stated to Global News: "We have been raising concerns with Wood's Homes about low staffing levels for some time to try to protect employees from being victims of violence."

On February 3, 1992, at the Ontario Glove Manufacturing Co. in Waterloo, Ontario, Patrick Dombroskie, a disgruntled employee armed with a rifle and a large knife, walked inside the building where he had been employed as a leather cutter for eight years. News reports say he was angry that he had not been asked to return to work after a second work performance suspension. Mr. Dombroskie was seeking out those individuals who he felt were responsible for his suspension.

The first victim was Greg More, 39, co-owner and vice-president of the family-owned business. Elisabeth Travassos, 43, a sewer in the plant, was killed second. Prior to his suspension, Ms. Travassos had complained to her supervisor Larry Strack about Mr. Dombroskie refusing to properly stack the leather pieces that she sewed. Both workers were paid based on the number of pieces they completed. The third victim was Mr. Strack, 43, who was shot outside while trying to flee the building. Following the murders, Mr. Dombroskie drove to police headquarters where he surrendered.

The majority of employee-driven violent situations are preventable. Incidents generally do not begin one day with someone brandishing a gun or a knife; that is actually the day the violence ends.

There have been a number of tragic workplace murder-suicides in Ontario over the past few decades that resulted in public inquiries. The intent of a public inquiry is to formally review an event, usually one resulting in the loss of life, to learn from the situation in an attempt to decrease or eliminate the possibility of a similar event occurring in the future.

One of those cases involved Theresa Vince, 56, who was a 25-year employee of Sears Canada in Chatham, Ontario. Ms. Vince was murdered at work on June 2, 1996. According to Western University's Centre for Research & Education on Violence Against Women and Children, Ms. Vince's tragic story unfolded as follows: "On June 2, 1996, Theresa Vince was murdered at her place of work, by her boss, the store manager, who also shot and killed himself. Sixteen months earlier she had made a complaint of sexual harassment and a poisoned work environment. For the majority of her time as an employee with Sears, Theresa loved her work, her co-workers and the atmosphere in which she worked. She excelled in her role and was described by many as 'highly competent' and 'the one who runs the store.' But things began to change slowly when the new store manager arrived. 'He treated her differently from the very beginning,' stated one co-worker. Almost everything we know about Theresa's experience was gathered from witness testimonies at a coroner's inquest into the workplace deaths. We know that Theresa's boss complimented her on her appearance. He stared at her. He phoned her on her extension '20 to 25 times a day' (in an eight-hour workday that's every 20 minutes) and called her into his office 'at least that many times.' He would follow her with his eyes when she walked by, even if he was engaged in conversation with employees and managers. He would follow her to coffee break and stare at her. He would take an extra-long route to the bathroom to pass by her desk. He told her, 'If he were married to her he would buy her a dishwasher.' He gave her expensive perfume and tried to kiss her. He frequently brought her up in conversation. He lifted his pant leg to show her his tan. He offered to rub suntan lotion on her back. He piled work on her. He would be mean and surly to her."

According to her daughter Jacquie Carr, who was 31 years old when her mother was murdered, Ms. Vince took the following action to stop the unwanted sexual harassment and inappropriate behaviour: *My mom had laid a complaint of sexual harassment 18 months before, to the regional human resources supervisor. She had been having trouble with some of his behaviours toward her for almost the entire time he was there in the store, so it had been going on quite a while. She was given a few choices. My mom could either go and speak to him and let him know that what he was doing wasn't okay and she would like him to stop, or she could write him a letter, or [the supervisor] could speak to him. She ended up talking to him herself. His behaviour just became worse. He didn't stop. Her way of managing it was very similar to what we know statistically about how people in her situation manage that kind of behaviour. She had mentioned a little bit to my older sister, but not very much at all. The person that she talked to the most was her sister. They were trying to handle it with coping strategies like staying away from him, trying to ignore it—things that we now know don't work.*

Ms. Vince's final attempt to eliminate the harassment was to take an early retirement. She was murdered two weeks prior to her last day.

Ms. Carr summed up her mother's experience in this heartbreaking comment: *Two months before she died, I watched my mother curl into a ball as she sat on the sofa—tears, one by one, rolled down her cheeks—all she could say was that she was under a lot of stress. It had been months since I had seen her smile. She couldn't sleep, she couldn't eat, she couldn't talk anymore—all she could do was curl up into her self-protective ball and wish for her hell to be over. She never made it to retirement day.*

Recommendations from the Theresa Vince Coroner's Inquiry were as follows:

To Employers:

- Consider implementation of confidential sources of emotional, psychological and psychiatric assistance, such as employee assistance programs.
- Educate employees on recognizing indicators of excessive stress or depression.
- Have effective workplace harassment and discrimination policies and procedures set out for employees.
- Follow the policies as written, with no distinction between formal and informal, written and verbal complaints.
- Train and update all employees on sexual harassment policies.
- Set boundaries of acceptable behaviour according to the Ontario Human Rights Code, sexual harassment cannot be acceptable—zero tolerance.

In 2001, Pat Hoy, a Chatham-Kent-Essex Member of Provincial Parliament, filed a private member's bill to amend the Ministry of Labour Act to include an employer's obligation to protect workers from sexual harassment. The bill was struck down four times.

Four years later, on November 12, 2005, Lori Dupont, a registered nurse at Hôtel-Dieu Grace Hospital in Windsor, Ontario—a one-hour drive from Chatham—was murdered at her workplace by her ex-partner, an anesthetist who worked at the same hospital. According to the coroner's report, Ms. Dupont's cause of death was loss of blood due to multiple stab wounds to her chest. Her murderer Marc Daniel died two days later after a self-inflicted lethal injection.

According to the inquest, the following is an account of the events of this tragic case:

In 2004, Dr. Marc Daniel met Ms. Lori Dupont in the recovery room of Windsor's Hotel-Dieu Grace. The anesthesiologist became obsessed with the nurse, pursuing her relentlessly, eventually persuading her to go out with him, and finally pressing her into moving in together into her newly acquired house (much of which he paid for).

Before and during this time, Dr. Daniel had harassed three other nurses in the hospital; he had broken one nurse's finger, had excluded another from the operating room and had verbally abused a nurse manager. These incidents triggered an investigation into his workplace conduct. As a result of the investigation, Dr. Daniel was required to sign a Memorandum of Agreement requiring him to:

1. *Go on probation,*
2. *Abide by the rules of the harassment policy,*
3. *Obey the Code of Conduct, and*
4. *Take anger management therapy.*

On February 27, 2005, Daniel injected himself with intravenous drugs commonly used to induce anesthesia. This was not investigated. The treating doctors in the acute psychiatric ward believed Daniel's explanation of using drugs to deal with the pressures of work. They did not believe Dupont and her mother, who claimed that the suicidal attempt was a tactic designed to control her behaviour. They told the doctors that they feared for the physical safety of Dupont and her child. Dupont broke up with Daniel while he was still in the ward.

On March 10, 2005, upon being discharged, Daniel requested a new psychiatrist and began psychotherapy with a psychologist, the only witness to testify that the attempted suicide was an aggressive act. Daniel also began to stalk Dupont at the hospital and at home. Her parents interceded to protect her at home.

On April 5, Dr. Daniel placed potentially embarrassing photos of Ms. Dupont on her vehicle parked in the hospital parking lot. He also confronted Ms. Dupont's father at his workplace, where he threatened to distribute the photos if he was not reimbursed for the funds he had provided for the house. She had returned most of the money but retained a small percentage for the hardship she had endured as a consequence of his conduct.

On April 8, Ms. Dupont attended a meeting of security, supervisory and legal personnel at the hospital at their request to discuss a strategy for dealing with Dr. Daniel following this incident. The employer cancelled

Dr. Daniel's security card access, asked him to get therapy and to pick up his mail elsewhere. Ms. Dupont sought a peace bond. A final hearing was not scheduled until after her murder.

During this time (June 2005), the Physician Health Program (PHP) intervened on Dupont's request. It provided a contract specifying that workplace monitors share certain information about Dr. Daniel with his psychiatrist. His psychiatrist, however, neither received nor requested such information in order to respect doctor-patient confidentiality. Dr. Daniel reported that he was ready to return to work, the psychiatrist sent a letter of recommendation to the PHP, which sent a letter of support to the hospital, which reinstated the doctor without consulting the nurses.

Upon returning to work, Dr. Daniel began harassing the nursing staff. He kissed one nurse on the cheek and offered to rub another's naked back. He continued to be hostile to the nursing manager whom he had verbally abused and the nurse whom he had excluded from the operating room. He intimidated Ms. Dupont by staring intensely at her, both in the recovery room and the lunchroom. One witness saw him body-check her in the hallway one day. The nursing staff feared that he was going to go "postal". The hospital testified that it did not discipline Daniel for his harassing conduct that breached the memorandum of agreement that he had signed in January 2005. This was because they were viewing his conduct as a symptom of a mental illness requiring treatment, not discipline.

In early November, a week before the murder, the PHP case manager was very concerned by her meeting with Dr. Daniel in which the doctor talked obsessively about Ms. Dupont. She requested that the psychologist reassess Dr. Daniel. Unfortunately, this did not happen before the murder-suicide.

Ms. Dupont lost her life on November 12, 2005, at 9:27 a.m.

I believe the Dupont case opened our eyes to the realities of workplace violence, not only in the province of Ontario but around the world. Most of us have a preconceived notion of the profile of a killer. We see a person who is "different" from us all, someone who may not have the ideal socio-economic status or education. We do not envision a highly educated physician who takes a nurse's life at nine o'clock in the morning.

Following Ms. Dupont's death, the Dupont and Vince families, the Ontario Nurses' Association and victim advocacy groups banded together. They relentlessly demanded justice for Ms. Dupont and individuals who were victims not only in the workplace but also in their homes. The issue of domestic violence was a fundamental factor in this tragedy, resulting in the employer's inaction.

The inquest found six main issues that are assumed to have contributed to the outcome of this preventable tragedy:

#1: "Confusion and indecision about how to deal with 'untouchable' doctor"

"Despite significant and documented complaints of serious disruptive behaviour problems and infrastructure of the Hospital Policies and bylaws by Dr. Daniel in the Spring of 2005, there seemed to be much confusion and indecision as to how to deal with this physician."

The murderer in this case was a physician. I believe that if the case details were identical but Dr. Daniel's occupation was substituted with any other position in the hospital, such as a nurse, ward clerk or environmental worker, the situation would have been handled much differently. An employee in a lower ranked position maintaining their employment at the hospital while behaving in such a violent and aggressive manner would have been unlikely.

#2: "Long history of disruptive Workplace Violence not considered in his re-appointment"

"Relevant behaviour issues and complaints were not identified during Dr. Daniel's re-appointment process at the hospital."

There was a long history of complaints spanning over the course of at least five years related to Dr. Daniel's inappropriate behaviour. This history only includes cases that were actually reported and documented. From my experience conducting workplace violence or harassment cases, management is often completely unaware of many of the incidents that are disclosed during the formal interview.

More often than not, victims hesitate to report any wrongdoing out of fear of retaliation, particularly when the perpetrator is in a senior position. Physicians hold the power in a hospital even over those assumed to be the senior leaders.

Several cases in which I have been involved where frontline workers or non-management employees were deemed to have broken the organization's mission, vision, values or code of conduct have led to severe discipline up to and including termination. If zero tolerance for violence is an organization's mandate, a foundation of its philosophy or a guiding principle, it needs to be applied to all workers regardless of their titles. The reality is that due to the financial agreement and non-employee status of physicians in a hospital, rules and regulations are more difficult to apply, although not impossible. Hospital privileges could be linked to expectations regarding the physician's privileges, solidified by an agreement stating the zero-tolerance consequences for breaching policies, particularly those pertaining to workplace violence or harassment.

#3: "Assessment of doctor's readiness to return to work based solely on his own word"

"Marc Daniel returned to work following the assessments of the PHP (Physician Health Programme) and his treating clinicians. Their letters of recommendation to return to work were based only on their interviews with Marc Daniel. There was no documentation of consultation by PHP with any of the OR nurses, the Hospital Administration or Lori Dupont."

Although it may be inconceivable how this could have happened, in work environments even today, decisions are made behind closed doors or negotiated around a table with limited input or consideration for the mental, emotional and physical health of complainants.

In one of my cases, a complainant went into work for an evening shift following a vacation to be faced with their physically aggressive peer who just returned from a weeklong, non-paid suspension for a physical altercation with the complainant. The complainant spent the entire shift without on-site management support in fear of another violent episode. When later bringing this scenario to the supervisor's attention, the complainant was told that the respondent had been punished and "paid their dues" with the suspension and so the complainant would just have to "deal with it." An hour before the complainant was to arrive at work the next evening with the respondent, they sent a resignation letter to management and never returned to the workplace.

#4: "Confusion about how to file a complaint or address the situation"

"It seemed like several people approached their supervisors or talked amongst themselves at the hospital regarding Lori's situation, as well as other incidents of Marc Daniel's abuse and harassment. However, it seems that several people were uncertain how to go about filing a complaint or addressing the situation effectively within the realms of the workplace code of conduct."

In most jurisdictions that mandate the reporting and investigation of workplace violence or harassment, there is an expectation that the employer will carefully lay out the steps in the procedure component of the document. Most policies that I have reviewed meet this criteria, however, in a number of cases, the process to report follows the organizational structure without deviation, particularly when the manager or supervisor is the alleged harasser. Oftentimes the procedure will simply state: "Report any inappropriate behaviour to your direct manager." What if that manager is causing the issue? If procedures are not transparent and do not specifically spell out the steps of each potential scenario, employees are at a loss as to what to do. In addition, there are certain positions, such as a physician, that would not fall into the category of employee, such as a mayor, council member or board member, whereby no action plan is outlined. This leaves staff vulnerable and those positions are viewed as untouchable.

#5: "Depression not viewed as a lethal risk factor for Lori Dupont"

"Dr. Daniel's depression did not appear to be viewed as a lethal risk factor for Lori Dupont. There seemed to be a focus on treating and managing Marc Daniel's mood and depression without dealing with his attitudes about women, relationships and abusive behaviours."

A number of pre-incident risk factors must be considered when reviewing inappropriate behaviours or communication. Violence is a pathway to a final act and a series of steps that lead to the end result, which is harm. According to the World Health Organization's Department of Mental Health and Substance Abuse, the following are risk factors for aggression:

- History of Aggression: including patterns of aggression (e.g., rare but very serious acts of aggression, frequent but less serious acts of aggression, aggression in specific circumstances such as response to specific delusions)
- Substance Abuse History
- Criminal History: violent and non-violent criminal charges
- Mental Illness: including links between symptoms and aggressive behaviour, and any current active symptoms
- Personality Disorder/Psychopathy
- Use of a Weapon
- Unemployment/No Meaningful Daily Activity
- Victim Access
- History of Non-Compliance with Treatment
- Hostile Attitudes/Threatening Statements and Behaviour
- Relationship Loss (e.g., death, divorce or separation from significant other or significant social support)
- Inadequate Community Alternative to Hospitalization
- Trauma History

- Risk of Danger to Self (suicide/self-injury)

#6: "Doctor's drug theft/misuse goes unchecked"

"Evidence was presented through Ms. Iovino-Hopper (a close friend of Ms. Dupont) regarding Lori's discovery of drugs and syringes in Marc's car, the responding EMS workers' discovery of drugs and syringes at Marc's final suicide attempt, Lori's mother's evidence regarding drugs and syringes found at Marc's first suicide attempt, and head of security's discovery of 30 syringes in Dr. Daniel's locker after his death."

The use of drugs and previous suicide attempts and/or self-injury is a prevalent risk factor regarding future aggressive behaviours or the commencement of violent acts against others.

As a result of the case details regarding Ms. Dupont's former relationship with Dr. Daniel, the inquiry resulted in the following recommendations pertaining to domestic violence:

To Employers:

- Design and implement policies, linked to training and actual practice, related to domestic violence, abuse and harassment in the workplace.
- Employees must be aware of the dynamics of domestic violence, abuse and harassment in order to identify it. They must know what to do when confronted with these issues in the workplace and be confident that if they speak to management, something will be done about the situation.
- Integrate skill-building programs in the workplace to ensure that professionals and non-professionals take appropriate action when faced with an incident of domestic violence in the workplace.
- Provide educational materials to support such training, including information concerning the legal responsibility to report such incidents.

- Integrate domestic violence awareness training into the orientation and ongoing professional development plans of all health-care professionals.
- Give Continuing Professional Development credits for training in the areas of violence in the workplace, harassment, bullying and domestic violence.

The inquiry recognized that "It is not enough to focus on mental health issues of employees who disrupt the workplace; their attitudes, relationships and abusive behaviours should also be taken into consideration. A trained workforce will be able to identify the signs of potential for lethal violence."

To the Legal System:

- Victims who submit peace bond applications should be kept in the loop about what is happening with their peace bond application.
- Evaluate the effectiveness of domestic violence training and monitor the extent to which it is being taken by the Crown.
- Develop an accessible process to give a voice to the concerns of victims, their advocates and the public at large concerning domestic violence.
- Create Domestic Violence Courts to focus on early intervention and vigorous prosecution or, alternatively, expand the hours of operation of the current court system to deal with cases of domestic violence.
- Domestic Violence Courts should deal with all matters relating to the case.
- Intentional court delays by the accused should not be tolerated.

Another highly publicized case involving a workplace murder-suicide occurred at Ottawa's OC Transpo in Ontario. This case illustrates the extreme effects bullying can have on an individual and workplace. On April 6, 1999, Pierre Lebrun entered the workplace with a hunting rifle and shot and killed employees David Lemay, Brian Guay, Clare Davidson and Harry Schoenmakers. The murderer was a former disgruntled employee who was allegedly constantly ridiculed by his co-workers due to a speech impediment. Mr. Lebrun was fired in August 1997 for getting in a fistfight with one of his alleged bullies, however, after union intervention he was later reinstated. He quit a few months later.

After shooting his former colleagues, Mr. Lebrun turned the rifle on himself. Mr. Lebrun's suicide note, left at his parents' house on the day of the shooting, was published in *The Globe and Mail* on January 11, 2000:

Mom and Dad, This is the most difficult letter that I have written during my life. I know that I'm going to commit an unforgivable act, and I'm going to cause you a lot of grief, but I have no choice.

I am tired, exhausted and completely backed against the wall. I fear for my life because of these retards from the union who are following me.

I am being followed, spied upon, humiliated from Vancouver, Kamloops, Kelowna and even Las Vegas—yes, I went to Vegas. They will never leave me alone. I can't go on living like this. They have destroyed my life. I will destroy their life.

I'm not asking you to forgive me, or even to understand me, but I'm asking you to tell the truth to the whole world so this doesn't happen again to anybody. OC Transpo and the unions can't hide from what they do to me. I know that everyone will say that I'm crazy, but to the contrary I'm very intelligent, too intelligent.

They will pay dearly for what they've done to me. The people who I hold personally responsible are: Daniel Besserer—store supervisor, Mike Price—his assistant, Dave Westerman—personnel director, Richard White—my last boss, along with many others. Don't rely on anyone, not even Richard Cantin, who is the regional government.

Some people had tried to help me: Liz Callagan—the EAP [Employee Assistance Program], Lois Emberg—job equity officer of OC, Peter Newgard

—equipment manager. Please send this letter to the media—TV, radio, newspaper—so they can tell the truth about me. I know that I have done things I should not have done. But all that I wanted was for them to leave me alone, not to bug me, but it was too much to ask.

They have spread lies, especially that I was a rat who denounced my own union members to try and have them stop laughing at me everywhere in North America. I never wanted it to come to this. But it was probably my destiny.

Your son who loves you a lot, Pierre

During the public inquiry, special attention was placed on the concept of psychological violence, which was defined as "bullying, mobbing, teasing, ridicule or any other act or words that could psychologically hurt or isolate a person in the workplace." It was noted that this type of inappropriate workplace behaviour should be focused on at the time it occurs rather than after a criminal act has taken place. Due to the fact that for years the murderer was allegedly harassed at work for a stutter yet ignored by management, 53 of the jury's recommendations were focused on employer-employee workplace issues. The jury specifically stated, "Evidence indicated that complaints in the workplace were not taken seriously and no action was taken."

[S]afety and security don't just happen: they are the result of collective consensus and public investment. ... We owe our children — the most vulnerable citizens in our society — a life free from violence and fear.

~ Nelson Mandela ~

Discrimination and Harassment in the Workplace

Over the years, the terms discrimination and harassment have become more commonly used. Legislative changes and the present education systems in Canada and around the world are training young people to stand up for their rights and the rights of those who are unable to do so for themselves. Words can carry a powerful punch even when there is no physical contact or attack initiated. Discrimination and harassment unfortunately occur in the workplace, however, oftentimes these terms are used incorrectly. For example, an individual may say, "I'm being discriminated against; I have to work this weekend." Is that truly discrimination? Perhaps, but it is more likely that the situation is an unfair practice that does not fall under the legal definition or meet the criteria of discrimination.

The term harassment can also be misused due to a lack of education or knowledge. Moreover, the term harassment may be a misinterpretation of performance management. Organizations often see grievances against management or senior leadership that, when investigated, are not cases of harassment, but rather management exercising its power to ensure that employees are providing competent services. On the other hand, in some cases the harassment could not be substantiated by a balance of probabilities (50 percent + one), however, the way the complainant was managed may be of concern.

One case I investigated involved a staff member who filed a harassment grievance against their manager. Apparently a number of staff members who worked weekends were taking an additional unauthorized 30-minute break. The situation was recorded on a security camera (staff were aware of when and where the cameras were installed). When meeting with the complainant about the grievance, the individual admitted that they took the illegal break. From their perspective, they were not grieving the case outcome or consequences, but rather the fact that out of four employees who were caught stealing corporate time, the complainant was the only one who had been financially disciplined. In addition, the complainant had no previous history of time theft or any other discipline on file.

Oftentimes, complaints against management that are deemed by the individual as harassment are not about the job requested or task assigned, but how the manager spoke to them. These complainants make statements such as, "They talk to me like I am stupid" or "They talk to me like they think they are better than me." Although legal harassment may not be substantiated, a case of incivility or a breach of a code of conduct may be a more accurate descriptor of the events leading to the complaint.

The Canadian Human Rights Commission defines discrimination as: "An action or a decision that treats a person or a group badly for reasons such as their race, age or disability." These reasons are protected under the Canadian Human Rights Act.

The Canadian Charter of Rights and Freedoms and the Supreme Court of Canada state that the following three inquiries may be used to determine whether discrimination has occurred (which should be applied by employers when making complaint determinations):

1) Differential Treatment

Was there substantively differential treatment, either because of a distinction, exclusion or preference, or because of a failure to take into account the individual's already disadvantaged position within Canadian society?

2) An Enumerated Ground

Was the differential treatment based on an enumerated ground?

3) Discrimination in a Substantive Sense

Does the differential treatment discriminate by imposing a burden upon, or withholding a benefit from an individual? Does the differential treatment amount to discrimination because it makes distinctions that are offensive to human dignity?

More specifically, prohibited grounds for discrimination include: race, national or ethnic origin, colour, religion, age, sex, sexual orientation, gender identity or expression, marital status, family status, genetic characteristics, disability and conviction for an offence for which a pardon has been granted or in respect of which a record suspension has been ordered. In a number of cases, an individual may be discriminated on more than one ground at the same or different times in the denial of goods, services, accommodations or employment. Moreover, a discriminatory practice or policy may be established by an employer (a person who or organization that discharges the obligations of an employer under the Employment Equity Act) that "deprives or tends to deprive an individual or class of individuals of any employment opportunities on a prohibited ground of discrimination."

Xenophobia is a hatred or fear of something or someone who is perceived as "foreign or strange." It is based on the notion that there is an "in" group and an "out" group, which manifests into a suspicion of the out group, resulting in the desire to eliminate their presence. Through history, we have seen the devastating effects of this phobia, including the treatment of Indigenous peoples by colonists, the Holocaust, the murder of black people by the Ku Klux Klan, the segregation of Japanese-Americans and Japanese-Canadians during World War II, and the segregation and persecution of the Muslim community following the 9/11 attack on the United States of America. Today, xenophobia appears to be growing at a rapid rate, despite the attempts of the in group to deny or downplay its existence.

In 1988, Peggy McIntosh, an American feminist, anti-racism activist and senior research scientist of the Wellesley Centers for

Women, published the article, "White Privilege and Male Privilege: A Personal Account of Coming to See Correspondences Through Work in Women's Studies." Her analysis began a dialogue about the dimension of privilege as it relates to power, race, class, gender and sexuality. A shorter version entitled, "White Privilege: Unpacking the Invisible Knapsack" was published in 1989. In her work, McIntosh uses the following metaphor to describe white privilege: "an invisible weightless knapsack of special provisions, maps, passports, code-books, visas, clothes, tools, and blank checks." As a Caucasian woman, she lists 46 of her own everyday advantages, such as:

- I can go shopping alone most of the time, pretty well assured that I will not be followed or harassed.
- I can be sure that my children will be given curricular materials that testify to the existence of their race.
- Whether I use checks, credit cards or cash, I can count on my skin color not to work against the appearance of financial responsibility.
- I can take a job or enroll in a college with an affirmative action policy without having my co-workers or peers assume I got it because of my race.
- I am never asked to speak for all of the people of my racial group.
- If a traffic cop pulls me over or if the IRS audits my tax return, I can be sure I haven't been singled out because of my race.
- I can do well in a challenging situation without being called a credit to my race.

Her book published in 2019, *On Privilege, Fraudulence, and Teaching As Learning: Selected Essays 1981–2019* is a collection of her published essays.

Prohibited Grounds for Discrimination

Race

According to the Canadian Human Rights Commission, race is a prohibited ground that is not specifically defined. Despite this, notions of race continue to exist in society and create differences among groups, therefore marginalizing them. This social construction of race is termed "racialization" and remains a potent force in society. Individuals may have prejudices related to people or characteristics that are racialized.

In addition to physical characteristics such as colour, the following characteristics are commonly racialized: language, accent or manner of speech, name, clothing and grooming, diet, beliefs and practices, leisure preferences, place of origin and citizenship.

One of my cases regarding racial discrimination involved an employee who filed a complaint based on perceived insults to their race. According to the complainant, who was born outside of North America, they brought their lunch to work to save money and, more importantly, because they liked their own cooking. They were employed at the company for two years and from the start of their employment until approximately two months after the complaint was filed, they had to deal with daily insults from colleagues at lunchtime. As with a number of other employees, they would store their food in the refrigerator and heat it up in the microwave before eating it. Each day, the other staff would make comments about the complainant's food, saying their food "stinks," asking if they could refrain from either storing their food in the refrigerator or putting it in the microwave, making comments about how "gross" the food looked, etc. Lunchtime became so stressful for the complainant that they started eating lunch in their car, even in the winter months, to avoid the criticism and disrespectful comments from their colleagues. Eventually through the support of a colleague, they filed a human rights complaint with human resources.

National or Ethnic Origin

According to the Canadian Human Rights Commission, the terms "ethnic origin" and "ancestry" are sometimes used interchangeably. Ancestry is closely related to from whom you have descended and an ancestor is usually more distant than a grandparent. One's ancestry may originate from more than one cultural group. Statistics Canada states that "ethnic origin" refers to the cultural origins of a person's ancestors.

Ethnic origin encompasses a wider range of characteristics than ancestry but also includes ancestry. The *Canadian Oxford Dictionary* defines "ethnic" as "relating to a population subgroup (within a larger or dominant national or cultural group) with a common national or cultural tradition." Ancestry and ethnic origin should not be confused with citizenship, nationality or language spoken. In the Ontario Human Rights Code, the ground of ethnic origin overlaps with the more commonly used term "ethnicity," which refers to a shared cultural heritage or nationality. Ethnic groups may be distinguished on the basis of cultural traits, such as language or shared customs around family, food, dance and music.

When I started my business full time, I also provided conference and event planning services to supplement my income. One of my specialities was assisting organizations with the planning of their annual general meetings. Many of my clients were multicultural agencies that serviced diverse groups of people. Most events were attended by 100 to 500 people. A common practice was to hire local community members to fulfil a number of roles, such as catering, decorating and on-site event support. As budgets were tight, one of the ways to decorate the space was to ask community members to lend their home country artifacts, traditional clothing or handicrafts, or gather posters from travel agencies to add colour to the festivities.

At the end of one such event, a few attendees wrote on their comment cards that they felt the travel posters adorning the walls were discriminatory. More specifically, they wrote that the posters were stereotyped depictions of a race or country used simply as a media tool for the travel agency and were in no way reflective of the actual country or its people. Initially, the planning group dismissed the comments as "one-offs" written by individuals who were unhappy with the agency's services or just had the need to complain about something. After a day of reflection, I brought up the feedback at our debriefing meeting and the others were very supportive. The issue was discussed with the diverse committee that reflected the community and a few conclusions were reached to support the comments raised. It was agreed that as opposed to a typical tourist poster, all citizens do not smile all of the time, wear the quality of clothes worn, eat the highly nutritional and varied diet, or enjoy a certain social activity like dancing or fishing. It was recognized during that conversation that there is poverty and a lack of social, economic and medical resources not only in our country but around the world, and those posters potentially represent an extremely low percentage of most people living in the community. It was an amazing learning opportunity for me and the other committee members; that what may have been done with the best intentions may actually have contributed to what we were so desperately trying to avoid.

Colour

According to the Canadian Human Rights Commission, "colour" is listed as a ground in the Ontario Human Rights Code but is an undefined term. A person's skin colour can be seen as a physical feature that is commonly racialized.

As a frontline worker, manager and consultant, I have witnessed and investigated many situations whereby a person of colour has been discriminated. Some of the situations have been blatant, some passive and, in many cases, extremely difficult to prove. Over the years, I have often heard the statement, "They're a racist." When querying as to what led the person to believe that someone is racist or requesting an outline of the incident(s) that led the person to this conclusion, I often hear, "I have no concrete examples, but I know they are racist."

I had a situation a few years ago when I was asked to be a keynote speaker at a conference that was a 4.5-hour drive from my home. As it was only a 45-minute presentation, I decided to fly there first thing in the morning and return later that day. To provide some context, it is important to know that many of my clients live over two hours away so depending on the duration of my work, I often stay over in hotels. As I don't always have the time or energy to go to a restaurant for dinner, I tend to carry supplies with me. In my computer bag, I could have everything from a fork, knife and spoon to a bag of protein powder to a box of cereal. On this trip, I went through the security screening at the airport and was stopped by a security officer to inspect my computer bag. Within seconds, the security guard pulled a steak knife out of my bag. I quickly realized that in my haste to catch my flight, I forgot to check my bag for anything that may be deemed dangerous or restricted by airport security. I explained that I carry these utensils because I often travel and eat on the road or in my hotel room. The security officer said he understood, however, I was not allowed to take the knife onto the plane. He further explained that security could keep the knife for me and I could pick it up when I returned later that day. I apologized and then proceeded to my gate. As I was walking away, I stopped and looked back at the security area. Suddenly a thought came into my mind. Right or wrong, I thought to myself, what if I was a different colour, race or gender? Would the outcome of the security officer finding a steak knife in my carry-on bag have been the same? Would I have been dealt with in the same respectful manner and allowed to board the plane? Those questions remain in my mind every time I take a flight. I believe the question of "what if" is an important and relevant one.

Religion

According to the Canadian Human Rights Commission, “religion” or “creed” is not a defined term in the Ontario Human Rights Code. The Commission interprets creed to mean “religious creed” or “religion.” It includes faith, beliefs, observances or worship. “To be recognized as a religion or creed under the Code, a belief in a God or gods, or a single supreme being or deity is not a requisite.”

One of our basic human rights is the right to have individual beliefs regarding religion. Although it is and should be honoured as a human right, it has been demonstrated around the world that religious beliefs and freedoms are much more complex than meets the eye. Throughout history, it appears that religion has been at the core of wars and the foundation of hate and destruction in most countries. Although there is much pride in Canada about the country’s openness and acceptance of diversity and different religions, the reality of the conversations in workplace hallways or around the dinner table can be quite the contrary. Discussions focusing on differences can create tension and animosity between individuals.

Organizations must be extremely cognizant of the diversity of their workers and how religious freedoms need to be incorporated into the workplace. Organizations have access to countless online or in-person training resources along with templates of policies and procedures to ensure that workplaces are inclusive. Although some issues such as religious holidays or the need for a place of worship within the workspace can be standardized, some issues may need to be reconsolidated once a concern has been raised to management.

I was conducting mandatory harassment education in an organization at the same time that a group of staff submitted a union grievance. The grievance was the result of a particular group of staff alleging religious discrimination. A new kitchen manager had recently been hired and during the manager’s orientation, it came to his attention that there were several safety concerns ranging from equipment not being shut down and secured properly to a lack of proper sanitation methods. Another safety issue that concerned the manager was that a number of staff members were wearing jewelry while working, specifically bracelets. According to the grievance, the manager called a department meeting and stated in the open forum that all jewelry, including bracelets, must be removed prior to commencing a shift. After the meeting, some of the staff members who wore bracelets at work approached the manager, stating that they felt singled out and "mocked" during the meeting. The group explained that the bracelets in question were religious bangles that could not be removed under any circumstance. The staff had been wearing these religious bangles in the workplace for years and were never questioned about them or asked to remove them. At this time, the manager stated that it was not his problem if the previous managers were "incompetent" and did not do a proper job. When questioned about the rationale behind the sudden need for the bracelets to be removed, the manager stated that the bracelets were a safety hazard that could cause injury to the employees. The staff members in unison stated that under no circumstance would they remove their religious symbols. They further questioned the manager as to why staff members were permitted to wear wedding bands at work, but the manager did not have a response to this question. As a result of reaching a stalemate, the staff members decided to file a group grievance against the manager and the organization for failing to allow religious freedom at work.

This case brought up many issues that the organization had to address. The main question being, how can religious freedom and health and safety be equally honoured? Does safety supersede religion or does religion overrule health and safety?

Age

According to the Canadian Human Rights Commission, "age" that is covered in the Code is 18 years or more. In my work over the years, I have faced a rising number of workplace harassment cases that are linked to the age of the complainant and respondent. As life expectancy increases and employment legislation is updated, the age defined for retirement has become arbitrary. Without being based on a physical evaluation of the individual employee, the practice is an ageist one.

I hear employees over the age of 40 complain that the younger employees do not have what they would consider a strong work ethnic and do not respect them for their years of service. On the other side, employees under the age of 30 complain to me that they are being "picked on" by the more senior employees. They accuse more seasoned workers of being "stuck in the past" and not interested in learning current technology, which in their opinion would result in greater efficiency. This increasing tension among age groups may create a very unpleasant, and in some situations, toxic work environment.

A company experiencing conflict within one of its largest departments contacted me a few years ago. The human resources adviser informed me that although the employer or the union had received no formal complaint, they had heard there was some disgruntled staff that could potentially lead to a grievance. It seemed that the issues became apparent when a new manager had been hired. The company mentor for the newly hired manager was also aware of the situation because in their monthly meeting, the manager raised concerns that direct reports were not following their direction, aggressively arguing against any new recommendations and displaying negative body language such as eyerolling and snickering behind their back. The manager did not want to make an issue of the inappropriate behaviour as they felt they had to earn the staff's respect and gain their admiration.

Rather than waiting for the issue to escalate, I was asked by my client to conduct a climate assessment for the department. Through this process, I met with all staff in private to ask them to rate and comment on the following departmental areas: morale, trust, respect, respect for the hierarchy, communication, teamwork, presence of rumours and gossip, top concerns, and solutions to problem areas identified. During the course of the interviews, it was revealed that the newly hired manager was approximately 25 years old whereas the vast majority of her direct reports were between 45 and 65 years old. It was shared by a number of employees that they had a hard time having "faith" in the abilities and competency of the new manager based on her age. Comments such as, "I am old enough to be her mother" and "I have sweaters older than her" revealed the ageist attitudes of the staff members towards the manager. As a result of the climate assessment report, education on workplace discrimination and harassment focusing on the concept of ageism was mandated for all departmental staff.

Sex

On December 6, 1989, at École Polytechnique in Montreal, Quebec, a gunman walked into a mechanical engineering class and demanded that the men and women go to opposite sides of the room. He instructed approximately 50 men to leave the room claiming that he was "fighting feminism." He shot all nine women in the room, killing six. For 20 minutes, Marc Lépine walked through the halls, cafeteria and into another classroom shooting women. In total, 14 women were killed and 10 were injured. Four men were also injured that day.

Some of the individuals who witnessed the massacre later committed suicide. In at least two cases, suicide notes confirmed that they took their life due to the distress caused by the massacre.

Let us remember...

Geneviève Bergeron, Hélène Colgan, Nathalie Croteau, Barbara Daigneault, Anne-Marie Edward, Maud Haviernick, Barbara Klucznik-Widajewicz, Maryse Laganière, Maryse Leclair, Anne-Marie Lemay, Sonia Pelletier, Michèle Richard, Annie St-Arneault, Annie Turcotte

Sociologist Allan G. Johnson defined the term misogyny as "a cultural attitude of hatred for females because they are female." This belief system is the basis of sexist prejudice and the oppression of women, which can be traced back to ancient Greek mythology. In recent years, the term "incel" (meaning involuntarily celibate) or the incel rebellion has emerged. This group of self-identified men is made up of males who are united by the public disclosure of their inability to "convince" women to have sex with them. Their shared philosophy is that women are considered extremely shallow and stupid. According to a *Vox* article published on April 28, 2018, there are only two types of women in the world of incel and both are "white, thin and attractive." Women are either considered to be "Stacys" who are ultra-feminine, attractive and unattainable and only attracted to hyper-muscular and popular men identified as "Chads"; or "Beckys" who are "average", women. "But while incels seem to believe that the untouchable (and seemingly nonexistent) Stacy will never sleep with them, they feel as though they are owed attention and sex from Becky," said the *Vox* article.

Although only a small percentage of incels are known to have turned violent, even one is too many. In 2014, Elliot Rodger, a self-proclaimed incel, killed six people and wounded 14 others in a stabbing and shooting rampage in Isla Vista, California. The manifesto he emailed to people he knew and the video he posted online stated that the act was "retaliation against women as a group for refusing to provide [him] with the sex he was owed." Inside the incel world, Mr. Rodger is considered a "hero." Alek Minassian, who in 2018 drove a van down the sidewalk in a busy part of Toronto, Ontario killing 10 people, praised Mr. Rodger as the "Supreme Gentleman" in his Facebook post.

According to the Canadian Human Rights Commission, the ground of "sex" is not specifically defined in the Ontario Human Rights Code, although it is generally considered to be related to a person's biological sex: male or female. Men and women receive equal protection under this ground. The ground of "sex" also includes a broader notion of "gender," which can be described as the social characteristics attributed to each sex. The Ontario Human Rights Code protects men and women from harassment and discrimination at work, including assumptions about their professional abilities that result from stereotypes about how men and women "should" behave, dress or interact. It was only recently that I read in the newspaper that organizations were no longer allowed to enforce women to wear high heels in the workplace.

Ontario's Occupational Health and Safety Act defines workplace sexual harassment as: a) "engaging in a course of vexatious comment or conduct against a worker, in a workplace because of sex, sexual orientation, gender identity or gender expression where the course of comment or conduct is known or ought reasonably to be known to be unwelcome" or b) "making a sexual solicitation or advance where the person making it is in a position to confer, grant or deny a benefit or advancement to the worker and the person knows or ought reasonably to know the solicitation or advance is unwelcome".

In the past, certain professions have been strongly associated with a specific gender. Occupations such as police officers, firefighters and physicians may have been assumed to be held by a man, whereas nurses, schoolteachers and office administrators were associated with women. Over the years, I have been exposed to a number of males and females who were fighting assumptions and stereotypes as they tried to gain respect in the workplace to fully perform their job.

Consider the following riddle (Stöger et al., 2004): *A father and his son driving together in their car have a terrible car accident. The father dies upon impact. The son is rushed to the hospital in an ambulance and is immediately brought to the operating table. The doctor takes a quick look at him and says that a specialist is needed. The specialist comes, looks at the young man on the operating table and proclaims: "I cannot operate on him, he is my son." How can this be?*

Frontiers in Psychology explains how this illustrates an example of a stereotypical gender bias: "Many people reading this text are confused and have difficulties solving the riddle. Their difficulties arise from attributing gender values to the characters occurring in the story. In the case of *father* and *son* the gender values are explicit as fathers and sons are definitely male. However, many readers attribute male gender to the gender-unspecified *specialist* as well which leads to an inconsistency in their mental model of the riddle. They think that the specialist is the boy's father although earlier in the riddle it is stated that the boy's father died. Thus, these readers have difficulties finding the highly plausible solution of the riddle that the specialist is the young man's mother."

Over two decades, I worked with emergency service personnel, which historically included a small number of women on the frontlines. In confidence and sometimes through a formal venue, I learned first-hand the plight of these women. One woman came to one of my training sessions and sat front and centre with no expression on her face for the entire three hours. She caught my attention in the sea of 50 faces because she was the only female other than me. Later that evening, I received an email from this woman, asking if she could meet me in private outside of her workplace and work schedule. This is not something I would normally do, but reflecting on the session and its dynamics, I agreed to meet her at the end of the week in a location that was approximately 25 kilometres from her workplace.

When I arrived at the chosen location, I stood there waiting for her. Minutes later, a woman standing about five feet away from me came over and said, "Hi Denise." I was taken aback because I did not realize this was the same woman who I stood facing for three hours only a short 72 hours ago. Out of her uniform and in civilian clothes, her appearance was significantly altered. With her hair down, wearing makeup and jewelry, a different person faced me. Generally,

I would not comment on a person's appearance, but in this case I am doing so to provide context to the situation. When we sat down, she asked, "You didn't recognize me, did you? I was watching you approach the restaurant and look right at me, but you didn't see me." I replied that I had not recognized her based on my memory of what she looked like in class. She went on to explain that this is how she looks when off-duty but would never consider wearing any makeup or looking remotely feminine when at work where her style can only be described as androgynous. She said this was one of the only ways she could defend and protect herself at work. She had been in the service for nearly 10 years and explained to me that every minute of her time at work she was simply trying to survive. From the moment she put on her uniform a decade earlier, she was told by her male peers and others that she would never "cut it" in the field. She was mocked about how she talked, how she walked and even how her uniform fit her. Personal invasive comments about her body were made in group settings and at times when she was alone with a peer or superior. From the start of her career, she made a personal commitment to never be alone with anyone if it was at all possible because she felt unsafe or was somehow being set up. During the night shifts, although it was acceptable to sleep if there was no situation that needed attention, she would not sleep. Before and during her shift, she would drink copious amounts of coffee and energy drinks to fend off drowsiness. If she really needed a few minutes of rest while at work, she would sit in a metal straight back chair against a wall. She had been groped, pushed and kissed without consent too many times to ever let her guard down. When she was not at work, she would spend hours in the gym, lifting weights until she nearly passed out. She said she had to be as big and strong as she possibility could to intimidate an internal predator or at least be able to try to fight one off. As I listened to her story over the next few hours, I felt like I was listening to a survivor of war. She fought off tears, which she told me was another one of her defences; never allowing herself to cry in front of others. She knew that this display of vulnerability would only be used against her as further proof that a woman had no right to perform the job.

At the end of her story, I asked her what, if anything, she expected or needed from me. I queried her reason for contacting me and requesting to meet. She simply said that for once she wanted to tell her story to someone who may actually understand her experience and, more importantly, not try to justify or downplay her experience. She told me that she knew from past negative experiences that she could never again go to her superiors, human resources, the union or an external body. She was tired of being dismissed and told to "ignore them," further stating that now she was "throwing in the towel." She expressed that her body was getting older and weaker and, for health reasons, she could no longer go to the gym for six to eight hours a day. Without the ability to keep up with her physical regimen, she felt unsafe to continue working in her chosen profession. She hoped that one day she could use her negative experience to help other women break down the "old boys' club" that dominated her profession. I told her that if at any time she needed to talk or required more formal assistance, she could contact me. At the entrance of the restaurant she asked if it was okay to hug me. We hugged and she walked away. I never found out her last name or heard from her again. With more women in traditionally male-dominated professions banding together to fight for equality since then, I can only hope that she continued to be strong and carried out her dream of assisting other women in similar circumstances.

Men in traditionally female professions also face their share of harassment and bullying. A number of male nurses have told me similar stories of being asked on a regular basis if they pursued nursing because they could not get into medical school or being faced with the assumption that being a nurse automatically makes them gay. Despite someone's intent, making an assumption about someone's sexual orientation is a microaggression. According to the

Merriam-Webster Dictionary, a microaggression is "a comment or action that subtly and often unconsciously or unintentionally expresses a prejudiced attitude toward a member of a marginalized group." Even if someone's assumption is incorrect, it does not negate the fact that the comment or statement is hostile or derogatory.

At the end of a training session, a male registered nurse approached me wanting to speak to me privately. Being the end of his shift and my day, we were able to have a conversation once all other workshop participants left the room. He started the conversation by saying, "I am glad that I am still here to tell you my story." Without any context to accompany this statement, I apologized and said I did not understand what he meant. He said he had "an awesome wife" and proceeded to tell his story. Coming from a long line of nurses and medical professionals, he was proud of his family and knew since he was a boy that he wanted to be a nurse when he grew up. Although the thought of becoming a doctor once intrigued him, he chose to pursue nursing like his role model—his mother. Shortly after graduating, he married his childhood sweetheart and landed his first job. He said that even in school and in his placements, jokes about being a male nurse and the stereotypes that go with it were widespread but tolerable. He felt that a good sense of humour was an important characteristic to have, particularly in a profession that often involved difficult and heartbreaking events. He had a difficult time when he left his first job because he truly felt a camaraderie with his peers. He also felt respected and gained a lot of knowledge from his manager. The new job he was taking was a charge nurse position, which would potentially lead him to his goal of becoming a hospital administrator.

On the first day of his orientation, a female nurse blatantly told him in private that she would not take orders from a man. She went on to say that men should not be nurses or in any other "feminine" role. Over the course of a few weeks, he had several negative encounters with the female nurse, ranging from aggressively correcting him in front of others, giving contradicting orders to her peers, improperly informing him of changes in patient conditions, and constantly having his clinical skills and decisions challenged. After being reprimanded in front of colleagues, patients and family members, his confidence began to wane. For 18 months, he walked on eggshells at work, started to suffer from headaches, chronic fatigue and bouts of depression.

Finally, his wife gave him an ultimatum: report the situation to his manager, quit his job or go to marital counselling. He chose the former option. The manager attempted to conduct mediation between the parties, but it failed midway, resulting in the female nurse abruptly leaving the session. A few days later, in a hallway alone, the female nurse said to him that in no circumstance would he be telling her what to do, let alone continue working there. She informed him that his "time was up" and firmly stated, "Remember and never forget who has the power on this unit." One of his female colleagues, another registered staff member with whom he was very close, got fed up with the treatment she was receiving by the same nurse and left the organization. Days after her departure, the female nurse started a rumour that he and the nurse who left were having an affair and was thus the reason for the nurse's resignation. The rumour quickly spread through the organization. When some of the staff heard the rumour, they were appalled and decided to "do the right thing" by calling his wife at home and telling her about his infidelity. One evening during his shift, he was confronted by three patients who called him a "pig." The staff had leaked the rumours to the patients.

When he arrived home from work, his wife was in tears at the kitchen table. Since she was eight months pregnant with their third child, he thought her emotional state related to her pregnancy. His wife told him that nothing physical was wrong with her, but she had received a very disturbing phone call earlier in the day from a blocked phone number. The female voice on the other line simply said, "Your husband is not who you think he is. Your husband is screwing one of the other nurses." He told me that after his wife said that, he thought he was going to black out. He told her that it wasn't true. Over the next week, calls to his wife were made several times a day with the same claims about her husband having an affair. He continued to deny the allegation and knew in his heart that the phone calls and accusations were directly linked to the threat from the female nurse in the hallway that day. He went in confidence to his manager to explain the situation and his theory about who was making the calls. Although supportive, the manager told him there was nothing she could do about the situation unless he had concrete proof that his colleague was making or facilitating the calls. A week later, his wife gave birth to their child. At the end of his story, he said to me, "Now what do I do? Do I ignore it and hope it goes away? Do I set up some kind of a sting to prove it is her? Do I put in a complaint to the college and let them deal with the situation?" He said he did not expect me to give him advice, he just wanted his story to be told. I asked him what he meant when he began his story with the statement, "I am glad that I am still here to tell you my story." He explained that he and his wife had been together since high school. During that time, particularly in his teenage years, he was not always faithful to her. The meaning behind his initial statement was that if his wife believed the caller's allegation about an affair, she might have left him and taken his two children and unborn child with her, and if that happened, he would have killed himself. The part that he had the most difficulty understanding was the fact that this female nurse hated him so much because he was a man in a position of power that not only did she want to ruin his career, she wanted to ruin his life. As a side note, I also hold responsible the other individuals who listened to the rumour, spread the rumour and called his wife.

Even business networking websites can pose a risk to women and even men. Professional networking is an extremely important marketing tool. Not only does it provide potential clients with the opportunity to learn about your work and experience, but it enables you to build a list of business contacts. Due to the nature of my work, when I first created a business profile, I was reluctant to post a photograph on my profile. I began seeing posts from women making comments like, "This is not Facebook" and "This is not a dating site." I discovered the meaning behind these posts when I started receiving messages not only through the site but also to my business email such as:

Thank you Denise for connecting back and how are you? Forgive me if I bother you. Your beautiful face and charming smile caught my attention and I could not resist to connect with you. I know this is inappropriate but I hope it does not offend you? Please I would like to know you and be your friend. Take care and have a wonderful day as beautiful as you.

Hello, how are you doing? Well I saw your profile and picture, I will appreciate if you would welcome a hand of friendship as we can talk and know more about our self in honesty. I will appreciate your reply. Thank you.

I suppose one may be flattered by such messages, however, I was not. It got me thinking, are profile pictures really necessary or are they another way to exploit someone? If pictures were not posted, would such messages like the ones above be sent?

A few years ago, there were several tragic cases of female real estate agents who were allegedly contacted by a supposed interested buyer, only to meet the individual at the vacant house and be assaulted and, in some cases, murdered. As a result of these cases, some real estate agencies removed the agent's picture from their advertising signs and business cards. So the question remains: Does a picture of a person make for a better salesperson or will it bring the highest bidder?

Sexual Orientation

Heterosexualism is a common belief and practice that assumes heterosexuality is the only natural and acceptable sexual orientation. We also live in a society that appears to assume heterosexuality as a default for someone's sexual orientation. The Canadian Human Rights Commission does not specifically define the term "sexual orientation." However, the Commission recognizes that sexual orientation is more than simply a "status" that a person possesses; it is an immutable characteristic that forms part of an individual's core identity. This ground encompasses the range of human sexuality from gay and lesbian to bisexual and heterosexual orientations, including intimate emotional and romantic attachments and relationships. "Sexual orientation" is the preferred term over "sexual preference" or "lifestyle choice."

Years ago, I received a request from a new client to conduct a harassment investigation. The scenario presented was that a manager in the organization inappropriately scolded an employee in front of other staff. As per protocol, I received the complaint and other complaint-related documentation. In one document, a manager had made a remark about the complainant, including a comment that was derogatory and generally used when referring to a man's sexual orientation. My client arranged for me to meet the complainant and union representative to conduct a preliminary inquiry. On the day of the interview, the complainant came into the meeting room with a union steward, shook my hand and declared, "Hi, I'm X and I'm gay." The union representative rolled his eyes and said, "Everyone knows that. Like she is really going to think you are straight." After a moment of uncomfortable silence, I said, "Hi, I'm Denise and your sexual orientation is not required or relevant to me unless you tell me differently." For the next 90 minutes, the complainant described his job duties, the history of his relationship with the respondent and the scenario that led to him filing a harassment complaint. During the time he was speaking, not once did he mention his sexual orientation or make any reference to homophobia.

At the end of the interview, I asked the complainant for his opinion regarding why the respondent shouted at him that day. Prior to his response, I was thinking that his answer would be either "Because I am gay" or " Because he is homophobic." However, he said, "Because the owners want to fire all of the full-time workers and just hire contract staff to save and make more money for themselves." As the interview was ending, I asked him one last question: "At the beginning of the interview, you shook my hand and told me that you were gay. Was there any specific reason that you told me that?" With a grin, the complainant said, "I told you that just in case you thought I was cute and wanted to ask me out." Lesson learned: never make assumptions or become biased regardless of the information that is presented to you. The case was substantiated in addition to the derogatory comment made by the manager in the written documentation.

The following is an email I received from a workshop participant who lived in an area of less than 1,000 people:

I have a problem at work that I've never encountered in my life. There have been a couple individuals from work that I've seen out and about in X that have directly implied that I am gay, and I have a real problem with that. Both of these people had been drinking. Both were with a large group of people at the time, most of which I have known, to some extent, for years. One of these groups were coworkers. Anyway, they were calling me a flaming homo, etc. in front of all these people.

I probably don't have to say I'm straight, but I will.

You need to understand I have no idea where these people are drawing this from, so it's very confusing and angering. The main reason I didn't beat them to a pulp at the time was because I didn't know until recently that Bill 168 means you can't physically stand up for yourself when you are in a work setting or function. I know you likely don't like to hear that, but at least I would have been able to walk around and still feel like a man.

I know these types of people probably have developed into their personalities largely based on parental influences and may feel personally inadequate, however that doesn't give them a licence to try to build themselves up by using demeaning language and actions against others. NOT JUST ME, BUT ANYONE!

I go to work these days and get snickers and chuckles from random people at random times for no apparent reason. People routinely look at each other and smile when I enter a room, and if I ask, 'What's so funny?' they just say, 'Nothing.' (Until recently, I tried to ignore it.) It's getting to be almost intolerable at times. I'm always paranoid at work.

I have talked to a counsellor about it, and tried to put myself above these people, however the innuendos are tending to get the best of me. I just recently talked to two union stewards at work about it as well, as I feel like I'm sort of running out of options. I asked them not to mention that I talked to them, but to simply ask people to act more appropriately if they hear of this type of behaviour. I'm pretty sure if people start thinking I'm telling on them, it will likely get worse if anything. This sort of stuff doesn't magically stop outside of work. These same people are in the community around me, and so they can be just as disruptive in my personal life as well, if they so decide.

It should be noted that regardless of a person's sexual orientation, they can file a discrimination case, based on the fact that the respondent is using derogatory slurs based on their assumption of sexual orientation.

Marital Status

Marital status is defined in the Ontario Human Rights Code as "the status of being married, single, widowed, divorced or separated and includes the status of living with a person in a conjugal relationship outside marriage" (that is, in a common-law relationship), including same-sex and opposite-sex relationships.

At the time of writing this book, the term "domestic partner" was the most acceptable term without making any assumptions. However, if an individual uses the terms husband, wife or partner, it is safe to assume that you may also use that term in relation to that specific individual's domestic situation.

Choosing to be single is a choice that an individual can freely make. The questioning of one's marital status is inappropriate and unprofessional in the workplace. However, if someone discloses their status, that is their choice but not an employment requirement or the business of anyone employed there, including management.

An opposite issue of martial status discrimination that is apparent in some workplaces is based on familial favouritism. Some employers have adopted an anti-nepotism policy, which prohibits spouses from working together or supervising each other. There is an assumption that these policies include all types of partnerships, including same-sex and common-law relationships. Scenarios that I have encountered in my work regarding domestic partners working together tend to exist in more rural areas. Family-run businesses and small-town business owners often have generations of families working for the same employer. If the rules and expectations are clear, challenges in the workplace between family members can be minimized. What tends to make situations more difficult for employers is when private family matters cross over into the work environment. Seldom does a situation that occurs behind closed doors stay behind closed doors. Oftentimes, rules are bent or broken when family members have a dispute that is either work-related or on a personal level. Familial or personal relationships in the workplace can be complicated and difficult to negotiate. One of my cases involved a complainant who was the ex-partner of the union president. The respondent was currently dating the union president, who was the sister-in-law of one of the managers.

How does an employer discipline and expect confidentiality to be upheld when employees live in the same house and sleep in the same bed? Can the consequences for a breach of confidentiality really be enforced when it is a case of "pillow talk"? Do employees with a domestic partner who is employed somewhere else face the same consequences when they go home from work and disclose organizational secrets or confidential information? Is sharing information about the company to a domestic partner who is not employed by the same employer exempt from the rules?

Gender Identity or Expression

Fortunately, the issue of gender identity and expression is slowly becoming less of a social issue, however, many individuals struggle daily with being accepted in the world, let alone the workplace, as themselves. Gender stereotypes are still pervasive in our society, although some industries are attempting to address this issue head on through public advertisements, internal policies and job advertisements.

The following definitions from the Ontario Human Rights Code are accepted according to the Canadian Human Rights Act, although each jurisdiction should be referred to for a relevant definition.

Gender identity: "Each person's internal and individual experience of gender. It is a person's sense of being a woman, a man, both, neither, or anywhere along the gender spectrum. A person's gender identity may be the same as or different from their birth-assigned sex."

Gender expression: "How a person publicly expresses or presents their gender. This can include behaviour and outward appearance such as dress, hair, make-up, body language and voice. A person's chosen name and pronoun are also common ways of expressing gender."

Trans or transgender: "An umbrella term referring to people with diverse gender identities and expressions that differ from stereotypical gender norms. It includes but is not limited to people who identify as transgender, trans woman (male-to-female), trans man (female-to-male), transsexual, cross-dressers, or gender non-conforming, gender variant or gender-queer."

Gender non-conforming: "Individuals [who] do not follow gender stereotypes based on the sex they were assigned at birth and may or may not identify as trans."

In recent years, I have been contacted more frequently about gender issues in relation to alleged discrimination and harassment.

Vernā Myers, an inclusion strategist, says, "Diversity is being invited to the party. Inclusion is being asked to dance." Preferred terms change and evolve over time. Workplaces are generally becoming more familiar and understanding of the importance of using inclusive language, although they still have a long way to go in adopting it in all areas of the workplace. Common language is not neutral, and it is tied to the culture and society in which it is used. On the other hand, inclusive speech/vocabulary and writing is respectful to all communities, by eliminating any racist or sexist language and avoiding stereotyping. Employers need to ensure that gender-neutral terms are not only used in everyday communications, but also reflected in the language and images used in policies, procedures, signage and written documentation. The pronouns "he" and "she" are being phased out and replaced with "they." Moreover, terms that demonstrate gender bias in a profession should be avoided. I find it interesting in the health-care world that managers will refer to "my girls" when discussing their staff and in the trades they tend to call them "the guys." In my experience, in both of those staffing groups, members of the opposite sex are also working in that field and, in most cases, within the department to which is being referred.

In training sessions when the discussion shifts to the critical need for individuals to be conscious of their language, I sometimes see eyes roll or smirks on people's faces. Statements such as, "We need to stop being politically correct all the time," or "People are so oversensitive," are commonplace. Gender-neutral language and inclusivity has nothing to do with political correctness or sensitivity, but all to do with treating everyone with dignity and respect. One must remember that the power of words lies in how they are received.

Descriptors of an individual are unnecessary unless they are relevant to the conversation. For instance, when a new employee is hired, it is not necessary to comment on the colour of their skin or their religion. However, the new employee's second language may be relevant to the discussion if it is an important aspect of their job, such as serving clients who speak that language.

A few years ago, I was invited to speak alongside a diversity expert to an organization that requested some education on how to attract females to their field and, more importantly, retain them. What brought this on was the revelation by a number of females in their exit interviews that they often felt ostracized from the majority of the leadership group, who were males, who used the term "guys" or "fellows" and had clients who refused assistance from a woman and requested a man when they came to do a job. The group of women felt that they were indirectly targeted and not treated as equals to their male counterparts. The dialogue that was stimulated in this group was challenging and allowed the participants to process some of their bias and unconscious assumptions.

Hiring must be completely free of bias in relation to the candidate's gender, sexual orientation, age, race, religion and other personal characteristics. The exception to this practice occurs when those characteristics are relevant to the job description.

An effective hiring process established in the 1950s involved blind auditions rather than having symphony orchestra conductors handpick their musicians. This helped to reduce sex-biased hiring and improve female musicians' likelihood of advancing out of the preliminary rounds. A screen was used to conceal the candidates from the judges, which produced the following results:

- Female musicians advanced to the next round by an additional 11%.
- During the final round, blind auditions increased the likelihood of female musicians being selected by 30%.
- According to analysis using roster data, the transition to blind auditions from 1970 to the 1990s caused a 30% increase in the number of females among new hires and contributed to a 25% increase in females in the orchestras.

This method is now the basic concept behind the current talent search TV show *The Voice* whereby contestants are provided with an equal chance during the blind audition component of the show. The judges are forced to base their analysis of the individual's vocal talent by using only their sense of hearing as opposed to visually seeing the person's appearance and physical characteristics. However, this selection process is only used for the first round of judging. Following this, both judges and audiences critique not only the individual's voice but also their appearance and style.

Harvard Business Review found that if a final candidate pool had only one minority, there was virtually no chance of the minority being hired. However, if there were at least two females in the pool, the odds of hiring one of them was 79 times greater. When it came to race, if there were at least two minority candidates in the pool, the odds of hiring a minority candidate was nearly 194 times greater. This is referred to as the "get two in the pool effect."

A useful resource for all job recruiters or hiring managers is a gender decoder for job ads, which can be found at gender-decoder.katmatfield.com.

Family Status

"Family status" is defined in the Ontario Human Rights Code as "being in a parent and child relationship." Men and women are equally protected under this ground. The ground of family status protects non-biological parent and child relationships, such as families formed through adoption, stepparent relationships, foster families, non-biological gay and lesbian parents, and all persons in a parent-and-child-type relationship.

The ground of family status also includes care relationships between adult children and people who stand in parental relationships to them. The protection extends to persons providing eldercare for aging parents or others in a parent-type relationship with the caregiver.

It seems that the ground of family status does not receive the same respect when breached as some of the other grounds, such as race, religion and sexual orientation. A common infraction based on family status that regularly occurs in the workplace involves weekends and holidays. The statement, "You should work this weekend [or on a specific holiday], you don't have kids," is frequently made. A participant in one of my training sessions revealed that the organization in which she works has an unwritten practice that vacation requests for the week of March break will only be considered if the person requesting the time off has children under the age of 16. Employees with either no children or children over the age 16 would not have their vacation requests for that timeframe considered. When I heard about this practice, I wondered how it would have been perceived, internally or externally, if it had pertained to a certain race, sexual orientation or religion? Would a human rights complaint or grievance be threatened or filed? What would be the outcome of such a practice? Family status is seen as equally important under the Canadian Human Rights Act, but often employers or employees don't treat it as such.

As with marital status, choosing to be childless is also an option and a conscious choice. Moreover, it can be a very private matter involving infertility and miscarriages. In one case, a woman's co-workers repeatedly commented about the fact that she did not have children. Little did they know that she had suffered three miscarriages in less than two years.

Another issue that has surfaced in the past few years is how organizations are (or are not) addressing changes in the traditional nuclear family. Increasingly, we are seeing lifestyles where individuals are having more than one partnership in their lifetime, which may bring with it step-children, step-parents, step-grandchildren and step-grandparents.

This issue was highlighted in one harassment complaint in which I was involved whereby the complainant felt that their employer was discriminating against their family status. Apparently, two of their biological grandfathers had died in the past year and when they requested time off for a third grandparent, their request was denied and they filed a discrimination grievance. Realistically what, if any, limit should be put on the amount of bereavement leave an employee can take, while honouring the family status and still running a business?

Genetic Characteristics

In 2017, the Canadian Human Rights Commission listed "genetic characteristics" as a prohibited ground to discrimination, but it does not provide a specific definition. The Canadian Coalition for Genetic Fairness states that "genetic discrimination occurs when people are treated unfairly because of actual or perceived differences in their genetic information that may cause or increase the risk to develop a disorder or disease." Moreover, this prevents employers from using genetic testing information to either hire, promote or terminate employees. According to the Government of Canada, in a survey conducted in 2003, approximately 90 percent of Canadians felt that insurance companies and employers should not have access to genetic information. As a relatively new prohibited ground, to date there has been a limited amount of cases filed and open to public review.

In recent years, there have been discussions regarding an employer's right to choose not to hire a smoker. The rationale presented is that employees who smoke will incur increased health costs for which the employer must pay. Individuals who choose to smoke are not considered a "protected" class. According to Forbes, this recently resulted in the company U-Haul announcing that they will no longer hire smokers in states where this is legal. This practice is viewed by some as "lifestyle discrimination."

Disability

The definition of disability is very broad. It includes any degree of physical, developmental, mental or learning disability. The disability could be present from birth, develop over time or be caused by an accident.

Throughout the years of conducting investigations, I have been exposed to cases whereby the complainant had a physical or mental temporary or permanent disability that was either common knowledge in the workplace or only shared with a certain number of people. Moreover, there have been a number of cases whereby an employee was injured at work and took time off to recover, only to come back weeks or months later on a work hardening program or under accommodation. Many complainants have tearfully told me that since coming back to work after an injury or illness, they have been bullied by their peers, called "a faker" or told that they are "riding the system" so they don't have to work as hard as others. I have found that most employees want to return to work and make a living to support their family. At the time of making the complaint, they have not only had to deal with their initial physical or mental health issue, but are now having to deal with being berated and forced to defend themselves at work.

One complainant told me that after returning to work following a workplace injury, they were accused by their peers of continuing to fake their injury because they had a "hot" caseworker. As a direct consequence of being ridiculed at work, many complainants go against their doctor's orders and end up further injuring themselves by pushing their limits and then need to take time off work a second time.

Unfortunately, some individuals with permanent, lifelong physical disabilities are also not spared from bullying. For months I was involved in a case of a young person who had a hearing impairment and was openly mimicked at work regarding how they spoke. In addition to being mocked, they also had to contend with a secret contest (that they learned of later) whereby some of the staff had an ongoing bet about who could get physically closest to them before they noticed them sneaking up on them. They were forced to always be on high alert to avoid being frightened at work. Apparently double points were given to employees who could make them jump or yelp when startled.

Employees experiencing acute or chronic mental illness can sometimes have even more difficulty in the workplace. The general public seems to be much more compassionate towards someone with a broken arm than someone dealing with a mental illness. Although society has come a long way in regard to acknowledging the importance of providing support for mental health, unfortunately there is still a negative stigma attached when a diagnosis is revealed or even suspected.

A case that particularly stands out for me is one whereby the complainant had recently been diagnosed with a mental condition. Although he had been struggling for years with physical symptoms, the mental diagnosis was not initially revealed. To feel supported at work, he disclosed his recent diagnosis to a few close colleagues. He also asked them to let him know if they noticed anything about his behaviour that seemed off or out of character so that he could monitor his reaction to his newly prescribed medication. A few weeks later, a peer who was not originally told, informed him that one of his confidants was telling others about his mental health issue. Infuriated, he confronted his confidant about the breach of confidentiality who denied the accusations and tried to blame someone else for spreading the information. During a meeting shortly thereafter, when the complainant disagreed with the manager about an interpretation of a policy decision, he overheard a colleague whisper, "I guess he didn't take his medication today." Over the next few months, an increasing number of staff became aware of his mental health condition and inappropriate comments were made more openly and frequently. The complainant began having panic attacks prior to coming into work, was unable to eat and started experiencing migraine headaches. Three months later, he went off work on a stress leave.

Conviction for an offence for which a pardon has been granted or in respect of which a record suspension has been ordered

According to the Canadian Human Rights Commission, a person cannot be discriminated against in employment because of a "record of offences," which is defined in the Ontario Human Rights Code to mean a conviction for:

1. "an offence in respect of which a pardon has been granted under the Criminal Records Act (Canada) and has not been revoked, or
2. an offence in respect of any provincial enactment."

Consider this scenario: A 36-year-old woman applies for a job as a receptionist at a sign company whose clientele is both individuals and small businesses. Customers can order products online or come into the office to have work customized by a graphic artist. At the time of her second interview, she discloses to the three-person committee that she has had two impaired driving charges: one 15 years prior and the second one nine years ago. As the job did not require a driver's licence, which she possessed, or to drive a vehicle, she did not think it would be an issue, however, she wished to begin her potentially new job with a clean slate and clear conscience. One of the committee members thanked her for her honesty and indicated that her previous driving charges were irrelevant to the position to which she applied.

Since she was the best candidate, she was offered the job, however, she was informed that she would be placed on a six-month probation period as opposed to the standard practice of three months. When she queried as to why a different practice was being applied to her, her new manager told her "off the record" that senior management wanted to ensure that she "wasn't a drunk" or "planned on coming into work hammered." The new hire was very insulted by the comments and greatly regretted having revealed a part of her past that was unnecessary. She chose not to address the issue on any level.

Approximately six weeks after she commenced her job, there was a non-work-related after-hours get-together with staff at a local pub to watch a sporting event. Although sports were of no interest to her, she felt it was important she attend to build comradery. After work, she went home to change her clothes and then took a taxi to the bar. More than a dozen people from work along with some of their partners attended.

The following day, when she arrived at work, a group of staff was standing by her desk in deep conversation. They immediately stopped talking when she walked in, muttered hello and walked away. Over the course of the next few days, the staff treated her differently than the previous weeks. She had a feeling that they were talking about her behind her back. The following day, she went into her manager's office and asked what was going on and why there was a sudden change in how she was being treated. After a bit of hesitation, her boss told her that a hiring committee member had observed the fact that she had taken a cab to the bar and made an assumption that she did not actually have a licence and was therefore deceitful during the job application process. To complicate matters, this individual had several close friendships within the organization and most likely shared their opinion with someone else, who then spoke to others.

She was very upset by the false accusations and being the topic of discussion. The following week, she arranged a meeting with her manager and informed them that if the gossip did not stop, she intended to file a formal complaint with human resources. That Friday at 4 p.m., while still on probation, she was called into human resources and let go from her position. She was told that the company decided to have co-op students from the local college do their placements at the front desk and fill the role of reception, therefore her position was no longer necessary. She was then escorted by security to her car.

She is currently unemployed and considering taking legal action against her former employer for discrimination based on a prior criminal conviction. Does she have a case?

During a training session, when discussing the issue of discrimination related to a criminal record, a man put up his hand and asked me, "Do you know what is worse than a thief? Way, way worse than a thief?" I responded that I did not know and he said, "An innocent thief, because once you get that stain on your clothes nothing will ever get it out."

Upon completion of the session, the man approached me and apologized if his comment was disrespectful or out of line. I told him that his question, as with all questions, are fine with me. He then provided me with the context to his comment. Apparently when he was hired, his ex-girlfriend's best friend was also working at the same company. Since he and his ex-girlfriend had gone through a bad breakup as a result of him cheating, the best friend took it upon herself to start a rumour that he was fired from his last place of employment for stealing. He reassured me that he had never stolen anything in his life. He then told me that he was quitting his job. The rumour had gotten the best of him and he felt his reputation was damaged and would continue to further erode if he stayed with the organization. His takeaway for me was that it did not matter if you did or did not break the law; when someone is intent on making others believe it is the truth then it is a difficult situation to overcome.

In both scenarios above, although not proven internally or in court, each case may potentially be a case of defamation. Defamation law may vary by jurisdiction, however, it is subdivided into two areas:

- Libel: defamation with a permanent record, such as an email, a radio or TV broadcast, a newspaper, a website posting, etc.
- Slander: defamation with no permanent record, such as a spoken statement or even a hand gesture.

To prove defamation of character, the complainant must first be able to prove that the accusation made against them is untrue. Secondly, they must be able to demonstrate that the misinformation or untruth has directly influenced or had a negative effect on their personal and/or professional lives. If those untruths spread to other future employers, the complainant would have a more difficult time trying to obtain and maintain employment.

One successful defamation case involved a Halifax, Nova Scotia woman who was awarded $52,000 in damages in 2016 based on a false accusation. In 2012, the complainant had enrolled in a policing program that required a firearm's licence. During the course of processing the application, the Department of Justice employee assigned to the case discovered that the complainant had previously worked at a Tim Hortons and during her employment, the coffee shop was the target of an armed robbery.

After reviewing the case, the Department of Justice employee was not convinced that the employee gave an honest version of events to the police at the time. As a result of this speculation, the department staff told both the college and the complainant's current employer that she was actually a suspect in the crime. Due to this false accusation, the complainant sued. Just prior to the case going to trial, the respondent admitted that the statements were false and they had breached privacy. The confession resulted in general, punitive and special damages being rewarded.

What Appears to Be Missing in the Human Rights Code

Size and Appearance

Growing up as a female, it quickly became apparent that the size of a girl's body seemed to be everyone's business. I vividly remember three girls my age in elementary school who were terribly bullied from kindergarten to grade six. All three of these girls were heavier than the rest of us. Somehow, children aged six and seven believed that larger kids were less important and unworthy of their friendship. One of the girls was also from the low-income neighbourhood. She spent most of recess sitting on a little wall by herself trying to defend herself from the cruel words of her schoolmates. I felt terrible about how she was being treated and somehow took on the role of her protector. I would sit beside her and try to keep the other kids away from her. I didn't understand why they were so mean to her when she did not do anything to bother or offend anyone.

In high school, the issue of appearance was further magnified, particularly for the girls who physically matured faster or slower than the others. The size of a girl's body—particularly the size of her chest—seemed to be a factor in her level of popularity with both boys and girls. At the time, I thought it was just a part of growing up and once I was out of high school, mental maturity would kick in and appearance would take on a less prominent role in friendships and work relationships. I quickly learned that was not the case.

Throughout my career, I have been mortified by the way that women gang up on each other and attack the one thing most women feel insecure about, which is the size of their body. In female-dominated workplaces, the "F" word gets used every day. Women call each other "fat," cows and pigs; words directed at another woman to hurt her. The number of women who have suffered from an eating disorder is off the charts. Boys and young men also have body image issues.

According to the National Initiative for Eating Disorders, in a Manitoba study from 2003 to 2005 of 565 10- to 11-year-old boys and girls, 12 percent of both boys and girls reported dieting to lose weight in the past year. Moreover, in a Nova Scotia sample in the same time period of 247 girls and boys in grades 6, 7 and 8, 24 percent of the boys in grade 6 compared to 14 percent of the girls were attempting to lose weight.

According to a February 2019 article in the World Economic Forum, "Obese workers often have lower starting pay and less hiring success—45% of employers say they are less inclined to recruit obese candidates. They are less likely to be regarded as able leaders or to have career potential, are more likely to experience bullying and harassment, and obese women are less likely to get customer-facing jobs."

It appears that weight loss is celebrated regardless of the reason for the loss. Without thinking it through, people are quick to say to someone, "Wow, you look great! You've lost so much weight." Perhaps this person is terminally ill. This comment would not be so obviously biased to the perception of what is considered an ideal body image if people also said, "Wow, you look great! You've gained so much weight."

Although clothing and grooming is included in the Ontario Human Rights Code under race, this can only be applied if the clothing or grooming is specific to the individual's racial background. Traditional clothes or regalia, in addition to grooming practices such as growing a beard, are sometimes predispositions to being bullied not only in the workplace but also on the streets. Some people will attack the size of someone's body, the shape of their nose, their teeth, ears, hairstyle, etc.

On *Britain's Got Talent* in 2009, millions of people watched in awe as British singer Susan Boyle hit the stage and sang "I Dreamed a Dream." Audience members and people around their televisions snickered and rolled their eyes as the 47-year-old took the stage. No one expected that when she opened her mouth, the voice of an angel would come out. Although shocked in the moment, the audience soon surrounded her with cheers and gave a standing ovation as she completed her audition. Little did Susan know that within hours, the media would feature her story on all major platforms. To my dismay, the coverage did not focus on her immense talent but rather on her hair, body size and communication style. How deeply disappointing; her talent was secondary to her physical attributes. Nicci Gerrard, a reporter for *The Telegraph*, summed it up perfectly: "Happiness doesn't come in the slip-stream of instant fame. There are no magic wands in life, and the story of Susan Boyle, which was sold to us as a fairytale come true, now reads like a lesson in sadness and shame. Her sadness and our shame."

Body Art

Over the past decade, body art (art made on, with or consisting of the human body) is becoming more prevalent in our society as a means of personal expression. The most common forms of this type of art are piercings and tattoos. Commemorative or memorial tattoos are also becoming part of mainstream culture as a way of expressing love or creating a permanent honorarium of a loved one. Ash tattoos (using one's cremated ashes mixed with ink) are also becoming more popular. An increasing number of people are opting to alter their bodies with procedures like plastic surgery, branding, subdermal implants, permanent make-up and aesthetic dentistry. There are also forms of self-expression considered by some to be more extreme, such as body shaping, i.e., waist or corset training, and mutilation, i.e., inserting metal spikes into the skull.

Employers must consider that tattoos and piercings are not only a personal choice but may also be a cultural tradition or hold some significance in countries like Samoa or India, or carry a religious meaning such as with Buddhism. If an employee has a cultural tattoo or piercing on a visible part of their body and another employee has a commemorative tattoo on a visible part of their body, should one, both or neither be asked by the employer to cover it up or take it out (such as an eyebrow piercing)?

In my work in long-term care, I have worked in many facilities that had residents who are Holocaust survivors. The mental, emotional and physical scars that those individuals have carried for decades never fade. I have been involved in cases where older adults, particularly those suffering from dementia, are triggered by a number of things, such as fire alarms, uniforms and the presence of a child's birth date tattooed on the wrist of a staff member. In those situations, some staff have been asked by management to cover their tattoo when providing care to that specific client so as to not cause any further turmoil to that client. As a result, some staff members have filed complaints against their employer arguing that the employer is disrespecting the employee's freedom of expression. So, the question remains, who is the judge of what is acceptable and what is unacceptable when it comes to someone's body—the employee or the employer?

Education

In most workplaces, there is a wide range of education levels not only between management and frontline staff, but also among peers. In many instances, employees have climbed up the corporate ladder in a seamless fashion. Nowadays, individuals are often required to take courses and earn certificates to keep the positions they have held for decades, let alone be considered for a new job or advancement. Although some employees may be grandfathered into a job and therefore not required to meet the present-day educational expectations, they are still at a disadvantage when working with or for someone who has higher credentials. In some cases, labourers have more education than the people to whom they report.

Technology has further complicated the issue, especially with the introduction of email and new software. Green organizations are being encouraged to go paperless regardless of the staff composition. For some employees, staying current and on top of new technology is not an easy feat. Oftentimes, there is an expectation that individuals will grow with the company and expand their skills and knowledge without customized training or education being offered to assist in the process. In addition, some individuals do not possess personal computer devices or cellphones due to their preference or financial constraints.

Unfortunately, these factors and the varying learning curve experienced by some employees could lead to a negative, toxic or bullying culture within the organization.

Employment Status

The tension between part-time and full-time employees seems to be present in some organizations. The term "part-timer" or "full-timer" are often used to refer to specific employees rather than being addressed by their names. The tendency for one group to blame the other for incomplete or incorrect work is commonplace in some organizations.

In one particular organization, there was unhealthy tension between the staff who worked full time and those who worked part time. At the end of an intense intervention, one of the tangible outcomes was a written commitment agreement between the two groups. The agreement included an expectation whereby the employment status of a person would not be referred to unless it was in context with what was being said or done. In all other cases, proper names were to be used.

I have also handled many cases whereby a full-time staff member has submitted a harassment complaint against a part-time employee stating that the respondent was attempting to harass the complainant to the point of quitting to secure their full-time position. I have observed this dynamic more often in rural areas since jobs are scarcer and employment opportunities generally only become available once someone retires or dies. In those areas, it is not uncommon for individuals to work for the same employer for more than 30 years, often starting as a student, then working part time and eventually becoming a full-time employee.

Agency or temporary staff also face harassment on a regular basis. Without proper training, they are often blamed for errors or incomplete work. I have had numerous complaints by these individuals who state that the disrespect and incivility they were subjected to resulted in refusing work requests from some companies, directly affecting their ability to make an adequate living to support their families and lifestyle choices.

In the end, anti-black, anti-female, and all forms of discrimination are equivalent to the same thing — anti-humanism.
~ Shirley Chisholm ~

Workplace Bullying

The term bullying is often associated with children and can have different meanings. On one hand, it is a very serious public phenomenon that is deeply and negatively affecting our younger population. It seems as though every day we are hearing around the dinner table or on the evening news, stories of children or youths taking their own lives as a result of being bullied and tormented in schoolyards, on the school bus or on social media. Parents may or may not see signs that their child is suffering as they silently carry the burden of being tormented by another child or group.

In 2012, a New Brunswick school district was the first in Canada to assign a full-time staff person to 'protect' a 12-year-old boy from being bullied for being overweight and gay. Unfortunately, that decision ended up further isolating the boy and causing more torment as his bullies then targeted him for being "babysat". As reported by the *National Post*, the boy said, "I don't really like it because I'm losing a lot of friends because she's there. She has to know whatever anybody tells me or whatever I say. I can't keep anything from her."

Shari-Ann Selvey was aware of her son's torment from the beginning. On October 7, 2019, 14-year-old Devan Bracci-Selvey was fatally stabbed outside his Hamilton, Ontario high school. Devan had been the subject of bullying since the second day of school. He was jumped and chased by a gang of older kids and his bike was stolen. The school was aware of the situation and his mother had been actively attempting to get a proactive response from school officials. The school board and the police both admitted they were notified of the bullying prior to the boy's death.

On the day of his murder, Devan called his mother to come pick him up from school after he saw one of his bullies, who was on suspension, inside the school. When his mother drove up to the school, she attempted to physically pull Devan into the car when the murderer stabbed him in the back. Devan died in his mother's arms. Two teenage brothers, aged 14 and 18, were charged.

A participant in one of my bullying training sessions tearfully told me that her 21-year-old son was bullied relentlessly as a child from elementary school to high school. She told me that her son was "mortally wounded" as a result of this childhood trauma. Her son had been in therapy since he was eight years old and she believes her son did not "amount to who he could have been" or possess the confidence he needs to "really make it in this world" because of being emotionally "tortured."

Another participant told me that her 10-year-old son had been in and out of psychiatric hospitals for the past three years for cutting himself as a way of trying to cope with the name-calling he was experiencing during recess.

One woman disclosed to me that a few years prior she was looking after her niece and nephew for a week while her sister was on a business trip. One night she left work at 11 p.m. and went to her sister's house where she discovered her 17-year-old nephew hanging in the basement. The note she found beside his body described his bullying experience and how he could not withstand another day of torment.

Over the past few years, it has been noted in obituaries of young people who commit suicide that the parents are opting to disclose that information publicly. Furthermore, they are openly using the word bullying and identifying their child's tormentor(s). It appears that these families want to open the discussion around bullying and suicide and place it in the lap of the perpetrators.

The following is an excerpt from a Pennsylvania teenager's obituary:

Miss Sadie L. Riggs, 15, of Bedford, took her own life on Monday, June 19th, 2017. … In an effort to debunk the rumors about Sadie's death we would like to share this information. Yes, Sadie took her own life, she hung herself. It is hard to fathom that someone so young could be so troubled.

Sadie was seeking help, she was in counselling and taking medication, but it was all too much for such a young soul to live with. If you take a minute and look at Sadie's family dynamics you will see that a large percent of the people in her life were not related to her by blood but she was sent to us by God who knew this child needed a family. Sadie had a tough life and until a recent incident at school she handled everything life served her. For a young lady so excited about going to the High School things sure went terribly wrong for her. For the bullies involved, please know you were effective in making her feel worthless. That is all between you and God now, but please know that it is not to[o] late to change your ways. Sadie's death has taken us to dark places, we will stick together and protect one another as we try to make sense of this tragic loss. To all the bullies out there, I just want you to know that as much as we despise your actions never, ever do we wish for you to feel the paralyzing pain that engulfs our bodies, a pain so severe that it makes the simple act of breathing difficult or the guilt that leaves us wondering what we could have done differently-or that struggle to remember the last words we spoke…Our hearts are beyond broken. Sadie, it was a privilege to have you in our lives and we will always love you. May you find peace in the arms of God and may we all be kind to one another. In lieu of flowers, the family of Sadie ask that you be kind to one another.

Some will argue that suicide is a selfish act whereas others believe it is a selfless act. When a suicide has occurred, the issue of mental illness is often used as a foregone conclusion. My question is and will always remain: What happened first, the mental health issue and then the bullying or the bullying and then the mental health issue?

We live in a world where people are labelled by their appearance; whether they are tall, dark-haired, light-skinned, big-nosed, etc. People can also be labelled by their personality traits; stubborn, lazy, arrogant, unpleasant, etc. Oftentimes, labels are used negatively. Rarely are labels used to compliment someone's personality; saying someone is nice, generous, thoughtful, etc. This may just be a realistic reflection of how our world has evolved.

Against my better judgment, I am going to provide a few labels that will guide the reader and provide clarity on the scenarios and stories that are shared in this book.

The definition of a bully can be extremely subjective. What one person perceives as a bully or a bullying behaviour can be completely different from another who observes or experiences the same behaviour. For the purpose of this book, I will be using the following definitions:

Bully: A person who habitually seeks to harm or intimidate another person directly or indirectly.

Target: A person who is the focus of a bully's attention. An individual who is "bullied." Sometimes referred to as a "victim" of bullying.

Bystander: A person who is present at an event or incident but does not take part.

Generally, when I am asked to conduct workplace bullying education or training for staff, it is either a proactive approach to teach the staff how to recognize and effectively deal with future incidents of bullying or a reactive session due to a past event, such as a termination because of bullying, an investigation or a high number of complaints being filed with human resources. If it is a reactive reason for the mandatory education, the staff are generally aware of the reason for the session because it was a high-profile case or it involved several parties. Prior to conducting any sessions with frontline staff, I recommend and conduct a seven-hour session for the management team. This full day allows the leadership team to become educated on legislation in addition to employer obligations and accountability. It also provides an opportunity for management to ask questions and explore case scenarios that they would not necessarily discuss in front of staff. Once this critical leadership session has taken place, I recommend to management that I meet alone with the staff to create a safe space to ask questions without management present. Theoretically there is freedom to have an open, confidential dialogue. I emphasize that the purpose of the session is not to vent about management. Moreover, I state that no case examples can be discussed during the session if the case in question is in the process of being investigated. The session remains confidential and I do not inform management of who said what or the specific content of the discussion. The exception to this rule is if I feel someone is a threat to themselves or others, then I immediately stop the session and alert management about my concern.

In one session on workplace bullying, I quickly felt the hostility in the room. To my knowledge, the session was planned as a proactive approach to provide staff with the tools to deal with the unfortunate reality that bullying can arise in the workplace. Seeing that there were no managers in the room (as per my request), I stopped and said to the group, "I am not sure what is happening here, but I can sense a lot of tension in the room." The room was silent for a minute and then a loud voice from the back said, "If no one else is going to talk, I'll tell her." This statement was met with more silence. So the person at the back of the room went on to explain: "We have all been talking about this session since we heard that we were mandated to be here. We don't understand why management would be so disrespectful to us and make us sit in a room for three hours and have someone present to us a subject intended for schoolkids; a session that they clearly don't think is relevant since none of them are being forced to sit here like we are." In response to that comment, I first stated that unfortunately the topic of bullying is not only applicable to young people but has recently been more openly discussed in the workplace and through various media platforms. I also informed the group that as far as I knew, I was simply there to present on an important topic. After fielding several questions from the group, there were a few internal questions that I could not answer so I excused myself from the session and proceeded to get the HR manager to come and speak to the group. I knew from experience that if the questions were not answered thoroughly to appease the audience at the beginning, my session and teaching would be discounted or ignored. The HR manager spent approximately 15 minutes providing the rationale behind the session and answering any follow-up questions. Once the manager left, I was freely able to present the information.

The participants' evaluations were positive and many staff wrote comments about how impressive it was that the manager took the time to explain to them why the sessions were necessary. Collectively they felt that they were communicated to in a respectful and transparent manner. My takeaway from that session was that never again would I do an introduction to a session as an outsider. Since then, I arrange with my clients for a member of the leadership team to attend the first 15 minutes of the session to explain the reason for the session, inform them of management's separate session, thank the staff for attending and answer any internal questions posed. Now the sessions run effectively and the transparency of management—even when it is explained that the session is a result of a negative situation—is greatly appreciated by the staff.

Another aspect that contributes to the success of a session is the setup of the room. To create a welcoming and non-intimidating space, I ask for the room to be set up in a U-shape with tables and chairs, if possible. Although it may sound like a moot point, in a session on bullying, rows are not conducive to a friendly, open environment. With a theatre-style layout, I can identify the targets of bullying right away. Oftentimes these individuals arrive early and alone to the session, scan the room for seating options and sit in the back row closest to the door. This way they can leave the room at any time without bringing attention to themselves. This strategic seating arrangement makes sense if you imagine being a target of bullying and having to sit in a row in front of your bullies, unable to see or hear what may be said behind your back throughout the session. Three hours of anxiety and paranoia with no means of escape is cause for many targets to skip the session or leave early. However, there have also been sessions where the target of bullying has sat as close to me as they can at the front of the room as if I could protect them from anything further happening to them.

Despite serious and devastating consequences of bullying, the term bullying is often used as a joke word. When I'm setting up training sessions, I often hear people make comments like, "You're a bully, you took my chair," or "You're a bully, you didn't bring me a coffee." These statements are usually followed by laughter. I do not say anything at the time, but I use the interaction as a teaching moment. I inform participants that although it is viewed as harmless banter, they should never use the term bully, particularly in the workplace, as a joke word.

One reason is that in many jurisdictions the term bullying is now recognized as a health and safety issue by governing bodies. So if the word is used incorrectly or as a form of humour, the employer may be legally obligated to conduct a formal investigation into the allegation of bullying. The other reason is that the word bullying should be seen as a powerful and serious term. If the word is repeatedly misused in the workplace and individuals call the other person a bully every time they disagree with each other, the word will lose its true meaning and power. This may result in a situation where the real targets of bullying are not taken seriously. This will ultimately saturate the word and allow workplace bullies to roam free within the organization with no fear of being investigated or sanctioned.

Koster Consulting & Associates—Workplace Bullying Study

What is the prevalence of bullying in the workplace? In my experience, people are often unaware that bullying is going on in their organization until they come to an education session on workplace incivility, harassment or bullying, or read a related article.

Over a two-year period, I conducted 2,500 individual surveys at a number of workplaces at their request. The survey results revealed to the client where the organization stood on the issue of workplace bullying.

The survey methodology was as follows: all staff members (frontline and management) who were presently working during the period of time the workplace bullying survey was conducted (with the exception of those individuals on a leave of absence or vacation) were requested to attend a mandatory seven-hour (for management staff) or three-hour (for frontline staff) education session on workplace violence.

The educational sessions were to provide employees with an opportunity to:

- Increase awareness of the differences between interpersonal conflicts, discrimination, harassment and bullying in the workplace
- Explore in depth the issue of workplace bullying and the effect on both an organizational and personal level
- Relate the issues presented to their own experiences through participating in self-reflection exercises
- Question assumptions, patterns of behaviours and workplace culture
- Increase a sense of empowerment when being bullied or witnessing inappropriate behaviour in the workplace
- Become aware of avenues for assistance

For the purposes of the education session and survey, workplace bullying (to be discussed in detail later in the chapter) is defined as: "a repeated pattern of intentional inappropriate behaviour, direct or indirect (aggressive or passive), whether verbal, physical or otherwise, performed by one or more persons against another employee or group of employees, which could reasonably be regarded as undermining the individual's right to dignity at work." (Source:

Code of Practice on the Prevention of Workplace Bullying under the *Safety, Health and Welfare at Work Act*, 1989)

All staff who attended the educational session were encouraged to complete the Bullying in the Workplace survey and time was set aside at the end of each session for survey completion. Clear instructions were provided and employees were offered assistance as required. The completion of the survey was not a requirement and participation was strictly voluntary. In addition, the survey was designed and implemented to ensure that all respondents remain anonymous with no avenues to identify individual respondents. Following the completion of the individual surveys, they were given directly to me for review, data input and report writing. No employees, including management or labour, had access to the individual surveys and only Koster Consulting & Associates personnel viewed the completed surveys.

It is important to acknowledge that the education sessions prior to survey completion were intended to provide accurate definitions and concrete examples of workplace bullying.

Survey Results

The survey uncovered that 29% of the 2,500 participants had experienced bullying in the previous six months and an additional 103 participants said they were "unsure" if they had.

The participants who had been bullied in the workplace were asked who the bully was in relation to their position in the workplace. Participants were able to name more than one bully. The top two positions identified included department co-worker (61%) and department manager (19%). Other positions included: member of council, senior administration, other department manager or supervisor, other department co-worker, direct reporting staff, and external parties such as outside service provider or service recipient.

The participants who had experienced bullying were also asked the type of behaviours they had experienced. Participants were able to name more than one behaviour. The top bullying behaviours experienced included: being subjected to the silent treatment (45%), exhibiting uncontrollable mood swings (36%), non-verbal intimidation (36%), falsely accused of errors not made (34%); and rumours or gossip of a personal or professional nature (34%). Other behaviours experienced included: thoughts, feelings and/or input discounted; satisfactory or excellent quality of work disregarded; singled out and/or isolated; verbal aggression; job performance falsely represented; retaliation after a complaint was filed; work and/or work credit stolen by bully; confidential information used to humiliate the target privately or publicly; sabotage; stalking or spying; and discriminatory, condescending or racial words/actions.

The top ways participants were affected by the bullying included: stress and anxiety, decreased confidence, tiredness, constant fatigue, headaches, migraines, decrease productivity at work and decreased self-esteem. Other effects included: sadness/depression; guilt/self-blame; irritability; anger; sleeplessness; nightmares; waking early; digestive/bowel problems; skin problems; poor concentration; increased alcohol, drug or tobacco use; and fantasies of retribution or thoughts of vengeance.

Of the participants who had experienced bullying, 62% indicated at the time of the survey that the bullying was still going on. In addition, of the participants who were still experiencing bullying in the workplace, 38% indicated that the bullying had been going on for more than two years.

The primary responses to the bullying situation included: talking to family/friends; discussing with colleagues; speaking to administration, human resources or management; and, if applicable, consulting with the union.

For those participants who had reported the situation to management, 32% said that action was taken and 20% were unsure if action was taken. Of those participants who indicated that was action taken to deal with the bullying, nearly 70% did not answer the question to indicate whether the action was effective, ineffective or made the situation worse.

The average rating regarding their satisfaction with the organization's response to their situation was 2.5 out of 6.

The survey also uncovered that 46% of participants had witnessed someone else being bullied in the workplace and 5% were unsure. Those participants were asked who the target was in relation to their position in the workplace. Participants were able to name more than one target. Department co-worker was the top target identified by respondents (66%) followed by direct supervisor/manager (15%).

The respondents who had witnessed someone else being bullied in the workplace were asked who the bully was in relation to their position in the workplace. Participants were able to name more than one bully. The top bully identified was department co-worker (67%) followed by direct supervisor/manager (13%).

The respondents who had witnessed someone else being bullied in the workplace were also asked the type of behaviour that they witnessed. Participants were able to name more than one behaviour. These top three behaviours were identified: mood swings, silent treatment and non-verbal intimidation.

Following the survey, specific recommendations and strategic directions were given to each organization based on their survey results. In addition, general recommendations included:

- Members of the human resources department and management team to review and discuss the survey results.
- Relevant parties (i.e., mayor and council, human resources, executive management team, union leaders, health and safety representatives) to participate in a strategic planning session to address the question: "Over the next 18 months, how can the organization continue to ensure a healthy (bully-free) working environment?"

- In order to ensure commitment, respect and transparency in relation to the survey process, all staff should be provided with a summary of the survey and strategic plan.
- Relevant parties to have a dialogue regarding the role of union leaders in the identification and intervention in member-to-member conflicts or inappropriate behaviours in the workplace.
- Ensure that both management and union leaders, if applicable, are actively involved in encouraging and supporting staff to report both internal and external violence/bullying that is both experienced and/or witnessed.
- Assure no reprisals will be made against reporting employees/ parties, and if retaliation occurs, sanction accordingly.
- Offer managers ongoing conflict resolution training for them to continue to monitor behaviours and be proactive in managing existing conflict situations before they escalate into a formal complaint.
- Ensure that all staff are given the appropriate information and training regarding any relevant new or revised workplace violence/bullying or related policies.
- Provide frontline staff who are faced with service recipients the educational opportunity to develop their skills, knowledge and confidence to deal with external people with aggressive and difficult behaviours.
- Offer internal and external resources to enable employees with personal problems or who have experienced workplace bullying to seek help and obtain support.
- Monitor and regularly review the issue of workplace bullying, including resurveying employees in 18 months to determine any trends and if the strategic plans were appropriate and effective.
- Incorporate workplace violence and bullying as a standing item on the following agendas: council, occupational health and safety committee, management team, department meetings, etc.

- Ensure that all relevant policies are applied and communicated to outside service providers, independent contractors and service recipients. Communication should include the organization's view on external and internal bullying, its commitment to the prevention of bullying, internal procedures for investigation and resolving complaints, and the consequences for making threats or committing violent acts on organizational property while conducting business or receiving service.

■

At the end of one education session, a woman came up to me and said, "Up until today, I never thought I could be bullied. As a matter of fact, I felt that in my 55 years I have never been bullied. At work there is one person who I just thought was difficult to work with. I have sporadic bouts of irritable bowel syndrome but I just realized in this session that I have diarrhea only on the days that I work with this person."

When bad or difficult behaviour is discussed, people tend to dismiss it as "interpersonal conflicts" or excuse someone's behaviour by saying, "Oh don't worry about them, they have always been that way." People tend to normalize negative behaviour rather than deal with it. By tolerating negative behaviour and its impact on others and the organization as a whole, it gives the bully additional power and sends a message to others that bad behaviour is acceptable. Unfortunately, some people think that if they ignore a problem long enough, it will eventually go away. This is a myth. Bullying is like a disease; the longer it is ignored and goes unaddressed, the more it spreads and more dangerous it becomes. The danger lies in the disease's ability to infect the entire body and, in some cases, ultimately cause death.

There is no universal standardized definition of workplace bullying. In education sessions, I will often have participants discuss the definitions of a personal conflict, discrimination, harassment and bullying. The exercise is usually more challenging than they anticipate. Groups tend to have the most difficulty differentiating between the definitions of harassment and bullying. Although the Ontario Ministry of Labour includes bullying as a form of harassment, it does not provide a definition for bullying. Over the years, I have reviewed a variety of bullying definitions that organizations have adopted. Within many of these definitions, the terms "power" and "status" are widely used and I have learned over the years that when people hear these terms they think bullies only exist higher up in the hierarchy of the organization. Of course, there are numerous cases where a manager or a person in leadership is a bully but it certainly is not a requirement for bullying. Nearly 70 percent of my case investigations involve peer-to-peer bullying, which can be among labour or management.

In one case, the union membership was split into two opposing groups that both submitted formal complaints about the other side. Individuals in upper management positions are not safeguarded from being targets of bullying. I have had cases where the CEO of a corporation has been bullied by the management team, senior executives have been bullied by union executive members and management leadership have been bullied by government-appointed officials. One executive director told me that when one of her managers enters her office, she has to sit down at her desk so that she can sit on her hands to stop them from shaking.

In some situations, the most junior person in an organization can have the most power. I was involved in a case where a hospital ward clerk was bullying a physician. Most people cannot even begin to imagine how this scenario could be possible. To create a picture of this situation, we first must understand the role of a ward clerk whose job duties include processing patients, completing necessary paperwork and coordinating patient assignments. Primarily, the clerk's role is to ensure the overall efficiency of a health or medical unit. In this particular case, the clerk performed her duties completely differently with her targeted physician than with the other medical professionals. From all accounts, the medical team was extremely impressed with her work ethic, competency and innate abilities to meet their needs without them even articulating them. However, the target did not receive completed paperwork from the clerk in a timely fashion, patient admissions and discharges were improperly communicated to the physician and telephone messages were not recorded or transferred. It appears there was an incident that occurred when they first started working together that set a negative tone for their future business relationship. According to the physician, he had questioned some of her processes and made suggestions on how to be more efficient. As a result of this confrontation, months went by where the physician received no communication from the clerk and thus spent most of his shift trying to figure out what was going on that day and what were the patient priorities. Eventually the physician took a stress leave. The ward clerk denied any wrongdoing suggesting that the physician had unattainable expectations, however, she did say that the physician thought he was "so much smarter" than her just because he had a medical degree.

Another case involved a frontline employee and a manager. There were ongoing performance issues with the employee, including arriving at work late or not coming in at all, not following safety standards and not following the direction of the lead hand. As a result of these issues, the manager began to follow the internal disciplinary process, which included informal counseling to discuss the employee's conduct, attendance and work standards. The staff member was told in detail which work areas needed improvement and was given the opportunity to explain their version of events. In addition, the employee received a written action plan to improve the areas of concern, which was signed by both parties. Following this agreement, the situation did not improve and the employee became increasingly belligerent towards the manager. After a number of unsuccessful attempts, the employee received a two-day work suspension for failure to comply with the signed agreement. Little did the manager or organization know how much power this individual held at the company. On the first day of his suspension, half of the employee's department members called in sick. On the second day, the staff members who were absent returned back to work and the other half called in sick. After interviewing all staff involved, one staff member told the manager in confidence that their peer had physically threatened to harm each one of them if they did not agree to systematically call in sick. The employee who stated this would not put anything in writing and threatened to file a harassment grievance against the manager if he ever questioned him again or disclosed to anyone that he was the one who informed management about the situation. All other employees who were interviewed simply stated that they were sick on the day in question and had the right to call in sick when necessary. As a result of the demonstrated power that the staff member had over his peers, the manager made a conscious decision to stop performance managing him. The manager felt that the work needed to be completed and the customer needs were more important than him exercising his managerial duties. He stated that he "had to pick his battles" and disciplining that particular employee was not one he was ever going to undertake again.

The term "control" that is included in most bullying definitions can also be misinterpreted. Control is generally perceived to mean the control that a manager exercises with their staff. As with power, control is not necessarily linked to a position in the organizational structure. For example, one tactic that is commonly used by bullies is having unpredictable mood swings. Complainants will often cite incidents where the respondent on one day is kind and respectful to them and then the next day will completely ignore them. The pattern is explained as the respondent being "hot" and "cool" varying throughout the week, over the course of a day or in some cases hour by hour. The complainant never feels safe and on days when the respondent appears to be having "a good day," the complainant is temporarily relieved. Groups of complainants or witnesses often describe the respondent as having a "flavour of the month" whereby they will relentlessly target one individual or group of individuals for a period of time and then suddenly shift their focus to another individual or group. There is a momentary sigh of relief for those no longer being targeted. Typically, this experience tends to be short-lived and the person or group will be targeted again days or even months later.

"When you are working here, you always have to sleep with one eye open at all times. You can never truly let your guard down," said one complainant. Some targets have stated that it would be easier to handle the bullying if they were consistently targeted, as the yo-yo effect of the bully's behaviour was much more difficult to handle. It seems that when you come into work, knowing you are going to be treated disrespectfully or openly humiliated is easier to handle than coming into work every day not knowing how you are going to be treated. One participant asked me in a session, "What is the difference between being a bully and just being an ass?" I thought about the question for a moment and then said, "Consistency. If you are an ass, you are an ass all day long."

For the past 20 years, I have used the following workplace bullying definition in my education sessions and recommended that my clients adopt it as it is the most accurate and sound definition I have come across. It has been suggested to me that I update this definition so that it is more current, but I have yet to find a better definition.

From Ireland's Code of Practice on the Prevention of Workplace Bullying under the *Safety, Health and Welfare at Work Act*, 1989: "Workplace bullying is a repeated pattern of intentional inappropriate behaviour, direct or indirect (aggressive or passive), whether verbal, physical or otherwise, performed by one or more persons against another person or group of people, which could reasonably be regarded as undermining the individual's right to dignity at work."

Breaking Down the Concepts of Bullying

In order to fully comprehend the meaning of bullying, the individual relevant concepts will be broken down below to provide clarity and further explain the bully phenomenon.

"Repeated pattern"

Generally, workplace bullying is a repeated pattern. Bullying is not a "one-off" behaviour that is offensive or disrespectful and it is not just someone having a "bad day." That said, a one-time unprofessional behaviour is unacceptable and should still be dealt with accordingly. Regarding harassment, some jurisdictions state that one incident of bullying can be deemed harassment. I find that single incidents are more often a case of incivility or a breach of the organizational code of conduct rather than bullying. Incivility is defined as a rude or unsociable speech or behaviour, or an impolite or offensive comment. Examples of incivility range from an individual not holding a door open when someone is knowingly right behind them or a peer not saying good morning or thanking someone when it is socially appropriate. These examples are considered low-level unacceptable social behaviour. Unlike bullying, these behaviours are ambiguous in that it is uncertain or vague as to whom the behaviour was directed at or there was no clear intent to harm a specific person. Someone not holding a door open could merely be that they did not see the person directly behind them just as failure to greet someone in the morning could be that they are late for a meeting or preoccupied and deep in thought.

In 1876, Henry Robert created a standard set of rules, called Robert's Rules of Order, to run orderly meetings with maximum fairness to all members. An excerpt from his rules reads: "During debate, and while the chairman is speaking, or the assembly is engaged in voting, no member is permitted to disturb the assembly by whispering, or walking across the floor, or in any other way."

Although more than 140 years have passed since Mr. Robert wrote his rules and much has changed in the world since then, how different is the ideal focus of our meetings now as opposed to then? I think most people would agree that we would like to conduct meetings as efficiently and effectively as possible. Personally, the part that says "no member is permitted to disturb the assembly" carries the most weight.

I have conducted numerous meetings and training sessions over the years and it still fascinates me that some organizations that claim to be run by rules and regulations allow individuals to break those rules on a regular basis. Meetings that are scheduled to start at 9 a.m. often do not start on time. Unless there is a legitimate reason for someone to be late, there is no reason to wait on those who choose not to come on time; it only punishes those who arrived on time.

This can also cause a cycle whereby the people who arrive on time no longer do so because they are wasting time waiting for others. In most training sessions, clients ensure that staff are there on time and people are prepared. However, I've stood in a room with less than half of the attendees for the training session, many of whom do not come with a pen or paper and, even worse, some who walk in 15 to 20 minutes late with a coffee in hand, not only disrupting the class by entering the room but sometimes actually waving to people or sitting down and talking to others. I figure if people have time to stop and buy a coffee, they could instead make an effort to be at the session on time. It is even worse when a leader is late as they are supposed to lead by example.

A breach of a code of conduct may be viewed as a more serious infraction than the previous examples. Organizations generally establish codes of conduct as a way to remind employees of the behavioural expectations when they are at work. The purpose of the code or a set of rules is to formally outline workplace rules and responsibilities, and in essence reflects the mission, vision and values of the organization. Most workplace employee handbooks outline the importance of integrity, collaboration and high-quality service. There is an expectation that employees will consistently use good judgment to preserve their employer's reputation. When staff are considering whether something might be in violation of the code, they may ask themselves if this behaviour or action is consistent with the code and whether it is ethical and legal. Common breaches of a code include being dishonest or lying about something (such as denying that you saw someone leave work early), using or "borrowing" organizational equipment for personal gain (such as taking a lawnmower from work to cut your own lawn or to cut lawns in your neighbourhood for profit), or using the company's internet during business hours (for instance, to check and respond to emails from customers regarding your personal family business). Although these behaviours and actions may be concerning, they are generally not a case of workplace bullying.

Bullies are not ambiguous or vague. Bullies will directly or indirectly target a specific individual or a group of individuals. Bullies are also fairly relentless and will go after the target on a repeated basis.

Bullying should not be confused with negativity. Charles Klein, author of the book *How to Forgive When You Can't Forget: Healing Our Personal Relationships*, shares an exercise where he asks an individual to describe what they see on a piece of paper with a red dot on it. Many individuals describe the dot. Klein explains that the dot is the pain and suffering people were experiencing. One of the things he taught people was that the white space signified good. The focus of the exercise was how individuals can shift their perspective from the negative to the positive.

According to an international allied group against workplace harassment, one in 30 people are bullies or have bullying tendencies. That means in an organization of 300, there are 10 bullies. From my experience, this is an accurate ratio. Although the number is low, both labour and management tend to focus on the 10 potential bullies instead of the 290 individuals in the organization who are good. People often get labelled as a bully when they have negative behaviours, but negativity does not define a bully. As a society, we need to stop obsessing on the negativity and spend more energy on the positive work and contributions made for the greater good. Constant complaints and negative attitudes can be the core of low morale in the workplace. Negativity should be viewed as a performance issue and have consequences to change the behaviour.

Personally, I believe that individuals are hired for two reasons: their skillset and their attitude. To gain the skills required for any occupation, there are colleges, universities and trade schools. Bursaries and scholarships are available in most jurisdictions. I believe that finding someone who possesses the skill to do a job is much easier than finding someone with the right attitude. The problem lies with employers focusing so narrowly on a person's educational background and work history that they fail to screen the applicant for the most desirable trait—that of high emotional intelligence. In short, emotional intelligence is the capability of an individual to recognize and understand their own emotions, in addition to understanding the emotions of others in order to guide their thinking and behaviour in a way that is appropriate to the situation or circumstance. The individual who truly fits comfortably within the organizational culture—ideally a healthy one—is more valuable than any education one may possess. Skills can be taught but attitude cannot. I would rather work with someone who has an amazing attitude towards learning and growing than someone with a series of letters at the end of their name who cannot communicate without offending someone.

Employers must take the time to select the right person for the job. Too many times I have conducted investigations into allegations of workplace bullying only to discover that the respondent does not possess the level of emotional intelligence to be successful in the job. I will hear managers say, "Well he is a little rough around the edges but really does a great job," or even more alarming, "We needed to fill the position and the choice that we made was the best of two evils." Understandably, organizations are sometimes in a difficult position to fill a position but what is the better scenario: dividing the job tasks between existing competent employees until the right candidate comes along or hiring someone who in the end is going to wreak havoc and create a negative environment for everyone around them?

Another scenario came to light in the Dupont-Daniel murder-suicide. Apparently at the time of the incident, there was an anaesthesiologist shortage in Windsor, Ontario, which was alleged to have been one of the factors in the hospital keeping Dr. Daniel instead of attempting to revoke his privileges.

Bullies have different core personality traits; some are negative in nature, some are positive and some are in between. Regardless of their core, a bully treats everyone the same (either positively, negatively or somewhere in between) but they treat their target differently and in an unacceptable way.

"Intentional"

In educational or training sessions, I am often asked, "Do bullies really know that they are bullies?" I usually turn the question around to the participants to get their opinion. In most cases, I get a balanced response: half of the individuals believe that bullies know exactly what they are doing and half believe that they don't. Too often I will hear, "That's just the way they are, they have been like that for years."

To be clear, bullies know exactly what they are doing. Bullying may be a core piece of their personality and consciously they may not be 100 percent aware of every move they make, but their intent is to control and eliminate the target from the organization. Bullies attempt to make their target's life miserable so that they either quit, go on a physical or mental leave, or make the target look incompetent so that they get fired.

One thing I tell individuals seeking advice on how to handle a bully is that if they are a complainant, the burden of proof lies with them. In other words, it is their responsibility to produce concrete evidence to prove that the respondent is targeting them. Surprisingly to most, it is not the job of the respondent to prove that they are *not* a bully. As part of my teaching style, I often ask participants questions or provide them with a case study. Regarding the intent of a bully I ask, "How do you prove intent?" Generally, people say it is proven through documentation. Yes, documentation is extremely important. The complainant should document dates, times and locations of incidents and include detailed notes of the event in addition to the names of any witnesses present.

People also commonly say intent is proven through witnesses. Yes, witnesses are important, as long as the witness has your back. Unfortunately, a reality of workplace bullying is that although employees will continuously talk in groups about the perceived bully, either on or off work time, due to the fear of retaliation, only one or a few, if any, will come forward with a complaint. A common scenario that occurs is when everyone sees what is going on, has directly witnessed a bullying behaviour and wants the bullying to stop, but when someone finally files a complaint, potential witnesses back down. Many times during an investigation, when interviewing primary witnesses regarding an incident that they allegedly knew about, they claim ignorance. Statements such as "I don't remember" or "I have no problem with anyone here. I just come to work and do my job" are commonplace. Due to the lack of support from those alleged witnesses, the complainant who came forward with goodwill is suddenly labelled as a "troublemaker." In a worse-case scenario, witnesses' non-compliance can also result in the complainant losing their credibility. They are often labelled "oversensitive" or told they "can't take a joke" or "need to loosen up and not take everything so seriously." An interesting concept to consider is whether witnesses are bystanders in the same way that bystanders are viewed as witnesses during a criminal investigation.

Although both documentation and witnesses can be invaluable, to truly determine if a person's behaviour has intent, they must be put on notice. I often hear from targets pertaining to the perceived inappropriate or bullying behaviours, that the individual "should know better" or that it is "common sense" that someone should not do what the bully does. I smile when I hear that things are "common sense." I think that if common sense was common we would not have signs in public washrooms that say, "Wash your hands" or speed limits on the highway that warn drivers that if they go over 50 kilometres per hour over the posted speed limit then the police may confiscate their vehicle. People also need to be aware that what is considered common sense or a courtesy in one ethnic group or country may not be seen as such in another, such as shaking hands and personal body space limits.

In order to be clear and determine intent whenever possible and only if they feel safe and comfortable in doing so, the target must tell the bully what the inappropriate behaviour is, how it makes them feel, how it is interfering with their job and ask for the behaviour to stop. Here is an example statement: "I feel disrespected every time you interrupt me when I am speaking to a customer and I would appreciate it if you did not do that anymore." It is recommended that when the speaker begins the conversation, they use the term "I" instead of "you." Starting with the statement, "You are disrespecting me when you interrupt me when I am speaking to a customer" will usually create defensiveness and may result in a negative altercation. The listener will immediately tune out before they even hear the rest of the statement. When coaching individuals on how to respectfully confront the bully or offender, sometimes they say they do not want to tell the person how their behaviour makes them feel (i.e., disrespected) because acknowledging it will give the bully more power. There is also the theory that explaining how it affects the person will reaffirm to the bully that they are getting under the target's skin. Those opinions are valid, however, without including the emotion or feeling in the sentence, the statement loses its impact. Consider the statement, "Stop interrupting me when I'm speaking to a customer." In addition to causing the receiver of the information to be defensive, it also appears that the person communicating is telling the other person what to do. A frequent response would be, "You're not my boss. Don't tell me what to do." By including the appropriate emotion for the context of the situation (i.e., feeling disrespected, afraid or unsafe), the statement takes on a whole different meaning. If an individual has no intent of making someone feel disrespected or afraid, when they hear the negative impact of their actions they will most likely cease that behaviour. Even if the individual completely disagrees with the speaker's perception, they will be conscious of the impact of that behaviour in the future.

In the case of bullying, there is ill-will intent. If the bully is approached by the target who states, "I feel disrespected every time you interrupt me when I am speaking to a customer and I would appreciate it if you did not do that anymore," the noted behaviour will most likely continue and in some cases escalate. In addition, if the bully has any followers, they may coach or negatively influence those individuals to also take on the behaviours that have made the target feel disrespected or fearful. Now the target is not only dealing with one person causing them distress but others as well. It is important that the complainant also documents the conversation when they put the person on notice, which will be important in the future should there ever be an investigation.

In situations where the target does not want to confront the individual about the behaviour due to fear or another negative emotion, someone else could have that conversation with the person; either that person's supervisor, manager, union representative or even a peer. Who delivers the message is irrelevant, as long as the respondent is clearly made aware of the concern and the desire for it to stop. It is extremely important that workplace harassment policies state that direct confrontation and discussion with the alleged bully is only an option and not a requirement in order for management or the employer to intervene.

"Direct behaviour"

Some bullies are very obvious and get directly in the target's face. They seem to get satisfaction from others knowing the innate power they have not only over the target but over everyone around them. When I have stated this in a workshop, I have had individuals say to me, "They don't control me." If that person did not control them in some way, they would not know who they were and would not continue the inappropriate behaviour or targeting. Being controlled is not necessarily being forced to do something; staying silent is another way of being controlled.

In most organizations, the majority of employees can identify the bully and the target, at least in their own department. Depending on the nature of the work, even customers or the general public can sometimes sense the negative vibes. These types of "obvious" bullies can be easier to handle because they are out in the open. I would personally choose a known bully over an unknown bully any day so at least I would know who to defend myself from.

This part of the bullying phenomenon is one that I have the most difficulty comprehending. We live in a society where someone will roll their car over on the highway and most witnesses will stop their car and call 911. Yet in cases of workplace bullying, people will watch a colleague mentally and emotionally deteriorate right before their eyes for a period of a few weeks to a year or more and not ask if they need any help. Human beings will run into burning buildings to rescue a stranger but will observe a peer having a panic attack or crying at work and walk away. The notion of "better you than me" seems to be prevalent in the workplace particularly when pertaining to bullying or harassment.

What is even more fascinating is that when a target is symbolically begging for help, the person will either directly say to them or indicate through their body language that they can't help because they must work there too. The workplace has become a battlefield; a game of self-preservation and survival of the fittest. Workplace harassment is the one type of violence where the victim is standing alone and the bully is surrounded by their posse or self-appointed supporters. Individuals tend to choose the team that is more likely to win to secure their survival rather than the most "ethical" team.

"Indirect behaviour"

Although bullies can be direct, from my experience most use indirect bullying by getting other people to bully the target for them. The way they accomplish this is by spreading rumours or gossip about the target. To remain undetected, they hide their maliciousness behind goodwill. Bullies will recruit gang members through deception and propagate a belief that is not true or only partially true. This is a form of self-deception and is always done with ill-will intent. The mistruths that are spread often lead to distrust and feelings of betrayal between the receiver and the target.

According to the *Canadian Oxford Dictionary*, gossip is defined as "informal talk or stories about other people's private lives that may be unkind or not true." Gossip often has negative speculation and rumour or talk of a personal, sensational or intimate nature. Generally, it takes the form of opinions, which takes on a life of its own as people add their own opinions as they pass on the gossip.

Rumours have three components: (1) they need to be based on real situations, usually of widespread interest, (2) they need to be believable and (3) they thrive best if they focus on something negative.

A "negative" rumour creates more interest and spreads much faster than a "positive" rumour. Society has contributed to this phenomenon. Results of rumours and gossip in the workplace include: wasted time and productivity as a result of excessive time exchanging gossip, circulation of false rumours and either heightened fear or falsely raised expectations, severe erosion of others' trust and staff morale in the workplace, hurt feelings and the possibility of reprisals, and worst of all, the creation of a toxic work environment.

The creation and circulation of a false truth is very different from an honest mistake. For example, consider an employee walking into a room and hearing another employee speaking in a raised voice to a client. The perception of the employee entering the room is that the other employee is "yelling" at the client. It may be discovered later that the client had a hearing impairment. Therefore, the individual who reported the incident to a manager for the alleged abusive behaviour towards a client was not being malicious but rather misunderstood or did not know the context of the situation. But as my mother used to say, "It is not what you say, it is how you say it." Tone matters.

Combating rumours and gossip is a group effort. For it to become virtually non-existent, individuals need to take personal responsibility and assess themselves before speaking about anyone else. More importantly, they must ask themselves, "What is my motive for telling what I'm about to tell?" and "Is this conversation in the best interest of the person it is about?" Also, "Is what I am about to say true? Is it harmless? Is it necessary?" The ability to self-reflect is important as individuals should consider how they would feel if someone said something similar about them.

An effective response to a person who wants to share information about someone else could be: "I'm uncomfortable talking about X when they are not present to tell their side of the story and when I hear you talk about other people and their situations, I wonder whether you talk about me to others. Let's hold off on this conversation until

X can be with us." or "Is this something X specifically asked you to tell me? If so, I'll be sure to let them know that you filled me in."

The most powerful and revealing question to ask someone when they are speaking about another person is, "Is what you are about to tell me something you would say if X were here?" If the person answers no to this direct question it would be well advised to discontinue the conversation.

Bullies have intent to cause harm. These individuals are very bright and usually master manipulators. They will not direct or command another person to unfriend or stop speaking to their target, but they can certainly cause the individual to not want to speak to them. Oftentimes when a bully is recruiting someone they will ask to speak to the individual in private. The conversation may sound like this: "I need to speak to you. It is really important, but you must promise not to tell anyone what I am about to tell you." The next part of the conversation is meant to convince the person that the bully has their good interest at heart. The bully may say, "I am only telling you this for your own good," or "I am only telling you this because you are my friend," or "You and I go way back and we have to stick together." Through this type of dialogue, it gives the receiver a sense of trust or a feeling that the other person is protecting them from something or someone. This way, the bully has created a scenario whereby the receiver is intrigued to hear what they have to say and feeling secure in the fact that they are protected and trusted. As part of the ploy, the bully has reinforced their position by making the person promise not to tell anyone, creating an intimate bond between them based on a private secret that they share. Once this bond is established, they have set a perfect trap to execute their plan. The conversation may then go like this, "You didn't hear this from me, but X is telling others that you are not doing a good job. They are saying that they are going to report you to management." When the receiver reacts, presumably upset or defensive, the bully will remind them, "Remember you promised not to say anything and if you do,

I will deny we ever had this conversation." That right there has put the receiver in a difficult position. They just received negative or false information about themselves that a third party (the target) is allegedly spreading to others but they have just promised to keep the information confidential. Usually this will cause a slow burn inside the receiver's gut. Then the next time the target approaches and tries to speak to the other person, they will most likely turn and walk away, leaving the target wondering what they did to the other person. The bully may go through the whole department and have similar private conversations with all staff about the target.

This indirect tactic may be used by anyone in any position, from frontline to manager to director. The impact on internal relationships can be devastating. If the bully is a frontline employee, they often attempt to recruit supervisors and managers. The core foundation of the deceit remains regardless of the party's position. Frontline bullies will often approach individuals with false or misleading information that causes the leader to become suspicious of the target. Consider a frontline employee knocking on a manager's door at the end of the day and saying, "Hi, I know you are really busy but I just need to talk to you for a minute. It seems like every time I work with X, supplies go missing. But you know what? This is stupid, I shouldn't have told you. I have no proof. Sorry to have disturbed you." The person then exits the office. A manager in possession of this new information will do one of a few things: (1) call the person back into the office to further explain what they meant by that comment, (2) tell another person in management or their direct report the information that was just shared, (3) begin to watch the target more closely or (4) begin to question the target's peers about the person's work habits or ask them directly if they are aware of the target stealing from the company. Regardless of what the manager does, one thing is for sure; they will put that conversation at the back of their mind until it is directly or indirectly brought up again. Say three months go by and suddenly the department's inventory is short or someone complains that they had something taken out of their locker. The first thing to cross the manager's mind is what that employee told them about the target and the conclusion may be that X is a potential thief who is now in a vulnerable position and may lose their job.

Everyone hopes they can remain unbiased and determine when someone is telling a falsehood or manipulating them. Managers may say they can remain fair and unaffected by gossip, however, we can all be fooled or misled. Most people tend to believe what someone is telling them is the truth. When these comments are made, it is usually quick, informal and downplayed by the bully. However, the information sticks in the receiver's mind, consciously or not.

I was involved in a case where a female staff member was bullying a male staff member. It appears that the female had intimate feelings about the male, which were not reciprocated. As a result, every time a new female employee was hired, within a few days the bully would pull the new woman aside and say something to the effect of: "I can't say much, but I wouldn't be in a room with X alone to save my soul." The female listener is most likely going to assume she is referring to sexual harassment or sexual assault. The bully has played on the fear that most women have regarding being assaulted. After hearing this warning, not many females would decide to make up their own mind about this man and be alone with him in a room. The falsehood of the conversation was a "sister" protecting another "sister" from the alleged male predator. Unfortunately, we all have weaknesses and vulnerabilities, and a certain type of person may use the things we fear the most against us for their own personal gain.

There is another component of this indirect tactic that is rather cruel. Oftentimes the bully will indirectly negatively influence a group of staff members to mistreat the target and then quietly sit back and watch the devastation they created. If that is not bad enough, sometimes the bully becomes the target's confidant. As the target becomes further isolated, the bully may approach them and ask how things are going, and when the target says they don't understand why everyone seems angry at them, the bully may say, "I know, I have seen people being mean to you. That's not right. Just know that I am here for you whenever you need me."

One complainant said to me in her harassment interview: "It was terrible when everyone turned against me for no reason, but what was more painful is that I just found out that the person I thought was my only friend was the one who started this whole mess." This individual was calling the bully at all hours of the night and disclosing all incidents that were happening to her, and the bully was actually coaching her and convinced her to file a formal complaint against the staff member who was mistreating her. The bully thought she would remain unnoticed because she was not the one directly mistreating the target. The bully also didn't realize that as a result of the investigation, the respondents told the investigator their version of events, which included the conversations with the bully about what the target had allegedly been negatively saying about them. In the end, the bully was identified as the root cause of the bullying situation. However, the respondents also had to take responsibility for their inappropriate actions and disrespectful behaviour, regardless of who started it or what was allegedly said about them.

Another disturbing component of indirect bullying is that the bully may also involve a patient, client or customer as part of their game. A simple statement to an external person such as: "If you need anything, talk to me, don't talk to them," or "Don't waste your time trying to explain it to X, they are new and don't quite get it yet," can quickly frame a person's opinion about someone. Although on the surface these statements may not be viewed as suspect, repeating them to a number of people can have a significant effect on someone's self-esteem and reputation. In addition, it is not just the words that affect a statement, it is the tone of voice and body language that is sometimes even more significant. Eyerolling, a slow shaking of one's head or a "tsk" at the end of a sentence can take an innocent statement and make it malicious.

Working as a consultant in long-term care facilities and the developmental disabilities sector has exposed me to many cases whereby a resident, client or family member is brought onto the side of the bully without even realizing it. Even people considered to be high functioning still have some level of vulnerability.

Often the clients who are more active and verbal are those selected by the bully as an ally. Consider a young person with an intellectual disability being faced with a seemingly kind and funny staff member who has always treated them well. Imagine the staff member saying to them, "Hey buddy! You are my best friend. You are my favourite person! If you want anything special or want to do anything fun, just ask me. But make sure that you never ask X, he is really mean." This type of statement about a specific staff member could be repeated several times to one or many clients. Now imagine one day there is a day trip that has been organized that the young person wants to attend but his friend (the bully) will not be working that day. The young person finds out on the day of the trip that they will be in X's group. Imagine what would be going through their head: "Oh no, I don't want to go with the mean person." The young person then says to their family that they do not want to go on the trip because X is mean. Family members and loved ones are strong, protective advocates and the first thought to come to their mind would be, "Mean?! What has X done?" Suddenly the family member is calling up management, telling them that X is abusive. As generally mandated by legislation, the organization takes immediate action by sending X home on a paid leave of absence and begins an investigation into an allegation of abuse or neglect. The train is now barrelling down the tracks picking up momentum and people on its way. If other clients and their family members have heard the same story about X, it is likely that with client and witness statements, that abuse will be substantiated. Once again, the bully wins the fight and the target is terminated, carrying an "abuser" label for a lifetime.

One of my cases was particularly heart-wrenching. A staff member in a long-term care facility was targeting one of her peers. Rumours, gossip and secret mockery were common occurrences. The situation was fairly overt: most staff, residents and their family members were aware of the tension whenever the two staff members worked together. One day, the daughter of a married couple living in the home in a shared room came for her weekly visit. Upon her arrival, one of the managers pulled her aside and asked to speak to her in private. There was a concern about her parents' behaviour for the past few days. Although they had different needs, the home was able to accommodate the couple and allow them to share a room. The husband had dementia, but he was mostly passive although quite confused. He was fairly able-bodied, getting around with a walker. He required limited assistance with his daily living activities. The wife was of sound mind, however, required a high degree of assistance with her daily living activities due to a number of medical issues and physical ailments. According to the manager, two days prior, the husband became verbally aggressive towards one of the staff members and yelled obscenities at her. This behaviour was unlike his regular quiet and compliant demeanour. The staff member who was being targeted had little to no interaction with the resident in the past. Around the same time this behaviour began, the wife started to cry and refused to leave the room or come to the dining room for meals. Like her husband, this was also a behaviour that had not been demonstrated in the past. The wife was extremely sociable and took great satisfaction in visiting the residents who had less cognitive and physical ability. Naturally, the daughter was concerned about her parents' new dynamic. She tried to gain some insight from her mother as to what had transpired to alter their behaviour. After spending some time trying to calm her mother down, she explained what happened. In the early morning two days prior, a staff member came into their room, pulled back the room divider curtain and began to speak to her husband in a whisper. Although the wife tried to intervene by asking the staff member what she was doing, the staff member ignored her. This naturally raised some concerns and made the wife very uncomfortable. As she strained to listen to what the staff member was saying, she heard the following conversation: *Joe, Joe how are you, how are you? Joe you know X, you know X? Joe, X hates you and thinks you are stupid. She says you're stupid. She hates you Joe, X hates you.* She could hear her husband becoming agitated, but the staff member continued: "Joe, X is in the hallway right now saying you are stupid. I am going to take you out in the hallway and you can tell her that she is stupid. You can tell her that she is stupid, Joe. Joe, you can say to her that she is fat. X is fat, right Joe? Say she's fat. And Joe, she is a slut. You call her a slut, okay Joe? Okay Joe?" According to the wife, this conversation went on for approximately five minutes. The staff member then took her husband with his walker into the hallway. At this point Joe started yelling, "You are stupid! You are fat. You big slut!" His wife could hear the targeted staff member outside the room trying to calm Joe down and bring him back into the room. In the meantime, the staff member who initiated the behaviour walked back into the room, abruptly pulled the curtains back and stared at the wife. Not a word was spoken for nearly a minute. The wife was terrified about what had just transpired and the silent message that she received from the staff member was not to say a word about what she may have heard. The daughter asked why her mother did not call her or tell one of the nurses what happened. Through tears, the mother said she was too scared because she relies on the staff to bathe, change and dress her. The mother also said she had witnessed that staff member in her interactions with the staff and other residents, and she was "mean and powerful." She worried that if she confronted the staff member or told anyone about what she saw, she and her husband would pay the consequences. Since the incident, she was too afraid to leave the room in case the staff member came back to try to get her husband to say or do something nasty, resulting in him being moved to a more secured unit. Her greatest fear was for them to be separated for the first time in more than 50 years. Therefore, in her mind they were old and vulnerable, so she had no choice but to keep quiet.

Over the years while working in social services and health care, it became apparent that the abusers of vulnerable adults or children were overwhelmingly also bullies in the workplace. Countless investigations regarding abuse or neglect have revealed, particularly during witness interviews, that the respondent created an environment driven by fear, which allowed them to break rules and regulations, steal from the organization and be unprofessional or abusive towards clients. Witnesses have disclosed that they knew of the bad behaviour for months or even years, but did not report it out of fear of retaliation from the individual. Many cases, such as the one previously cited, are a situation of resident abuse in addition to bullying. Despite the fact that co-workers were afraid of the staff member and her erratic behaviour, in the end they were also subjected to the consequences of failing to report prior behaviours to management. Had the initial behavioural concerns been brought forward, many residents and staff members could have been spared the torment that they experienced. Moreover, the staff could have also been charged with neglect for leaving the residents in harm's way.

It is an interesting dynamic when I talk about indirect bullying tactics in my presentations. Often when I am speaking, I will see a participant's face drop as they realize they are being bullied or part of a bullying gang. I have observed staff suddenly look at each other, panic-stricken. In one management group session, all of the managers realized simultaneously that one of the 40 people in the room had pitted the managers against each other. Most of the managers were not speaking to each other, only to realize that they were pawns in the bully's game to gain complete control of the leadership team, resulting in total control over the staff. Sometimes we just need someone to connect the dots for us and then everything becomes clear.

Bullies are like puppet masters working behind the scenes; in many cases the performance is seamless, the creativity is brilliant and the final performance has an everlasting effect on the target who plays every scene over in their mind for years to come.

"Verbal"

Verbal bullying tactics include yelling and screaming, name-calling or the silent treatment. In my experience, yelling is more common with males and managers, and the silent treatment is a tactic chosen primarily by women.

In one harassment case, the complainant was a registered nurse who was continually called "stupid" by a physician at patient care conferences in front of patients, family members and colleagues. She said to me that she had two choices: "follow the doctor out to the parking lot with a baseball bat" or "never again say a word in a care conference." She chose the latter option. As I was listening to her, I thought what a shame; the registered nursing staff often know the most intimate and important details about the patient, and in this case she decided never to share her knowledge, experience and expertise again. Understandably, the complainant was saving herself from internal stress and public embarrassment but as a result, patient care would suffer.

In another case, a male executive leader referred to the one saleswoman working with a group of males as a "bitch" in weekly sales meetings. As a single mother of a young child, she felt that "keeping her mouth shut" and receiving a regular paycheque was more important than her pride or "biting the hand that feeds her."

Although being the subject of someone's yelling can have a powerful effect, the silent treatment is sometimes even more devastating. Individuals in the workplace can go hours, days or even months where the bully and perhaps others do not acknowledge the target's existence. A complainant said to me in an interview, "I would rather be punched in the face than X [the bully] pretend that I am not standing in the room." The feeling of being invisible often leads the target down a path of isolation, self-doubt and, in more extreme cases, self-loathing.

"Physical"

Like many types of violence, it can start out subtly through verbal or psychological abuse and may eventually become physical. If the bully's "non-physical" control or intimidation is having little effect on the target, the bully will often become physical. In a female-dominated workplace, the likelihood of the situation becoming physical is less than in a male-dominated sector. However, physical bullying is not restricted to punching and slapping.

Consider a scenario where a co-worker comes into work every day, slams the office door and the kitchen cupboard when making their morning coffee. Later that day, the co-worker returns from a meeting and throws a file at the wall. At the end of the day, a colleague requests a set of keys for the safe and instead of coming over to their desk and handing them to the person, the keys are thrown across the room, hit the desk and land on the floor.

One complainant working a night shift asked their bully to borrow a pen. With unnecessary force, the bully threw the pen at their target striking them directly in the eye. This final physical act was the catalyst for a workplace violence complaint that was filed by the target after many months of torment.

It is more difficult to prove that these types of physical bullying were done with ill-will intent, however, if the desired effect is to intimidate and control the work environment, it could potentially be considered physical bullying or acts that create a toxic work environment. A more obvious physical case involved a kitchen staff member who was unaware that her bully heated a cast iron frying pan on high, which she received with her bare hands resulting in second-degree burns.

"Otherwise"

According to the Royal Canadian Mounted Police, many forms of bullying can be considered illegal offences in most jurisdictions, including:

Criminal Harassment: "Repeated tormenting online, with texts, phone calls, and/or emails causing the other person to fear for their safety."

Uttering Threats and Extortion: "Threatening to share someone's personal information to others if they don't do what you want them to do."

Assault: "Threats or acts of non-consensual force, violence, bodily harm, or destruction of personal property."

Identity Theft/Fraud: "Creating a fake online profile to ruin someone's reputation."

Defamatory Libel: "Spreading rumors about someone."

In addition to verbal and physical tactics, other tactics used by bullies or their followers include vandalizing property, graffiti or sabotaging others' work. One complainant was publicly humiliated at work when the biweekly staff schedules were posted in the lunchroom and her name was circled with red pen and the word "bitch" written beside it. Another male employee had to have his schedule removed from an open staff area because whenever it was posted, someone wrote "ass kisser" next to his name. So there are endless possibilities to the situations that can occur.

Another individual left their lunch locked in their car for fear of what the bully might do to their food if it was left unattended in the staff refrigerator as this was a known behaviour of the bully whenever someone would cross them. They told me of situations where used band-aids, tampons and condoms were found in staff members' lunch bags. To exacerbate the problem, apparently on several occasions when the issue was brought to management's attention, the target was told not to bring their lunch to work and suggested to buy their lunch instead. The fact that management did not take the issue seriously or investigate this public health risk placed the onus on the target to deal with the situation. The complainant's solution was to bring a cooler of ice every day and leave it in the trunk of their car. In another case, a bully continuously unplugged a refrigerator that had the target's medication in it.

Several unrelated targets who did not work in the same organization or geographic area told me about situations where their bully would use the company vehicle as a weapon in their game. In all cases, part of the job of these individuals was commuting from one location to another with another staff member. The vehicle used was either a personal vehicle or company-issued one. Stories were told of the bully demanding to do all of the driving when working with the target. The bully's mood was quickly revealed based on their driving habits that day. On a good day, the driver was calm and abided by the traffic rules. However, on a bad day, the driver would usually drive well over the speed limit, through red lights and take corners at an unsafe speed. In all cases, the target did not say anything to the bully at the time because their safety and well-being were at the bully's mercy.

Setting someone up to fail is another bullying tactic commonly used in the workplace. When arriving at work, a target may spend a significant amount of time at the beginning of their shift looking for work-related supplies or equipment that have been hidden on them, trying to figure out passwords that are constantly being changed without notification or looking for keys for rooms and filing cabinets that have been unnecessarily locked. Targets often come to work early to locate or reorganize their workspace before their official start time. Out of fear of retaliation, targets often do not alert management or the union of the situation, and these issues will persist until either the bully slips up or the tactic is discovered by someone else. In some businesses, a lead hand or crew supervisor may be on duty and have the expectation of being the leader but realistically has no power to exercise any authority. A common error that organizations make is giving a frontline worker in a unionized position the title of supervisor while still being a union member. Simultaneously being a frontline employee and supervisor does not give the person the credibility that is required for the position to be effective. This scenario may lead to the downfall of the individual in that position as it could put a target on their back for incivility or bullying behaviours.

Another one of my cases involved a frontline employee who worked midnight shifts during the week that started at 11 p.m. and ended at 7 a.m. One night, a manager on call received a call from the lead hand who said there was an environmental issue that required immediate attention. The manager arrived at the workplace at approximately 10:45 p.m. As the manager drove into the staff parking lot, he witnessed what he believed to be a staff member standing by the trunk of a vehicle taking tools from the car and loading them into a buggy. The manager then watched the staff member leave his trunk open, take the buggy into the staff entrance and return to the vehicle with an empty cart. The manager watched the staff member make three trips to the car, into the building and back again. This scenario did not make any sense. The last time the staff member went to the car and locked it, the manager emerged from his vehicle and confronted him. Being late at night, the staff member was surprised to see the manager and appeared nervous. The manager surmised that the staff member must have been stealing tools from the workplace. However, it did not make sense that the staff member was taking tools from his car and bringing them into the building as opposed to taking tools from the building and putting them in his car. After a few minutes of questioning, the employee broke down and told the manager what was going on. Apparently the employee had been hired less than one month prior as an external candidate for a low-level supervisor position. He explained that since his first day of work, he had been harassed by his peers for being the "newbie" and allegedly taking a job away from the internal employees. Name-calling and pranks such as locking him in the washroom or out of other rooms occurred on every shift. Within a few days, the tools required to do his job started to go missing. When questioned about their whereabouts, he was told to "find them yourself, newbie." The employee became so stressed that he was not eating or sleeping properly. Still on probation, he felt that his only option was to bring in his own tools from home to be able do his job. Therefore, the tools that the manager saw the staff member taking out of his car and into the building were his personal property. The situation was only discovered and rectified because the manager had unexpectedly arrived at the workplace to deal with the emergency.

Some bullies will go to great lengths to sabotage their targets. A frontline employee I encountered was secretly buying their own supplies because other staff members were hiding supplies at the end of their shift. It was discovered during the investigation that supplies were being hidden above the ceiling tiles in the staff room.

To add insult to injury, the effects of bullying and harassment may also follow the target home. One target disclosed to me that her bully showed up on her wedding day with a car full of uninvited guests and paintballs. To obtain proof for her employer, the target installed cameras on her private property to protect herself from her bullies who vandalized her property in the middle of the night.

In another case, in a health-care environment a target was terrorized on the night shift when their bully would pull a call bell in a patient's room and when the target would answer it, the bully who had crawled under the bed would grab the target by the ankle.

Other tactics included hiding in closets and around corners and jumping out at the target randomly. On some shifts, the target would be startled four or five times and then not again for weeks. This caused fear for the target with every step they took and got to the point of taking a leave of absence due to anxiety. When I met with the target, they told me that due to the situation, they now sleep with the lights on.

"Performed by one or more person against another person or group of people"

The following excerpt is from an email I received from a target who read an article about a presentation I gave:

It was interesting to know that others suffered similar situations as I have in the workplace. I do not know if you have run into workplace harassment where not only employers ignore it but unions participant in it (even by pressuring management to join in) against the very people they claim to represent. I gave the union countless opportunities to stop it and at best they ignored it and at worst joined in spite of their "policy" of zero tolerance to workplace harassment. I went from floor reps to the national president. They did not want and feared to deal with it. The head bully had not only recruited others but had a long history of bullying others. He was formerly related to one of the managers and had befriended many union leaders. He bragged regularly that they will not touch him because he has too many friends in high places. I eventually gave up on turning this horrible situation around by isolating myself from anyone that I suspected may cause me more trouble.

A bully needs enablers to be truly effective and powerful. Most bullies recruit at least three people to be part of their "gang." As referenced in the email above, participants in a bullying situation can include a wide range of players from all levels of the organization. The more participants, the stronger the bully becomes and inevitably the weaker the target. I have been involved in many situations whereby the target has been on probation when the bullying occurred. In many cases, the target either leaves early voluntarily or fails to pass their probation period.

"Which could reasonably be regarded as undermining the individual's right to dignity at work"

In most professions, the focus is on customer satisfaction, which is achieved by treating external "customers" with dignity and respect. All organizations I have encountered have told me with great confidence that violence and harassment in their workplace is unacceptable. The term "zero tolerance" is widely used within the walls of most organizations. Any staff member who is rude, belligerent or disrespectful to a customer is usually automatically sanctioned; sometimes mandated to attend an anger management program, enrol in a basic communication course or even terminated.

When I hear the term "zero tolerance," I challenge it. I believe that no organization is completely free of violence or harassment. Bullying behaviours imposed by staff against staff, regardless of the organizational positions, are tolerated every day. If a staff member acted the way they do with each other towards a customer, they would automatically be sanctioned or dismissed. It is forbidden for an employee to give a customer the silent treatment, a cold stare or call them a jerk. However, the truth is that employees at all levels do that on a regular basis to each other and those behaviours are tolerated. For an organization to claim that it is free of violence or harassment, it must include everyone, not only customers or the general public.

When an individual starts a new job, generally they are filled with anticipation fuelled by happiness, nervousness and some uncertainty. When they sign the employment offer, they are certain of a few things: (1) they will receive financial compensation for the work completed, (2) they will be treated with dignity and respect by their peers and management, and (3) they will remain gainfully and gleefully employed by the organization until they decide to find work elsewhere or retire.

In jobs or professions that deal directly with external customers, unfortunately there is a significant chance that some inappropriate, rude or abusive behaviours may come from the public and be directed at employees. Most employees realize that customers are not being paid and are not bound by a signed code of conduct that stipulates both expectations and sanctions for breaching that code. That said, due to several recent high-profile workplace violence incidents involving irate customers or estranged domestic partners, an increasing number of organizations are posting signs in public areas stating there is zero tolerance for violent or aggressive behaviours towards employees. These signs further state that if an individual exhibits such behaviour, they may be refused service or removed from the property by security or the police. So the question remains: Why should bad, aggressive or bullying behaviours be accepted among employees? Is it unreasonable for an employee to expect to be treated with respect by their peers? Indignity and disrespect occur every day in the workplace.

One complainant said her workplace bully pulled down her pants and underwear in a public waiting room. During the investigation, the respondent explained that the incident was "just a joke" and the complainant should not be so "oversensitive." Any time a situation or incident occurs, the questions should be (1) Does this behaviour model professionalism? And (2) Is it acceptable to exhibit this behaviour in a business environment? A common workplace definition of harassment states that the act of harassment is "engaging in a course of annoying and provoking comment or conduct—that is—or ought reasonably to be—known to be unwelcome." The term "ought reasonably to be" refers to what the reasonable person would deem appropriate. Would a person reasonably believe that pulling someone's pants down in a public work environment is acceptable?

Would a person reasonably believe that calling someone a "bitch" is professional? When that test is truly applied, the decision-maker's internal bias or the organization's culture are no longer factors; only the nature of the act is judged. This is a far better principle to apply than one or more person's personal feelings regarding a workplace situation or what they deem to be humorous.

It must also be noted that we live in a multicultural and multi-denominational world where a variety of social norms exist for different situations. It may be assumed in all cultures that it is inappropriate to pull someone's pants down in public but what about more subtle actions? For example, let us examine the hand gesture of making a fist. Depending on the context, a fist may be interpreted as a threat in some situations and in others seen as a positive symbol of solidarity. Eye contact is another body language act that has different meanings. Growing up, I was taught that making eye contact was the proper and respectful way to communicate with someone. However, in other cultures, establishing eye contact is viewed as disrespectful and dishonest or a sign of threatening or aggressive behaviour.

I have been involved in some interesting cases regarding the interpretation of words from different cultural backgrounds. In one case, a staff member who was under 30 years old filed a complaint about a staff member who was over 50 years old from another culture. The older staff member was allegedly referring to the younger staff member as "girlie." The complainant perceived this title to be extremely disrespectful and diminishing. After the investigation, in which harassment was unsubstantiated, I conducted a mediation between the two parties primarily because they had to work with each other on the same shift. The purpose of the mediation was to air their differences and mutually agree on how they would interact in the future. The younger staff member explained that the term "girlie" made her feel disrespected. The older staff member, who had shown a tough exterior throughout the process, started to cry. When she composed herself, she explained that she used to call her daughter "girlie" as a term of endearment in their home country. She said the other staff member reminded her of her daughter because of her age and mannerisms. Once the context was explained, it no longer held a negative meaning for the complainant. The mediation was a success and ended with the two parties embracing.

The Players: Bully, Target and Bystander

Below is, in my opinion, a brilliant letter I received from a workshop participant:

Dear Denise,

Rather than silent appreciation, I'd like to express how much I appreciate your bringing a ray of sunlight into a dark area, which pervades this society of ours, as well as many others. Since "charity begins at home," we need to start with our own workplaces and homes, and if others wish to learn from us after observing positive results, well & good. But too often, the "help" we give others is contaminated with all the same unholy dynamics, and even more-so. Books like The Ugly American *have attempted to deal with some of this stuff.*

Too often, manipulative people readily isolate, attack, and go on to persecute others, and too often "innocent bystanders" are drawn into it, to the extent that they are unable or unwilling to intervene effectively. And as you mentioned, often the "bullied" are not only the most "sensitive" people in the workspace (or home), but also the most creative, talented, and devoted. They are often so unfamiliar with the bully's tactics, so "naive," or perhaps unwilling/unable to believe that anyone could be so wrong and mean-spirited, that they fail to respond early and positively, during the critical period before the bullying becomes well-established. And by then, the "bullied" one is traumatized and becomes even less effective in responding (unless very adept, well-informed, and/or properly "coached") and the bully has succeeded in recruiting "fellow travellers" and active enablers, some of whom "go along" in order to avoid being bullied in turn.

It's not just the "Kitty Genovese" stories (though they abound): it's the daily misery of so many workers, not only in the health care field, but in almost every walk of life. Not all bullies and abusers are sociopaths/psychopaths. So much the worse when they are. (Many spouses have found out, too late, the true nature of their supposed "better half," and even the police and the legal system are often instruments far too clumsy and inefficient to provide any real protection from a determined schemer, out to harm and to harass.)

The lessons of Robert Hare (one of the more in-depth researchers and authorities on psychopathy) and many others who have written about these phenomena are simply not learned, not remembered, not given the prominence they deserve, not even in the penal system—what to speak of the overloaded health care, school, and social support systems. Far too often, bullies and abusers have a free hand, for years at a time. The cost, by any standard, but especially from the standpoint of "quality of life" (a concept now well established as a prime measure of the effectiveness of health care interventions), is enormous.

Regarding the monetary dimension, I am sure that the cost in lost productivity can be measured, provided that information can be accurately gathered, and that this will eventually be a prime motivator on behalf of reform—money talks, after all.

A broadening of the definition of harassment would be desirable, from a legal standpoint, i.e., de-coupling the issue of bullying or abuse from a specific, identifiable "challenged" or easily identifiable characteristic. After all, the real issue is the intent to harm, and persistence in inflicting it, as opposed to the specific characteristic which the perp has seized upon. I consider this a laudable goal, and would be willing to provide help, time and vitality permitting. Not sure how to help—I'm not a lawyer (Thank God! Though I was advised to study both law and medicine), and therefore cannot help with statutes and precedent, etc.

My feeling, after 6 decades of watching the world improve in some ways, but in others, move closer to the precipice, is that until we treat pregnant *mothers and fetuses gently and with respect, stop treating newborns like unfeeling pieces of meat to smack on the back at birth and puncture (in the newborn ICU, for example) without any anesthetic, and on & on through home, daycare, school, apprenticeship/college, workplace, marriage, & old age, then we are not going to get anywhere on a political and international level. And if we keep up the level of mutual disrespect internationally, we can kiss our a** goodbye, before many generations.*

Some want to colonize Mars. Look what a mess we're in here—just imagine how much "fun" we could have with 2 or more planets!

Well, I didn't intend to send you a long letter, just a short note. Good luck, and don't stop. Except to recharge your batteries & take care of home, of course.

When it comes to harassment or bullying in the workplace, there are one of three groups that an individual will fall into: the bully, the target or the bystander.

The Bully

As mentioned previously, the bully may be known within the organization due to overt behaviours and actions or is not openly identified due to the indirect or passive tactics the bully is using. One individual who wrote to me after attending a session defined bullying as: "A coward who tries to rule his/her weaker fellows by cruelty or threats: to rule with bluster and threats—to be noisy and overbearing.... Those who have no insight for humanity. Deep down they are cowards, lonely souls who get by in life brutally destroying another human being. They strive to break the spirit, then the body and mind."

A workplace bully has one desired outcome: to eliminate the target from the organization. Elimination can come in one of three ways: bully the individual until they quit, torment them to the point where they need to go on a physical or mental leave, or set the target up to look incompetent so they get fired. The means to this end is first through control. The bully controls the target through intimidation and direct threats, but even more likely through turning others against their target.

The following is from an email I received from a target who attended one of my sessions on his experience with a bully:

X takes no responsibility for his actions, he simply makes excuses for them. He told me this is the way he is and he is not going to change. I consider this a threat. He tells me not to take things personally but takes things personally himself. X has not learned to change what he is doing wrong and as such, we have no reason to believe his behaviour will change. This unsafe working situation has not changed because X's attitude has not changed. I cannot feel safe in my workplace with this unresolved situation.

There are many theories about what makes a bully a bully; from being tormented by bullies in the playground, to never being taught the true meaning of civility, to being mentally ill. There are types of bullies that are narcissistic, attention seekers and sometimes just plain mean. One thing that we all must agree on is that we all have bullying tendencies. Every human being has the capacity to behave in a way that is less than civil. As adults, if we are honest with ourselves, we can all remember a time after an incident when we were not proud of how we acted. We all have a certain tolerance level and bad days. However, that does not make a bully.

The characteristics possessed by bullies are relatively consistent and core qualities of that individual. At the far end of the spectrum, according to Robert D. Hare and Paul Babiak in their book *Snakes in Suits: When Psychopaths Go To Work*, a psychopath is defined as a person with "a personality disorder rooted in lying, manipulation, deceit, egocentricity, callousness and other potentially destructive traits." The authors state that one percent of people in the United States of America are psychopaths, however, out of the total number of managers in the workplace, three percent are psychopaths.

Personality disorders must be diagnosed by mental health professionals. Oftentimes, the term "psycho" is used to describe a bully in the workplace. Regardless of a medical diagnosis, the difference between a chronic bully and someone occasionally displaying a bullying behaviour is very different. Imagine being in a situation whereby someone at work is constantly correcting you for perceived errors for a prolonged period of time. Out of frustration, you may reach a point where you step out of your normal professional mindset and lash out at the person by saying, "You need to cut me a break! You are not my boss and you need to get out of my face." After that, you quickly exit the office and slam the door. Within hours or even minutes you revert to your natural disposition and feel guilty, remorseful and embarrassed about your outburst. You may send the person a text or email to apologize or seek them out to make amends. An apology is made, the incident is not repeated and it is soon forgotten.

After such an incident with a bully, they would feel that they righted a wrong, were justified in taking such a stance, or proud for speaking their mind and putting that person in their perceived place. If the incident shook up or intimidated the other party, similar behaviour will be repeated to gain more control. This person never reverts to a different frame of mind, but rather has feelings of justification and passive or aggressive acts of control will continue when they feel it is necessary.

Oftentimes when discussing a bully's tactics, such as tampering with someone's computer, hiding supplies or setting up a plan to sabotage someone's work or reputation, people look at me with wide eyes and say, "Really? How much time do these people have?" Unfortunately, the stories are real and so are the consequences.

Bullies tend to attack or increase their bullying behaviours at times when they deem the target to be vulnerable. Complainants have told me of coming back from a bereavement, maternity/paternity or medical leave only to be faced with extreme bullying behaviours. One particular case involved a male manager who was targeting a number of female employees. The targeted group was between the ages of 20 and 45. The investigation was conducted and the allegations in most of the cases were substantiated. As a result of the inappropriate behaviours, the manager was terminated. A few weeks after the case was completed, I received a call from the HR liaison who told me that after the manager was escorted out with his personal items, his desk was cleared out for the new hire and while going through the drawers, they discovered a sophisticated excel spreadsheet that had a list of all of the female staff in his department, their ages and the dates they were menstruating. When the staff members were questioned about how he would have known this intimate detail, they disclosed that every month he would joke with them in a staff meeting and ask who was currently on their period. When cross-referenced with the dates of the complaint allegations, the incidents coincided with the staff members' cycles.

Not all cases of bullying are this methodical, however, we all have bullying tendencies to some degree. Therefore, self-reflection exercises are extremely valuable tools if the individual is honest when completing the exercise. The book *Mean Girls Grown Up* by Cheryl Dellasega is an insightful resource regarding the roles that females take in the playground, which then translates into how they behave as adults. I have adapted some concepts to create an exercise that has been useful in training sessions to allow participants to look at their own bullying tendencies in the workplace. A rating system of 1 meaning *Not like me* to 5 meaning *Very much like me* is used to respond to the following statements:

1. I am more likely irritated than intrigued by others.
2. I use defamatory language when I speak about certain individuals.
3. I always want to be in charge, calling the shots and making plans without asking for input from others.
4. My work "style" tends to intimidate others.
5. I constantly think about how I will attain or maintain a position of power at work.

6. Some people tend to "avoid" me.
7. I often forget to apologize when I knew I was wrong, believing that it didn't really matter.
8. I tend to shut out people who provide feedback on my performance or behaviour.
9. Being the best at work, no matter what the cost, is all important to me.
10. I have deliberately schemed to exclude or sabotage other people at work.
11. I tend to gossip about other people, believing that it is harmless.
12. When I hear gossip about other people, I repeat it.
13. I have been referred to by others as aggressive or a bully.

During this part of the session, participants are told that their honesty is extremely important and they will not be sharing their assessment with anyone else. Their results are personal and will only have power if the assessments reveal areas of improvement and the individual has the desire and ability to work on those areas. There is no final total to the exercise in order for a person to determine if they are a bully or not. Instead, I ask participants to reflect on questions that they have rated three or above. Critical areas from my experience focus on #12 and #13 related to gossip. Through all my case experience, rumours and gossip are the demise of individuals and in some cases entire organizations. If an individual came to work, did their job and did not discuss others with ill-will intent, the levels of morale and civility at organizations would greatly increase.

An additional exercise can be completed with the same set of questions. Once each participant completes the assessment, it is given to five or more of their direct co-workers or in the case of a manager to their reporting staff to complete based on their perception of that person. It is critical that this exercise is only done in a closely supervised manner due to the fact that it can have a negative outcome and be used as a bullying tool. However, if used properly it can provide some interesting insight to each individual. The perception that one has of themselves versus how they are perceived by others can be radically different. Statement #4 *My work "style" tends to intimidate others* is one where a discrepancy may occur. The individual may feel they are extremely approachable and have a good-natured style, while others may perceive them to be difficult to approach or inconsistent in their style. The point of the exercise is to allow for perception and reality to be intertwined and for a discussion and potential internal growth to occur, bringing the parties closer together.

The Target

One target sent me the following email:

I have never heard of anyone referring to bullying as some kind of disease, but over the past five decades of my life I have watched bullying become crippling and sometimes deadly. There seems to be no cure but what I have discovered is that this disease cannot be spread by coughing or sneezing. It is not spread from animal to human and no amount of handwashing can stop it. This disease has been most known to attack young people and schools are hit the hardest, where school grounds become battle fields. This disease has now spread into our computers. … As a child I became exposed to those who had this disease and it has crippled me physically, mentally and emotionally. I would carry scars of bullying for years to come and death would become a friend. I believed back then that when I turned to adulthood, I would no longer be exposed to those around me with this disease and I would be freed from the years of hell and the bullying would stop. When I stepped into the world and into the workplace, I soon learned that it was all a myth that the disease was only amongst the young. I was so naïve to have believed that. What I have learned about this disease when found in adults can become far more painful than I ever could have imagined. The verbal abuse and the cruelty from bullies could often leave the bruised co-worker feeling alone and depressed. Most times a worker has to turn to outside help because of fear of other co-workers finding out and they become blacklisted. I know first-hand the scars I carry each day due to bullying from a few co-workers. I am one of those people that can honestly say thank you to God each and every day for my job. I love it with great passion, never taking one blessing for granted, for I am part of this great team. I did not get this far in life without a lot of struggling and those who continue to try and break me through your bullying. Well I stand tall knowing that you are cowards and my heart aches for you because you are so sad and crying for help inside…

Sometimes "victims" of any type of violence may be seen as weak or somehow deserving of what happened to them. The myth of "victims chose to be victims" is still prevalent in our society. Individuals with that frame of mind must ask themselves, who would *choose* to be ostracized, criticized or psychologically beaten? The profile of a target of bullying is often surprising to the general public but even more so to the people who are targets themselves.

Let us cast our minds to the playground. Think of the children who were bullied. Think of the qualities they possessed. We could go to any school in the world, have all of the students stand against a wall and pick out the children who are at a greater risk of being bullied. This is a sad commentary of the current state of the world. If we were to guess who may be bullied, we would most likely choose the poor child, the heavy child, the child whose skin tone does not match the other kids, the child wearing different clothes or the child with the crooked teeth or large ears. However, there is a group of children who get bullied who do not fall within those stereotypical categories and cannot be identified simply by looking at them. Those invisible students are the ones with a high grade point average, generally labelled geeks, nerds and the teacher's pet. They are the nice kids, the popular kids and the kids who share their lunch with the kids whose parents couldn't afford to send a lunch. And who are the children who are bullying those kids? The bullies tend to be the ones with the low grades.

A New Zealand study conducted in 2015 revealed an 18-percent increase in exam results when grades were not posted for other students to see. A mother approached me after a session and shared with me the struggles her son had with bullying at school. According to his mother, this boy was extremely bright and everything he touched turned to gold. Since he was a young boy, he was able to retain information immediately and repeat it years later verbatim. This innate ability made school very easy for him; he would usually score between 95 and 100 percent on his tests. Like many schools, the school he attended had a practice whereby after the tests were marked, the teacher would read aloud the results to the entire class. Personally, I am not a fan of this practice. I think students should have tests passed back and be given the option to share their grade if and to whom they wish. In the case of this boy, after several tests with nearly perfect marks, he began to be bullied for being "too smart." He endured name-calling and physical aggression particularly on the day or a few days after receiving a nearly perfect grade. As a defence mechanism, he started to deliberately write wrong responses or leave several questions unanswered on his tests. Failing a test became his new challenge. His parents saw a dramatic decrease in his average and received a call from the school after their son walked into a test, signed his name on the attendance sheet, wrote his name on the top of the test and walked out of the room. A meeting was arranged with the parents, student and guidance counsellor. At this meeting, the boy was defiant at first but then broke down and told them about the bullying. He said he didn't want to be smart anymore, just average like the other kids. Through several meetings and counselling sessions, it was decided that the boy would write the test as he would have prior to the bullying and the test would be marked and mailed back to the parents. When the marks were read aloud to the class, a fake test and grade between 70-75 percent would be given to the boy. At the end of high school with a 97-per-cent average, the young man had his pick of any university. Although this story had a happy ending, it made me question whether the solution fed into the bullying pattern and put the onus on the student to "play along" to make the bullying stop. I wonder if this student's bullies were held accountable for the verbal aggression and physical attacks in which the boy was subjected. What about the psychological damage that may have become apparent years later?

Now if we take the general profile of those schoolyard bullies and targets and put them into the workforce, they are the exact same groups of people. The staff who are the most competent are the individuals who are targeted by the least competent individuals. The target is going to outshine the bully so the bully must diminish the target to narrow the competency gap. Staff who are less competent also get bullied. Regardless of a person's work performance or competency level, no one has the right to bully someone else.

Most targets of workplace bullying are the most competent employees in organizations. The bully seeks out a certain type of individual who has many characteristics that the bully does not possess. Bullies are driven by two things: jealousy of abilities and relationships. The target generally has the following qualities *prior* to the bullying: proficient, devoted, intelligent, authentic, trustworthy, dependable, independent, inspirational, ability to master new skills, well liked, sensitive, willing to share knowledge and experience, and has high moral standards. Targets who work on the frontline are often called "ass kissers" because they have positive and productive relationships with management or senior leaders. That employee is often the individual who volunteers to be on a committee, work late or clean up the boardroom after a meeting without being asked. When I speak to a target after they have filed a complaint, they are tired and sad. I hear comments like, "I was the one who started the Friday potluck," or "I was the one who organized staff birthday parties on my own time." Sadly, they would also tell me, "I don't do that anymore. Doing anything extra did not get me anywhere but in trouble. Now I just come to work, keep my head down and do my work. I am no longer trying to make this a nice place to work." What a shame. Here is a person who was invested in the organization, showed initiative and leadership, and who lost the desire to contribute beyond their assigned job duties because someone or a group of people couldn't stand the fact that this person was not like them. This person was a gift to the organization.

This is an example of the crab mentality, which simply means if I am not happy then you cannot be happy. It is a metaphor that describes a behaviour pattern that has been observed when crabs are placed in a bucket. Although one crab could escape, the other crabs will sabotage their effort by pulling that crab back into the bucket. The same thing will happen with humans if they are working with a certain type of individual or group of individuals. The individual or group will see a confident employee who willingly and openly wants to succeed. Out of envy, spite or a badly directed competitive spirit, this person will be hampered by others and pulled back into the "bucket."

Once bullying begins and the target's competency and self-esteem are attacked on an ongoing basis, the target's stronger characteristics slowly fade away. Over time, a once competent and capable individual may become weak and incompetent. Workplace bullying is like domestic violence; if the abuser has adopted verbal or non-verbal tactics, both are extremely powerful. Repeatedly being told that you are stupid, worthless and no one will love you will lead to believing those things to be true. Similarly, in the workplace if a person is told on a continuous basis that they are incompetent, not fitting in and will never make it in their profession, they tend to start to believe it. Self-doubt and a negative inner voice can turn a once confident and strong individual into a shell of their former self.

The feeling of self-doubt affects everyone differently, however, in some professions doubting one's abilities and losing confidence can be deadly. I worked with a firefighter who disclosed that as a rookie, he was being harassed daily by his peers and senior leaders. He was constantly called a "punk" and told he was only good enough to wash the truck. Even when cleaning the truck, he was criticized. He knew he had to earn respect but as weeks and months went by and he was constantly being told he was incompetent, he started to lose his confidence. He started questioning himself on the scene of a fire and spent hours afterwards playing the scene over in his mind—even the situations with a positive ending—trying to figure out if he did everything right, obsessing about things he thought he could have done better. A turning point for him was arriving at an active fire scene and as he prepared to enter the building, he hesitated. The next day he went to the doctor and took himself out of work "for the safety of the public." He felt that he had lost his edge and didn't know if he could continue on his career path to becoming a fire chief. He went back to work a few times and tried to move forward, but he was too far gone in his negative thinking. Eventually he resigned from his position and after his marriage ended, moved back into his parents' house.

Two things need to be present for bullying to be successful: (1) the target's sensitivity, vulnerability or weak spot and (2) a gang to follow them.

I believe all adults have a weak spot. It could be their appearance, education, family history, etc. Sometimes we disclose our insecurities to others only to have them used against us in the future. One of my main weaknesses that causes me stress and anxiety is having to do mathematics or work with numbers. I was raised in an era where calculators were seen as a great gift but never used in the classroom. I have struggled with math my whole life. Now knowing that, if anyone wanted to make me look bad, they would simply need to give me a budget or numbers to crunch and I would most likely fail at the task or require great assistance to complete it.

Picture someone with a learning disability. Their employer may never know about that disability. I have met many people over the years who have comprehension or language issues.

Years ago, I was working with a group of individuals around team building and identifying and responding to workplace bullying. The group was composed of mostly women who did manual labour. For most of these individuals, English was not their first language and they had been working in the same area of the company for more than 20 years. After my session, three women approached me to tell me they were recently told by their manager that due to changes in health and safety standards, they were now required to pass a written test pertaining to some key components of their work. The level of anxiety these women were experiencing was extremely intense. One woman was the spokesperson while the two other women stood back and had tears running down their faces. I was not quite understanding the issue. When I asked them about their concern with management's request, I was told that the three women were illiterate in English. They were able to read English at a very basic level but could only identify words related to their workspace, such as "wash your hands," "danger" or basic tasks that were written on the daily assignment sheet. These women had postponed the written test for months and only had one more week to write the test or be suspended. Their manager had no idea they could not read beyond basic words. The woman told me that the group would buy and share a newspaper every day and pretend that they were reading on their breaks so no one would know they were illiterate. Now they feared for their jobs and felt that disclosure of their illiteracy would result in their termination. I spoke to these women for a few days and encouraged them to speak to their manager about the dilemma and request that the written test be conducted verbally. With great fear and little hope, the three women had a meeting with their manager and revealed their best-kept secret. Their manager was extremely supportive and allowed the test to be read and answered by each employee while someone else recorded the answers on the test sheet. All three women passed the test with flying colours.

Things could have turned out differently if their manager was a bully. Firstly, their manager could have insisted that the test be done in the exact same manner as the rest of the staff, which would have resulted in a failing mark and potentially a dismissal. Secondly, even if the manager allowed for the test to be completed verbally, they could have used this new information to negatively influence the future of these women.

The last update I received from the women was that their manager was in the process of looking at funding a literacy program that they all could attend, in addition to any other employee who was interested. It had also been suggested that the manager should see if there were any other employees with the same issue and potentially bring the course to the workplace and build it into the employees' work hours.

The second factor is a gang. A bully needs other people who will either willingly play the bullying game with them, go along with the bully out of fear of becoming their next target or be unwittingly manipulated in joining the gang. Another term used in this scenario is "mobbing." The late Tim Field of the Tim Field Foundation stated that mobbing "involves a group of people whose size is constrained by the social setting in which it is formed, such as a workplace. ... The group members directly interact with a target in an adversarial way that undermines or harms them. ... Throughout the mobbing experience, the target is deceived into fighting, blaming and trying to hold accountable the minor bullies of the mobbing group rather than the chief bully."

The mob mentality is a powerful force that targets an individual who is going against the grain of organizational culture. Demonstrated in a passive or aggressive way, the end goal is to further isolated and intimidate the person who poses a threat to the organization's status quo. Being conscious of the potential or actual mobbing will put the target in a better position to defend themselves and not be taken further down the road of destruction and self-doubt. Only internal strength and the support of strong allies will empower the individual to continue to fight the battle that at times can appear to be an impossible feat.

The Bystander

The bystander effect is also sometimes called the "Genovese syndrome" after Kitty Genovese, whose 1964 murder in Queens, New York sparked social psychologists to study the bystander effect. Ms. Genovese, who was 28 years old, was coming home from working at a bar around 3 a.m. She parked her car approximately 100 yards away from her apartment building and began to walk towards the entrance. Winston Moseley approached her, and when she ran from him towards the front door to her building, he chased her and stabbed her.

Ms. Genovese screamed and cried out for help, and a neighbour yelled for Moseley to leave her alone. Mr. Moseley ran away. Ms. Genovese staggered towards the back door of her apartment building, but a locked door prevented her from entering. She collapsed on the ground near the door. Mr. Moseley returned and stabbed her several more times, raped her and left her for dead. A witness who heard Ms. Genovese's screams during the second attack finally called the police, who arrived too late. Ms. Genovese was dead.

Several of Ms. Genovese's neighbours heard her cries from their apartments, but reports vary as to how many of them, if any, called the police. After her murder, *The New York Times* ran a story with the headline: "37 Who Saw Murder Didn't Call the Police." A later investigation found a few witnesses and most of them didn't realize the cries they heard were for help, and none of them actually saw the entire attack. Probably a dozen people heard Ms. Genovese cry out, but many of them thought it was rowdy drunks coming home from a bar.

In the case of bystanders, one must realize that after a tragedy occurs, we cannot change past events. Bystanders or those who make a conscious decision not to become involved or intervene in a situation must unfortunately live with that choice after the fact. Deciding not to act is in fact making a choice. As activist and Holocaust survivor Elie Wiesel states, "We must always take sides. Neutrality helps the oppressor, never the victim. Silence encourages the tormentor, never the tormented." By virtue of doing nothing, the bystander is allowing the behaviour to continue.

To add to the tragedy of the Ottawa OC Transpo murder-suicide, one of Mr. Lebrun's former co-workers and confidants committed suicide three months later due to the shame and guilt of not informing others of the disturbing comments made to him by the murderer. The following is an excerpt from his suicide note written in July 1999 (published in *The Globe and Mail* on January 11, 2000):

"I have been unable to sleep well since the shooting at OC. The gunman, Pierre, had talked with me to greater length about it, and where to be for a better shot at some managers. As it turned out he shot himself at this location in the loft. I feel guilty as hell for not telling anyone. Who was I to know if he would do it or not?"

During training sessions, using *Mean Girls Grown Up* by Cheryl Dellasega, I have adapted a similar approach with bullying tendencies as when assessing bystander tendencies. Using the same 5 point rating system, participants are asked to honestly rate themselves (1 = Not like me to 5 = Very much like me) regarding the following areas:

1. I don't express my thoughts or feelings out of fear of repercussions from others.
2. I go along with what some people say even if I don't want to.
3. I will do almost anything to avoid conflict with other people.
4. I am often frustrated internally about how people treat me.

5. I often witness inappropriate behaviours towards others and don't challenge that behaviour.
6. I am often upset with myself for not speaking up for those who do not have the strength to speak up for themselves.
7. I often sit in silence when I hear people speak with ill-will intent about someone else.
8. I often pass on rumours or gossip I hear from others.
9. I am often overly nice to people who intimidate me in order to stay on their good side.
10. I sometimes enjoy "watching" controversy between other people.
11. I have refused to assist people who have approached me for help when they were being treated badly by another person.

As with the bullying assessment, the responses are not tallied up or shared; they are simply left for the individual to ponder and, if necessary, make positive behavioural changes. For me, statement #11 is the most important as the consequences to that choice can be deadly.

One of my most heartbreaking cases involved a small organization in a rural area. After more than 40 years, the CEO was retiring. As part of the succession plan, the organization started to recruit a new person for the position months before the CEO's official retirement date. It was both an internal and external recruitment whereby potential candidates were brought forward to a selection committee. After an extensive search, an internal employee was offered the position. Although this person had limited management experience, as a 20-year employee they had extensive knowledge of the business and its clientele. Shortly after starting in their new role, I received a phone call to assist with the transition. Apparently the new CEO was not only experiencing stress from the steep learning curve, but disrespect from the staff in both the management and labour levels. Insubordination was a common occurrence in addition to blatant disrespect. I was hired to provide the individual and management team with some strategies to deal with this transition, in addition to harassment and bullying training to the staff. Within three months of taking on the new position, the CEO committed suicide.

As a result of this sudden loss, supports were put in place for the staff and family members and a celebration of life ceremony was organized for the entire community. The CEO was a popular and well-established community member. The business was shut down on the day of the funeral and hundreds of people attended the ceremony. It was an extremely emotional day that ended with a very powerful statement. The mother of the deceased, who was in her 70s and had to be assisted up to the podium, said one sentence, "You people need to be ashamed of yourselves." The mother then left the podium under her own strength and walked through the crowd of mourners, pointing out every person who worked at the company and walked out of the building.

There were two primary bullies in this case who spent months tormenting the CEO. Out of the nearly 20 people who worked there, no one seemed to care that this person had unintentionally lost 30 pounds in three months and was coming into work in the middle of the night to catch up and learn about the position's roles and responsibilities. Apparently when the CEO begged the staff to help with their job transition, they were blatantly told, "You wanted to be the boss, I guess you're gonna take what comes with it."

Although I always try my best to be unbiased, in this case the mother was right, the staff should be ashamed. The CEO's physical and mental struggles were clearly identifiable to anyone watching. After their death, the conversation turned to who was to blame, the target's mental status and how some martyrs were saying they "could see it coming." My question to them was, "Where were all of you when you 'could see it coming' or the detrimental effects of disrespect, incivility and bullying?" This question may never be answered to an acceptable degree, however, they have to live with the emotional consequences of at one time being in a position to potentially intervene to a time when nothing can be done other than send thoughts and prayers to the person's devastated mother and loved ones.

It takes a warrior's courage to acknowledge that your point of view matters, that your truth matters, that your gifts matter, and that your presence on this earth matters. You don't have to earn this right; it's yours as part of your birthright.

~ Debbie Ford ~

Bullying: The Technological Evolution

I have had a variety of reactions from participants when conducting training on the topic of workplace bullying. I have seen both men and women sit in a workshop or training session and become increasingly emotional. The issue of bullying cuts to the core of humanity. Participants become emotional for a number of reasons; it may be that they are presently being bullied in the workplace and feel like I am talking about them or they are being bullied at home. Although in the session we are talking about workplace bullying, this phenomenon unfortunately is a mirror of domestic violence. Individuals have said to me, "I can't believe it, I felt like you spent three hours describing me and my situation." One woman told me I had just described her ex-husband, another said I had described her 14-year-old daughter and another said she was being bullied at home by her adult step-children.

People tend to get emotional with this topic if they were bullied as children. One man left one of my sessions and started hyperventilating in the hallway. Once his peers calmed him down, he told me that the topic of childhood bullying was too intense for him; that as he was listening to me he felt as though his childhood bully was in the room calling him names and punching him in the stomach.

For individuals who were bullied as children, they will never forget that experience. Even when they are elderly and their memory may be fading, they will still remember the name of their bully. Even individuals who were not bullied, years later when they see their elementary or high school picture, they can still remember the names of their best friends and the bullies who terrorized their schoolyard. Everyone else in the picture will be a blur. We remember those who impact our lives in either a positive or negative way.

People can also be sensitive to this topic if they have children, grandchildren or nieces and nephews who are presently being bullied in the schoolyard. Bullying in my generation seems to have been a more manageable situation than what young people are dealing with today. When I was in school, if a child had an issue with another child, one of them called a fight and after school they met at the back of the school for a bit of a scuffle, and then they avoided each other for the rest of the year. They did not have text messaging (or even cellphones), Facebook, Instagram or Twitter. Now individuals at a very young age can torment others on a variety of social media platforms sometimes to the point of suicide. What is deeply disturbing is often the individuals involved have never met each other and do not even live in the same country.

Technology has become a tool to spread hate and destruction with the touch of a finger or snap of a picture. From verbal disagreements, to physical altercations, to the use of social media, both child and adult bullying has evolved over several decades. No longer do individuals need to gain strength physically or mentally to berate or threaten another person. Incivility and criminal activity can now be conducted with the click of a button or creation of a website or Facebook page. Manifestos and live streaming have taken the world of bullying and violence to another level. The fact that cellphones are now being given to primary school children for safety reasons ironically brings with it more danger and exposure to inappropriate ideas and images than ever before.

In addition, emojis are the new sexting. According to technology influencer Ariel Coro, teenagers are now using emojis as a new secret language for sexting. Some examples of this code language include:

Strawberry = vagina

Rose = vagina or virginity

Camera with flashbulb = send me a naked picture

Film camera = sex tape

Negative roll film = send me a picture of your private parts

Camel = having sex

Technology and the internet have taken bullying to a new level. No one is truly safe from a bully's grip. Through cyberspace and social media platforms, the bullying and harassment game can now be played 24 hours a day.

Those who live in Canada may remember the heart-wrenching case of Amanda Todd, a teenager from British Columbia. As a young girl, Amanda was just trying to fit in with her peers and thought the online world may bring her some much-anticipated friends and supportive allies. Seeking acceptance, Amanda was lured by a false sense of anonymity and seemingly innocent gesture at a time when sexting was relatively unknown. She connected with an online predator who was later discovered to be a man in his 30s. After repeated requests, Amanda succumbed to the pressure and sent the perpetrator a topless picture. From that moment on, her life changed forever. She was bribed, exploited and bullied for the remainder of her short life. Amanda switched schools but her stalker found her friends on Facebook and sent them her picture. The bullying escalated to the point of Amanda attempting suicide by drinking bleach, resulting in hospitalization and a rapid increase in the bullying behaviours.

On September 7, 2012, Amanda posted a nine-minute video using flash cards. In this raw video, she detailed her situation and asked for help stating, "I have nobody." On October 10, 2012, Amanda committed suicide and millions of people worldwide had viewed her vulnerable self.

This case exposed the dark side of the internet, the concept of sexting and, more importantly, the world of online sextortion. A man living in the Netherlands was charged in connection with Amanda's exploitation and ultimate death in addition to a number of other similar criminal acts he committed against other young people across the globe. See the Amanda Todd Legacy Society (amandatoddlegacy.org) for more information.

Another tragic case of teenage suicide occurred two years prior to Amanda ending her own life—that of Tyler Clementi, an 18-year-old man living in New Jersey. As described on the Tyler Clementi Foundation website (tylerclementi.org):

Tyler grew up with a passion for music. Tyler began playing the violin in the third grade and became an accomplished violinist. He performed in numerous orchestras and was awarded with several accolades for his musical contributions.

Tyler was also an enthusiastic bicyclist and unicyclist.

By combining his knowledge with creativity and talent, he taught himself to play the violin while unicycling. He understood that we all must learn to embrace unique qualities in others and in ourselves.

The summer after his high school graduation, Tyler was learning to embrace his gay self. He had just begun the important journey of coming out to close family and friends. Tyler was brave and honest about who he was, but this was still a difficult, vulnerable time for him.

In August of 2010, Tyler began studying at Rutgers University where he was excited to learn, grow and have the freedom to live openly as a gay man.

He began playing violin at the institution's high level orchestra. Only a few weeks into his first semester, Tyler's musical gifts earned him a seat in an orchestra comprised primarily of upperclassmen and graduate students. Tyler was one of only two incoming freshman who made the graduate school orchestra.

Within weeks, Tyler became the victim of a horrible act of cyber-harassment, a type of bullying or cruelty that takes place using the internet.

One night, Tyler asked his dorm mate, Dharun Ravi, for some privacy because he had a date. Ravi agreed but what Tyler didn't know was that Ravi was planning a horrible act of humiliation; he secretly pointed his computer's webcam at Tyler's bed, and then left.

The camera captured Tyler in an intimate act, as Ravi invited other students to view it online. Many students at the university contributed to this invasion of privacy by not reporting or stopping what was happening to Tyler.

Tyler discovered what his abuser had done when he viewed his roommate's Twitter feed. He learned he had widely become a topic of ridicule in his new social environment. He also found out that his roommate was planning a second attempt to broadcast from the webcam.

Several days later, Tyler Clementi ended his life by jumping off the George Washington Bridge. He was eighteen years old.

In April 2013, Rehtaeh Parsons, a 17-year-old student from Halifax, Nova Scotia, was taken off life support three days after she tried to hang herself. Rehtaeh was bullied relentlessly for more than a year after allegedly being gang raped at 15 years old. Police confirmed that a photograph of her having sex with one of the teenage boys was sent to friends. Her mother Leah Parsons wrote on her Facebook tribute, "Rehtaeh is gone today because of the four boys that thought raping a 15-year-old girl was OK and to distribute a photo to ruin her spirit and reputation would be fun. Secondly, all the bullying and messaging and harassment that never let up are also to blame. Lastly, the justice system failed her. Those are the people that took the life of my beautiful girl."

Over the past 10 years, I have been involved in numerous cases involving the internet and social media. Text messaging is now one of the most popular stalking tools. Most people over the age of 12 have a cellphone. Work is no longer a place to concentrate on the task at hand without being interrupted by personal issues. Before cellphones became a necessity and perceived right of employees, an intercom was used to page someone if they received an external call and handwritten messages were taken. Communication with friends or family was restricted to breaks, lunch periods and after work. Cellphones serve a purpose when used properly, however, they can also wreak havoc. I have had cases where complainants have had their picture taken without permission, sometimes in change rooms and washrooms, and then these photos were posted online.

Another trend is employees posting work grievances or complaints online to either embarrass their target or make a point to their employer. An employer's expectations of confidentiality are breached daily. Employers are now creating social media policies to protect the workplace and the employees from online content that may be inappropriate. Professional networking websites are being used for venting purposes whereby employees publicly call out their employers in an open forum either as a last resort or with malicious intent. The question then becomes: When does the use of an individual's personal social media account become their employer's business?

More commonly, companies are creating strict policies regarding how it wishes to be portrayed. Employees have been sanctioned or terminated due to an inappropriate picture of them online wearing a company hat or T-shirt. Some organizations believe their employees have a right to their private lives, however, they are also considered to be representing the organization at all times, even when they are not at work or on company time. The best advice is when leaving the workplace, remove any uniform or articles of clothing such as a hat or jacket that has any identifying information about the place of employment prior to attending any social situation that could put the employee in a compromised position. A workshop participant told me that her co-worker was allegedly terminated from her job because her Facebook profile picture showed her taking shots of tequila while on vacation. The photo was taken while the employee was off work, however, as stated by the manager, her place of employment was included on her Facebook page.

Another workshop participant described to me through tears the daily taunting that she received from a bully at work. Her body size was attacked every day in the workplace and being called a "fat pig" was not unusual. One evening while she was on Facebook, she received a friend request from her bully. Although cautious about the intent, she felt she was being paranoid and thought this may be the bully's way of apologizing to her for how she had been treating her. Reluctantly, she accepted the request. A few days went by and everything seemed fine both at work and online. Then she saw that the bully had posted a picture on Facebook of a pig with a caption that read, "This looks just like X. I didn't know she had a sister." The target was devastated not only to see the post but also to read all of the offensive comments posted by strangers and some of her co-workers. Shortly after that, the bully posted a picture of a truck dumping garbage into a hole with a caption that read, "It would be great if X was at the bottom of that pit." Although the target did not tell many people what was going on, when she did, the person's immediate response was for her to unfriend the bully. The co-workers who commented on the pictures now completely avoided her at work, while the others who saw the posts silently shook their head when they saw her. She said she did not unfriend this individual because she would rather know what was being said about her online. The fact that the bully had ill-will intent when making the friend request took the bullying to a whole new level of malice.

A few years ago, I recall seeing a very disturbing video online. The video showed a dog that was hit by a car and another dog straddling it in traffic to protect it from further harm. The individual who shot the video from the sidewalk was talking at the same time as filming. The gist of his talk was that human beings needed to be more like the dog that rushed to the aid of the injured dog. There were dozens of comments calling out the person who posted it for filming the incident instead of intervening. The video is a sad commentary on the state of our world, particularly in light of technology.

Technology has created this phenomenon of digital bystanders who would prefer to take a picture or video of a disturbing or abusive act instead of coming to the victim's aid. It seems that any incident that occurs at work or in public is now filmed and sensationalized. The irony of the situation is that staff demand privacy yet oftentimes will grieve the employer for installing cameras or a GPS system in a company vehicle, and at the same time fight to have the right to carry their cellphone and use the voice record or camera as they see fit.

Photos and videos of workers sleeping or talking on the phone when they are supposed to be working is regularly shown on the evening news. I hear from managers that they are concerned that every conversation or meeting with an employee is being audio recorded or secretly videotaped. This is not only an invasion of the manager's privacy, it may also be a confidential matter, such as a discipline meeting or private staff forum. Moreover, depending on the type of business, such as social services or health care, personal client or patient information may be misused or made public. When a recording is later played, it is often out of context or potentially edited with malicious intent. A rule of thumb to live by is to assume that you are always being recorded in some format.

When conducting an investigation, in some cases I have been warned by my client about a person's history of secretly audio recording conversations or meetings on their phone and so I will ask the individuals in the room if they intend to tape the interview. Theoretically, I have no problem with the taping, but I do have an issue with the confidentiality, in other words where the tape will end up if it is recorded on an individual's private cellphone. Will the recording be shared with other employees or outsiders? I was involved in a case where a criminal act resulted in the physical injury of a client. At the time, a quick-thinking employee photographed and filmed the injured party. The police were called and confiscated the individual's cellphone as part of their investigation. In a similar case, it was nearly three months before the cellphone was returned to its owner. This created a great deal of stress for the individual once they realized that not only did the police have the information they needed for the investigation, they also had access to everything else on the cellphone.

The Continuous Professional and Personal Aftermath

Everyone has a story to tell either of themselves or someone close to them who has faced this epidemic. I have witnessed entire organizations become increasingly sick and symbolically die because of one individual who is a bully. Organizational trust, morale, communication, teamwork and quality of service dies a slow painful death. New and previously unaffected staff members quickly become affected and either join in on the destructive behaviour, become a target or leave the organization.

Gender also has a unique effect on the bullying phenomenon. In one case, a man in his early 20s, a new graduate, worked two shifts for his new employer. After his second shift, he resigned, stating he did not think he would be "walking into the gates of hell." He was not referring to the customers, but rather his peers. Until this new job, he had always worked in a male-dominated field. In his brief exposure to a female-dominated workplace, he said he never imaged that women could be "so mean to each other." He decided that he was "safer" working with men, so returned to his old job, which paid him significantly less money and had no benefits.

In another case, a young woman was one of 16 students who graduated from a local college. Six months into her current job, she started having issues with a peer so she reached out to her former guidance counsellor who shared that 10 of the 16 female students who graduated from the class worked less than three months in the field due to stress and feeling as though they did not fit in.

One workshop participant sent me an email following the session she attended and in part wrote:

Let me start off by telling you that when I first knew about this course, the date and the time of my expected attendance, I immediately became anxious. I worried and I stressed, wondering if the woman that bullied me three years ago would be in this course at the same time as me. I intentionally arrived 25 minutes early so I could have a seat and check out the parking lot to see if her car was there. I thought that if I got a seat before she did (IF she was in the same class) then it would be a little more calming for me to have her enter the room than have myself enter the room with her already present among colleagues. I did not sleep very well the night before, worrying that she would be there and worried about the comments, remarks and "looks" she would intend for me.

In another workshop, I presented in a theatre-style room that seated approximately 50 people. The desks and chairs were bolted to the ground. As I began presenting, there was a woman sitting directly in front of me in the middle seat. She was intently listening, often nodding her head in agreement to the bullying phenomenon. Several times her eyes would well up with tears. About halfway through the session, another woman in the back of the room raised her hand and asked for clarification on a point I had just made. As I was listening to the woman speak, I could see the woman's face in the front row completely drain of its colour. As I responded to the question, the woman in the front row stood up, bent over as to not block my view and left the room. She never returned to the session. At the end of the session, I was packing up my equipment when there was a light knock on the door and the woman entered the room. She apologized for abruptly leaving the session and proceeded to tell me that she had gone to the high school in the small town where I was teaching where she was terribly bullied by another girl for four years. She was relentlessly mocked and called names daily. She believed that due to the bullying and stress she was under, she only received average and below-average grades. Now 20 years later in a mandated training session, she heard her bully's voice for the first time. Although she knew they were employed by the same organization, which employed over 300 people, they worked in different departments and on opposite shifts. Through tears she explained that when she heard the voice from the back of the room, she felt like she was in a time warp, sent back to the 1990s. When she left the room, she vomited and did not have the courage to come back. She wanted to thank me for validating her high school experience.

The physical reactions of targets that I have seen firsthand, heard about from others and felt when I've been personally targeted are indescribable. Some survivors of workplace trauma have referred to having a form of post-traumatic stress disorder (PTSD). In one case, an organization had a manager who, in public places, was physically aggressive with staff. From the outside, this may have appeared as a joking gesture. While smiling and talking to the staff member, the manager would slowly start to squeeze their arm to the point of leaving bruises. No one was safe in this environment.

I was contracted to work with the management team following the termination of this senior manager. When I arrived at the building on the day of the training, I was directed by reception to go to a meeting room where the leadership team was waiting for me. When I arrived at the room, I knocked and opened the door. In the room were a group of people staring blankly at me and looking extremely nervous. I actually thought I had entered the wrong room. Once it was confirmed that I was in the right place, everyone introduced themselves, but I could sense a very tense environment. Respectfully, I asked the group if they were prepared for me to conduct the training. One of the participants became extremely emotional and said, "It is her. It is like she is still in the building after three months. This is ridiculous that she still has such a hold on a group of grown-ass adults." I had no idea what her statement meant, although I did receive a briefing regarding the incidents that led to the senior leader's termination. The woman elaborated and said they were all chatting with each other as they waited for me to arrive. As I walked down the hall in my high heels, they could hear the clicking of my shoes. Apparently the only person employed at this organization who wore high heels was the senior leader, so it was easily identifiable when she was coming in your direction. Since she left, no one had worn high heels until the day I arrived. The fear that struck them as I walked down the hall was more than they could handle; it was as if they were having flashbacks. For the first hour of the session, we had to debrief about their experience before any of the training could take place. If we had not done that, no one would have listened to what was being said. I believe the negative power of the manager's physical behaviour and the click-clack of high heels will stay with those individuals for a very long time.

According to the Mayo Clinic, PTSD symptoms may start within one month of a traumatic event or sometimes years after the event. Symptoms are generally grouped into four categories: intrusive memories, avoidance, negative changes in thinking and mood, and changes in physical and emotional reactions.

Symptoms of intrusive memories may include:

- Recurrent, unwanted distressing memories of the traumatic event
- Reliving the traumatic event as if it were happening again (flashbacks)
- Upsetting dreams or nightmares about the traumatic event
- Severe emotional distress or physical reactions to something that reminds you of the traumatic event

Symptoms of avoidance may include:

- Trying to avoid thinking or talking about the traumatic event
- Avoiding places, activities or people that remind you of the traumatic event

Symptoms of negative changes in thinking and mood may include:

- Negative thoughts about yourself, other people or the world
- Hopelessness about the future

- Memory problems, including not remembering important aspects of the traumatic event
- Difficulty maintaining close relationships
- Feeling detached from family and friends
- Lack of interest in activities once enjoyed
- Difficulty experiencing positive emotions
- Feeling emotionally numb

Symptoms of changes in physical and emotional reactions (also called arousal symptoms) may include:

- Being easily startled or frightened
- Always being on guard for danger
- Self-destructive behaviour, such as drinking too much or driving too fast
- Trouble sleeping
- Trouble concentrating
- Irritability, angry outbursts or aggressive behaviour
- Overwhelming guilt or shame

I have always believed that bullies just don't rob the target of their work life, they also rob them of their home life.

Unfortunately, most people who have been in the workforce for more than a few years have worked with someone who they would consider to be extremely difficult or unpleasant. We live in a world of differences, which is a good thing, however, these differences can make it challenging to work with certain people. There is a distinct difference between working with a bully and someone who has a defiant personality. When working with someone who is constantly challenging decisions, ideas or beliefs, an individual may go home and vent to friends or family about how this person made the day extremely long and tedious. However, as the person moves on to other activities, thoughts of this person begin to leave their mind.

One just needs to debrief or complain for a moment and then they do not think of that person until they have to face them the next time at work. This is the reality of the workforce; we cannot always be surrounded by people who think or act the same as us.

On the other hand, working with a bully brings a whole different dynamic to the interaction. When a target leaves the workplace, they bring the bully home with them. The bully is in the car with the target, in the shower, in bed and on vacation with them. The bully is constantly on the target's mind regardless of what the target is doing. As a result, the target's family members are also deeply and negatively affected. One workshop participant told me in confidence that he had recently returned to work following a medical leave and that he was being bullied at work, however, he thought he was coping. He went to work, came home and supported his family. One day he returned home from work and went straight to bed. A few minutes later, his four-year-old daughter came into his room and said, "Daddy?" He bolted up from bed and screamed, "What the fuck do you want?!" As tears rolled down her face, his daughter pointed at him and said, "Daddy, you're a mean man." The next day he went to his doctor and requested a stress leave.

The following excerpt is from an email I received from an individual who attended one of my workshops:

My family has struggled with a situation for almost a year now, and still suffer the repercussions of what I believe is the work of a bully. I don't know if anything can be done to remedy a situation like this "after the fact," but I am desperate after helplessly standing by while this has repeatedly assaulted my family member and their family as a result of the outcome, which was the loss of employment. Not only has it left them under financial stress, more seriously it has left them a shell of the person they once were—a confident, happy and productive individual. … The personal assault didn't end there. They since applied for other positions, expanding their search geographically. It seems they have been blackballed because although they have excellent references and a wealth of knowledge and experience to offer, they cannot get a job. What does one do after investing this much of your life into your career?

Targets go home and generally do one of two things: they either bully their family or shut them out. The target may miss meals, dinner parties and sometimes holidays because they are so emotionally drained from trying to survive or defend themselves against their bully that all they can do when they are at home is try to recharge their battery and gain enough strength to go back to work the next day rather than calling in sick.

One individual told me her story and how it has affected her life for over a year:

I was working in the same department for the past 10 years. I worked with a woman who was recently transferred back into the department from another department. This woman targeted me from the beginning.

Without getting overly personal, I was married and my marriage fell apart due to infidelity from him. This woman was aware of the fact that my marriage was suffering. This woman spent many times call blocking her phone calls, sitting outside my home waiting for my husband to leave and would make the call to me, disguising her voice or simply hanging up when I answered. She was attempting to make me think "she" was the voice of the mistress or hang up and make me wonder or panic. She was doing this while at work knowing I would be coming to work at 3:00 and was interested to see the "frame of mind" I arrived to work in a scattered state, falling apart minutes after I had arrived. I had a co-worker that sat by daily and witnessed this woman and her actions. This woman continued to "set me up" on a daily basis … going as far as cancelling external service providers, just so I looked bad that they did not show up, knowing it was my handwriting on the calendar that had booked them.

Eventually, I had started to stick up for myself … which was probably a very bad move for me to do. She put her games into high gear one day. I got a phone call from the main office informing me I was suspended until further notice due to a complaint of a co-worker and client. To make a very long story short … FINALLY … the co-worker I spoke of earlier was present when this woman was telling our client what to say about me to my boss. This woman had been manipulating an innocent man. All of this went on for the course of 12-15 months ... from the day of the first complaint to suspension. I was found innocent of my suspension. It had gotten so bad that I changed all of my shifts to opposite of hers, was prescribed anti-depressants and literally cried and vomited while being at work. I had my lawyer involved and it was only because I had nowhere else to turn.

As of today, I am happily still employed in that organization. However, on a daily basis someone tells me that "she" has just driven by the house. She continues to stalk me while I am at the workplace and continues to trash talk me on Facebook.

Absenteeism is the most common symptom of bullying. Organizations must stop putting employees on the absenteeism performance monitoring system without finding out why the person is calling in sick in the first place. Of course, there will be those who abuse the system. However, there will also be targets who call in sick because they are sick from anxiety or suffering from a mental or emotional issue caused by their bully.

Looking at the hundreds of targets I have worked with over the years, by the time they speak up about the issue or I am called to assist with the situation, I would estimate that approximately 65 to 70 percent of them are on some kind of absenteeism or probation program. The actual reason they have been away from work so often is because they are working with a bully. In workplaces where the employees work shifts or on some sort of rotation, I can review absenteeism records and identify the bully and the target based on the pattern of call-ins. Company schedulers have a wealth of information given to them every day about bullying situations. Employers may not even realize what is going on until they speak to the person(s) in charge of staffing a workplace. When schedulers call to see if an employee can pick up a shift, they are often asked who is working that day or who is in charge. Depending on the name(s) that is given, the person will decide in that moment if they will take the shift. It is simple to determine what is going on if the scheduler or manager keeps track of who is called, the questions being asked, the answers and if the employee takes the shift. I've had clients tell me they are implementing a new monitoring tool or having trouble staffing a work area, but they are only looking at the numbers as opposed to the real reasons behind it.

On many occasions when I raise this point with a client or in a training session, I have both labour and management tell me, "No, they don't come in because they don't want to work the hard shift or in the more challenging area," or "They don't want to work with the lazy person." Granted, these are legitimate reasons to not want to come in, although most people could always use more money. When an employee is called in and hears the perceived "lazy" person's name, they may roll their eyes or shake their head but take the shift anyway knowing they will be frustrated and exhausted at the end of the day. However, when the employee hears the name of a bully or harasser, a completely different set of emotions sweeps over them. The person's stomach flips, anxiety starts to kick in and they know there is no way they can spend one extra minute with the person who is tormenting them.

I regularly challenge organizations to dig deep into the root cause of a high level of sick time to determine the core reason. One example is when a new manager is hired. I have been involved in cases whereby employees have not missed work for years only to start calling in sick once a new manager or supervisor is hired. Not everything that happens at work is a result of bullying or harassment, but it should not be overlooked as a possible explanation for sudden performance changes. An individual who misses work can harm the bottom line of some companies or affect the annual budget for non-profit organizations. It also impacts co-workers who are required to pick up the work of the absent employee.

In one case, a man who was being bullied contacted me for advice. He was not coping well with being bullied at work, particularly because his bully was his manager and part of his concern was that his manager was a woman. He told me that if a male manager was treating him this way, he would deal with his concerns head on but the fact that it was a woman posed an internal challenge for him. A month went by and I received a message from him that he was in the hospital. Apparently, he got into a car accident on the way to work. Later, in confidence, he told me what had really transpired. He said he was on his way to work and, like most days, the closer he got to work, the more anxious he became. In a split second, he made a decision that he said he later regretted. He accelerated his car and drove deliberately into a tree. He was very clear in telling me, "Denise, I did not want to kill myself. I just needed to mess myself up a little so I could get a few months of a break [from work]." I was shocked when I heard his confession, but I also understood his rationale.

Around the same time, I was part of another investigation where a complainant told me that they almost always had to pull over on the side of the road during their drive to work because they suddenly needed to vomit. This was caused by the dread of going into work and contemplating what the bully might do to them that day. Another person told me that if they saw the car of the bully in the parking lot, they would leave and call in sick. Another person told me that they were going to have a surgical procedure done that wasn't necessary just to get some time off work and get away from the bully.

On November 18, 2017, Corporal Nolan Caribou, 26, committed suicide while at CFB Shilo in Manitoba during a training exercise. Allegedly, Cpl. Caribou had informed his supervisors a year prior that he was being bullied. He had reported that in addition to being called names and his locker being defaced, he was subjected to ongoing ritual hazing, organized fighting described as a "fight" club and harassment. Cpl. Caribou's mother Freda Caribou says her son was harassed and denied opportunities because he was Indigenous. The torment for Cpl. Caribou turned deadly.

Sometimes when I relay these scenarios in my training sessions, I see the eyes roll. There have been times when a participant has raised their hand and said, "That is ridiculous! How could anyone get to the point of intentionally trying to harm themselves or having surgery that they don't need?"

People should not judge someone or prescribe what that person should or should not have done. Most people cannot afford to quit their job; they have bills to pay and in many cases a family to support. There are single parents, parents supporting children on a poverty line minimum-wage job, individuals funding their education by working part time only to be in debt for years after graduating, and individuals sponsoring a family member in another country to immigrate. The thought of voluntarily leaving their job does not even come to mind when contemplating an issue at work.

Concern this scenario: a single mother in her 50s working as a labourer in the same non-unionized company for over 30 years with a grade 10 education is being harassed or bullied by her manager. Do you tell her to quit her job? Do you tell her to file a complaint with the Ministry of Labour or human resources? Do you advise her to go back to school and get a better education? Do you tell her that social assistance is a better choice than working in a toxic work environment? Do you tell her to hire a lawyer? Now picture that you are this woman. Would you choose any of the above options or would you come to work every day, keep your head down, try to stay out of the manager's way and continue to get a paycheque every two weeks?

Even as a consultant, all I can do is provide my clients with options and recommendations, but at the end of the day, they choose what they consider to be the most feasible or the best of two evils. My client Norma chose to go back home and there was nothing I or anyone else could do to stop her or take away her decision-making power. As the saying goes, everyone is fighting their own battle, a battle that you may never know about.

I receive many investigation requests from rural areas because it is difficult to find anyone internally or even in the community who is unbiased. The most complex and heartbreaking cases tend to be the ones in rural areas where people work and live in the same community.

The following email that I received from a participant who attended one of my training sessions demonstrates this point:

[Your session] made me realize that I am still being bullied by an ex-family member who also works at X. Like you said, my story is like The Jerry Springer Show. *This is the only time I wished I lived in a huge city like Toronto, because I can't get away from them and their gossip anywhere. We are always connected to someone that knows the situation. I have learned how to change how I react to them and all the stuff that they have put me through. But deep down it still affects me every day as there are children involved and they use them as pawns. After months of counselling I realized that I can't change that person and that I'm not the bad guy in this story.*

My story *began when this person and a family member split up. We keep thinking that some day they will see the light and realize that they are a bully and that the stuff they have done to my family is totally uncalled for. But here we are still in the same situation. I did go to management, they listened to our stories and things were better for awhile but they continually gossip about whatever is going on with the family, even as recent as a week ago. They are smart, and personally doesn't go off on me at work anymore, but eventually all the stuff they say comes back to me somehow. I do avoid them as much as I can at work, but a day doesn't go by while I'm working that I don't think about it. They will be nice to me for awhile and then just when I let my back down they turn on me. I have let so much go by, but I feel they will never let it rest at work, as they thrive on all the attention they get from all the followers. I know I can't fix what I have let happen but I need some advice on what to do now. What can*

I do about gossip? I know that I have to document but they say it to me directly, will it just be hearsay? I don't feel that any of my personal life or my family's should be discussed at work.

After listening to your session I realized that I will never stop them unless I step up to the plate. They don't sabotage me personally but they have almost broken my family member. As I write this I have to stop myself from crying, when they hurt I hurt. Almost every day they verbally abuse my family, doesn't let us see the kids and now they are turning the kids against us. The police have been involved, CAS has been involved many times, a file is open on them right now, but that person still comes out smelling like a rose. My family member isn't innocent, but they try their best not to do anything in front of the kids, but they are so frustrated at this point that sometimes they handle things wrong. This person has put the kids in the middle of this at least 80% of the time. My light bulb moment happened when you said that a bully's kids will grow up to be bullies themselves. One child is so angry and the other one cries a lot and is always sick. I feel so guilty that I can't or don't know how to help them.

Never doubt that a small group of thoughtful, committed citizens can change the world; indeed, it's the only thing that ever has.

~ Margaret Mead ~

Taking and Assessing a Complaint

Individuals in leadership positions may not realize the importance of receiving and taking a verbal or written complaint from someone who has come forward for the first time. The initial complaint taken is of the utmost importance as it will be the foundation and basis for any future follow-up, particularly if an investigation is the outcome of the complaint. When a person comes forward immediately following an incident, they tend to be highly emotionally charged and having not had time to process or methodically state their concerns, they tend to just blurt out their story. The first time they tell the story may be considered the pure truth, in that it should not be viewed as suspect and everything from that point of disclosure until the last statement or document will be compared to that initial statement. Any changes, additions, omissions or deviations will be cross-referenced with the original statement. This process will assist the investigator in determining the credibility of the complaint and the witnesses as the investigation process transpires.

I recommend that employers provide proper and intensive training to supervisors, managers, and health and safety representatives on how to receive a meaningful complaint. This training should be provided to any manager or internal leader, such as a lead hand or charge position, on all shifts and in each physical location.

It is recommended that the individual who is initially approached by the complainant take the complaint regardless of the reporting structure or the relationship between the parties. Receiving the complaint does not mean having to deal with the complaint or taking responsibility for further action or follow-up. Once a complaint is documented, it would then follow the appropriate internal complaints procedure. I have heard of numerous situations where a complainant came forward to a manager who was not their direct report only to be told to go to their direct manager. It is logical to assume that the complainant knows the typical protocol, however, has consciously decided not to approach that individual for a variety of reasons, including the manager may be the person with whom the complainant has an issue, the manager may be away or viewed as "too busy" to take on the complaint or the complainant does not feel safe or comfortable with the manager. When someone comes forward to a manager who is not theirs, it is generally due to a trust or respect issue. If an organization has a healthy work environment, the managers should not have any problem with their reporting staff speaking in confidence to another manager. It is only workplaces that have issues or appear to be toxic that do not allow this practice. Once the complaint is taken, the recipient will proceed to the next steps, such as referring the issue to human resources or the reporting manager.

All complaint recipients must follow the same process for all complaints regardless of the complainant's history or the recipient's perception of the complainant. Moreover, anyone in a labour or management leadership position needs to take every complaint seriously as well as offer the same support to all complainants. When an individual comes to a manager's office, two biases will present themselves: the manager's opinion of the complainant and the manager's opinion of the subject of the complaint. Regardless of the manager's view, they must remain as unbiased as possible during the process of receiving the complaint. Due to the amount of stress that is generally felt by an employee when bringing issues forward, the manager needs to encourage the complainant to talk about the incident or their concerns.

Although in most cases the recipient wants to be supportive when receiving a complaint, oftentimes the questions posed to the complainant may actually deter the complainant from proceeding. Questions such as "Do you really want to do this?", "Do you realize that this is a very stressful process and may take a very long time?" or "Do you think the situation is that bad that you have to make a formal complaint?" may cause the complainant to second-guess themselves or feel as though they are being oversensitive or dramatic. This may cause the complainant to retreat to the same situation, which may get worse and lead them down an even more difficult road.

When an individual comes forward with an issue, the recipient must consider the complainant's well-being. Oftentimes the complainant has spent days, weeks or even months finding the strength or reaching a breaking point before they finally come forward. The complainant may be in a fragile or emotional state and need extra care. A common joke with managers is that everything happens at the end of a Friday or the beginning of a long weekend. Although some managers think employees do it deliberately to mess up the manager's schedule, in my experience it is done for another reason; the complainant usually wants to unload the issue and not have to come back the next day and potentially face the person they are complaining about. It is also not uncommon for a complainant to make a complaint the day before they are going on vacation because they are hoping that by the time they come back, the situation will be rectified.

Offering resources to complainants such as counselling resources is critical. This may include the organization's employee assistance program (EAP) or external resources. Unfortunately, regardless of what the employer tells them, there are still employees who believe that an internal counselling service is not confidential and their concerns will be shared with leadership. In addition, managers should not act as "counselling" staff unless they have been formally trained and it is part of their job description. Managers could spend hours in discussion with the complainant with no advancement of the issues presented. There may also be potential liability if the wrong advice is given and there is a negative outcome.

It is critical to involve the complainant in solutions addressing their concerns and notify the complainant of the complaint status.

The biggest issue that I hear from complainants after they have filed a complaint is that they have not been kept abreast of the complaint status, including whether the respondent has been notified or even if anything is being done to address the issue. This was apparent in the Koster Consulting & Associates survey whereby a number of those who had been bullied were unsure if the action taken was effective. This is most likely a result of a lack of communication from management to the complainant.

I was contracted to deal with a harassment complaint pertaining to one department staff member against another. When the complaint was presented to management, the manager told the complainant that the issue will be dealt with immediately and they did not need to worry about working with the respondent again. The complainant came back to work on the Monday only to walk into a staff meeting and be greeted by the respondent. As a result of the unexpected encounter, the complainant had a panic attack and ran out of the building into the parking lot where they were hit by a car. Fortunately, they were not physically hurt, however, the emotional damage resulted in the staff member taking a three-month stress leave.

If a complainant voices concerns about their physical well-being, the complaint recipient must implement security measures immediately. Unfortunately, when an individual articulates to a manager or even a co-worker that they are fearful of another employee, oftentimes that individual is labelled as "paranoid" or told that they are "overreacting." All fears must be taken seriously and immediately referred to the appropriate authorities, such as human resources, an internal or external threat assessment team or the police. Lastly, complaints must be followed up and include concrete actions.

Fears are oftentimes related to employers and unfortunately not always acted on. On March 26, 2012, in a medical clinic in Newfoundland, 49-year-old receptionist Stephanie Chaisson was murdered by her husband. Ms. Chaisson's estranged husband, Luke Chaisson,

54, had entered the clinic and told a witness to leave the building. Following this, shots were fired. Ms. Chaisson died and the shooter had a self-inflicted wound. He later died in hospital. The rifle that was used was not registered.

Two months prior to the incident, the police were contacted and were investigating the harassment of Ms. Chaisson. Mr. Chaisson was arrested with the condition that he was not to contact his estranged wife. The murder happened one week prior to his scheduled court appearance.

Co-worker and nurse Lori Chaffey, who was in the clinic when the incident occurred but eventually escaped and called the police, stated that Ms. Chaisson had told her about the stalking, telling CBC News, "She had slept with a bat, she had asked for help, she had a restraining order on him. We had been in other places prior to that—he had been there. If we went out anywhere socially, he would show up. He easily found her."

She said that as she heard the shots being fired, "As a nurse I had heard and seen things over the years, and even what she had been telling me, I never really truly understood the gravity of how bad it was. … At that moment, I understood the gravity of what her life had been like and her fears."

According to Ms. Chaffey, the workplace had a number of safety concerns that were identified to the employer, however, were not addressed. She said "… it wasn't a safe facility."

There may be a situation whereby more than one person comes forward with the same or similar complaint simultaneously. It is important for the complaint recipient not to interview the complainants together or take complaints as a group. All complainants should be dealt with separately and best practices should be applied equally to each. The main focus of receiving the complaint is to determine outcomes based on each complainant's presenting issues. When a group of people is allowed to "complain" or report an issue together, there tends to be one or two spokespeople and a few people who sit there and nod their heads. This may result in the complaint appearing to have more people involved, when really there are one or two complainants and others who are either witnesses to a situation or acting as a support system. I have also run into situations whereby an individual, when interviewed as part of the complainant group, has informed me that they did not have any concerns, however, they were told that because they are a union member they must attend the meeting when the complaint is filed. Moreover, I have had employees who have signed complaints or issue forms only to later reveal that they did not have an issue but were pressured by their peers or somehow compelled to sign it.

For a complaint to be given and received in a way that is most useful and forthcoming, the complaint recipient must follow a consistent and diligent process when accepting complaints. Prior to hearing the actual complaint, the recipient must set the foundation with the complainant so that they understand the internal complaints process and are not misled about the outcome of their complaint. Complainants must be aware that once the recipient has knowledge of the complaint, appropriate action will be taken. The complainant must also be aware that due to legislation or organizational policies, their name may be brought forward should it be deemed appropriate or legally required.

One case that stands out involved a manager who kept an issue to themselves instead of following the proper internal process. Three staff members complained to that manager about their direct reporting manager. Months went by where that manager kept notes and supported the staff who begged them not to take their concerns to a higher level. Finally, the complainants went to human resources and filed a formal complaint. At the end of the investigation, the manager who was the respondent received one-to-one coaching and the manager who was supporting the staff who did not report the incidents was terminated.

CARE Model™

As a result of dealing with dozens of cases whereby the employer allowed the complainant to dictate the complaint process, I developed a complaint process model called CARE, which stands for Confidentiality, Accountability, Retaliation and Expectations. The model suggests that the following areas should be discussed by the complaint recipient with all complainants, regardless of their position or professional background, *prior* to them giving names or specific details regarding the issue(s) or person(s) being discussed. In addition, the employer must mandate all leaders to follow the same process to ensure consistency of practice. If all leaders do not follow the prescribed process and the complaints process is challenged at a later date, the employer may be found to have treated employees unequally with potential favouritism or targeting

Confidentiality (C)

When making a complaint, due to embarrassment or fear of retaliation, the complainant often indicates that they do not wish the complaint recipient to tell anyone else about their complaint or use their name. Before the complaint is made, it is critical that the complaint recipient immediately informs the complainant of the parameters of confidentiality. The recipient should assure the complainant that their issues will be kept confidential to the best of their ability, however, at no point should they promise the complainant that they will keep the issues raised confidential beyond what is reasonable.

The complainant should be fully aware that issues presented may be brought forward to the appropriate parties if deemed necessary by the recipient. Appropriate internal parties include human resources, senior management or union leaders. External bodies that may be exempt from confidentiality include legal counsel or the police.

In addition, the complainant should be cautioned that in order to preserve the integrity of the complaint process, they will be mandated from that point on to also keep confidential the issues presented and not discuss their concerns during or after the complaints process with anyone, including co-workers, co-complainants or any other staff member.

Accountability (A)

According to the *Cambridge Dictionary*, accountability is defined as "the fact of being responsible for what you do and able to give a satisfactory reason for it, or the degree to which this happens." Regardless of the recipient's reluctance in pursuing their complaint, the employer has the responsibility to ensure that due diligence is followed regarding any complaints received. It is imperative that the complainant is aware that once the recipient has knowledge of a situation that they will be held accountable to act accordingly.

Retaliation (R)

One of the primary hindrances to a person coming forward with a complaint is the fear of retaliation. Retaliation is defined as "to hurt someone or do something harmful to someone because they have done or said something harmful to you." However, by receiving an internal or external complaint, unless under some kind of privilege such as a lawyer or physician, once there is knowledge there is accountability, which leads to liability. In response to this fear, the recipient must ensure that the complainant will be free from any retaliation from the individual who is the subject of the complaint or any third party. Whistleblower protection is a necessary part of any successful complaints process. According to the *Cambridge Dictionary*, a whistleblower is "a person who works for a company or organization that tells an authority about something illegal happening within the company or organization." All internal workplace violence and harassment policies, in addition to general complaint policies, should clearly indicate the employer's commitment to the protection of the complainants and the sanction for any threat or intimidation to said parties. The complainant also needs to be reminded that they must not be party to any form of retaliation towards the respondent or any witnesses.

To solidify this concept, the complainant must be informed that if they encounter any retaliation as a result of their complaint, they should bring it forward to the proper authority. It is also recommended that the appropriate party check in with the complainant on a regular basis following their complaint to ensure that no retaliation has taken place. This is important because in some cases of post-complaint retaliation, the complainant does not bring the subsequent inappropriate behaviours of others forward for fear of even further duress.

Expectations (E)

Prior to the complaint being discussed, it is important that the complainant is asked about the steps they took prior to discussing their concerns with the present recipient. The following questions need to be asked:

- Have you spoken to anyone else about this issue or concern and if so, who?
- When were they spoken to?
- What was the previous process for their complaint?
- What was the outcome of the complaint?

Also, to determine the complainant's expectations, they should be asked the following question: "What do you hope will come out of our conversation today?" By asking this question, the complaint recipient is made aware of the complainant's state of mind and therefore will potentially be able to predict how the rest of the discussion will unfold. For example, if the response is, "I want them fired immediately," it may be determined that anger and intense frustration is the overriding emotion. On the other hand, where the response is, "Please just make it stop," it may reveal feelings of desperation or hopelessness.

Following the completion of the CARE process, the complainant needs to be asked if, in light of the information presented regarding confidentiality, accountability, retaliation and expectations, they still wish to make their complaint. If the complainant wishes to proceed, only then will they begin telling their story as to what brought them to the recipient.

It should be noted that all aspects of the CARE model must be agreed to and if not, the complaint process must not continue. It is important that the recipient does their best to empathetically support the complainant to move forward in the present or at a future date. Depending on the situation, if the complainant does not wish to continue at the present time, the recipient should follow up with them following the initial approach to determine if the complainant had a change of heart and wishes to proceed.

The following is an example of a CARE script:

Thank you for coming to speak to me today regarding an issue or concern that you have. Before you proceed in explaining to me what brought you here today, I need to tell you about a few parameters regarding our conversation.

I am here to support you, however, I need to speak to you about the issue of confidentiality. In my role, I am accountable to ensure that the workplace is free from any unsafe health and safety practices or inappropriate behaviours, including discrimination, harassment and bullying. Therefore, it is important for you to know that whatever you tell me I will keep confidential to the best of my ability. That said, if you disclose an issue to me that I believe needs to be addressed in another forum, I will have to act accordingly because once I have knowledge about a situation, I am required to act. Exceptions to the confidentiality rule are human resources, the manager, legal counsel, union leaders or the police.

In addition to me staying within the boundaries of confidentiality, it is important that you also keep confidential the issues presented and do not discuss them during or after the complaints process with anyone, including co-workers, co-complainants or any other person on staff. That said, if you wish to have support from your union in this process you have the right to do so.

One of the primary hindrances to a person coming forward with a complaint is the fear of retaliation. I want to assure you that the organization will protect you from retaliation from the individual you are complaining about or any other third party while on organizational time and property. Not only should you be free from retaliation, I must remind you that you also should not be party to any form of retaliation against anyone.

Therefore, if someone retaliates against you as a result of this complaint, you should bring the issue of retaliation to me or the proper authority. To monitor this, I will check in with you occasionally to ensure that you are safe from retaliation.

Before we get into the content of your complaint, I need to be aware of the steps you have taken regarding this issue prior to coming to discuss it with me. Can you tell me if you have spoken to anyone else about this issue/concern? If so, with whom and when did that discussion occur?

If the complainant discloses that they have discussed the issue with another party (namely a manager or human resources), the following questions must be answered: *As you have stated that you have talked to ________________, what was the previous process to deal with your concern and what was the outcome?*

I have one more question to ask before we proceed: What do you hope will come out of our conversation today? If the complainant's response is "nothing" or "just want to vent," the recipient must review accountability again.

Now considering the information presented regarding confidentiality, accountability, retaliation and expectations, do you still wish to make your complaint? If the complainant wishes to proceed, they will begin telling their story as to what brought them to the recipient. If the complainant does not agree to any part of the CARE model, the complaint process must not continue. On the other hand, the employee must be reminded that they are legally obligated either by internal policies or external legislation to report any code of conduct breaches or illegal behaviours.

I understand that what we have just discussed can be overwhelming, however, I need to ensure that you understand the complaints process prior to speaking to me. This is not done to discourage complaints but to ensure our accountability in dealing with issues. I hope that at some point you will come back to me or another person of authority with your issue so it can be dealt with and you can feel more comfortable in your work environment.

It is important for the complaint recipient to takes notes during the discussion to capture an accurate picture of the issues presented. Moreover, the purpose for notetaking is to show interest, confirm that the complaint is being taken seriously and verify the complaint. Any complaint documentation should not be recorded in a journal or daily diary as it may, depending on the issue or incident disclosed, be later subpoenaed by a civil or criminal court of law. Therefore, there should not be any notes included that are irrelevant or confidential to any other employee or sensitive organizational intelligence.

The recipient should inform the complainant that notes will be taken during the process to make the complainant feel more comfortable. I highly recommend that no computer or electronic device is used in this process. The time that the CARE process takes will completely depend on the complainant; in some cases, the introduction may take between five and 45 minutes. Therefore, once the individual agrees to proceed with their complaint, if the recipient stops to log into their computer or search for the appropriate form, the complainant will have idle time to think and may in fact change their mind and no longer wish to proceed. For the same reason, it is equally as important that the recipient does not answer or make any phone calls or leave the room prior to the complaint being disclosed. A notebook and pen are the only tools required to take the complaint.

Regardless of the complainant's or recipient's opinion of the severity or seriousness of the complaint presented, the recipient must keep in mind that all notes may be disclosed to an arbitrator or legal counsel if it proceeds to a formal internal or external level.

Once the stage has been set for the complaint process and the complainant has agreed to the CARE parameters, they will then be given the opportunity to share their concerns. It is advised that the recipient uses the free recall method to obtain the best information from the complainant in a way that causes the least amount of stress. Free recall is a person's uninterrupted narrative of an incident, situation or concern.

Oftentimes when individuals make complaints, they present issues in a way that bounces back between the past and the present. Sometimes this is evident during the free recall if they substantiate incidents with dates or time periods, however, it may not be so apparent when they only focus on incidents and do not indicate a timeframe. It is helpful if the recipient can get the complainant to repeat their complaint in a chronological fashion. A guided question for the recipient to ask that may assist in this process is: *Now that you have explained the concerns that brought you to speak to me today, I am going to ask you to try to tell me your story in a chronological order. It would also be helpful if with each issue presented you tell me the names of those involved or a witness to the situation.*

It should be noted that complaints are valid and need to be taken seriously even if the complainant cannot remember exact dates of incidents. Dates may become important if the complaint becomes an investigation of discrimination, harassment or bullying.

Use the following questions to help the complainant with date recall: *Although you do not recall the specific date of the situation, do you recall the time of year that it occurred (i.e., winter, spring, summer, fall) or any significant organizational issue that was going on at the time (i.e., budget, special event, etc.)?*

To begin the free recall process, the recipient may ask the complainant the following question: *Can you please tell me the concerns that brought you here today?*

Once the complainant has completed the free recall process and told their version of events, the recipient now has the opportunity to ask specific questions to explore certain points further, seek clarity or gather additional information. It is helpful for the recipient to use the interviewee's exact words to draw their memory back to a specific point. For example: *You stated earlier that when you came into the meeting "the room seemed very cold and suspicious." Could you please clarify what you meant by that?*

Following the free recall and follow-up questions, complainants will be requested to provide a written statement regarding their concerns. There is a higher success rate of receiving written complaints when they are completed at the end of the complaint process rather than the person leaving with the expectation that a written statement will follow later. The written statement should be completed on sheets of lined paper in pen and dated and signed by the complainant.

If the complainant leaves the recipient after making a complaint, they often become more fearful of retaliation and less likely to provide the complaint in writing. If the complainant wishes to provide a written statement at a later date, the recipient should accept their wishes, indicate this in their notes and follow this up with the complainant the next day.

If the complainant sends the written statement electronically, the recipient should print and save the electronic version of the complaint including the email message. When requesting a written statement, the recipient must be able to articulate the reason for the request in a way that is accepted by the complainant: *Now that you have told me your story and areas of concern, as I mentioned earlier, I am now going to request that you provide me with a written statement of what we just discussed. Although this may seem like a redundant exercise, I need you to write out your issues in your own words to ensure that I have all of the information recorded accurately. In addition, by providing a written statement, you will be assured that your complaint will be taken seriously from all parties hereafter.*

Sometimes the complainant may request to read the recipient's notes and sign off on them. This is not an ideal situation as the complainant may try to edit the recipient's notes possibly out of fear of retaliation or an attempt to minimize the incidents so that the recipient does not take any further action. To avoid this scenario, the recipient should request that the complainant write their own statement. If they decline to do so, the recipient should allow the complainant to sign the recipient's notes with the parameters that no information shared will be deleted but new information may be added. It should be noted that the more information that any party verbally shares or writes in their statement regarding their version of events, the more opportunities there are for a statement comparison and creditability testing.

The recipient should be conscious of literacy issues and if the literacy level of the complainant is known to be low, the complainant may be assisted in completing the written statement if necessary. Assistance may include the complainant dictating the statement to the recipient. At the end of the statement, it should read: *I, ____________ (complainant), have requested that ____________ (recipient) write out my voluntary written statement regarding the above complaint. Signed ________________ (complainant).*

If the complainant does not wish to provide a written complaint, the recipient should add to their own notes: *Complainant was offered and declined to provide written statement.*

In a time when everyone has a cellphone, opportunities for capturing incidents or post-incident interactions/outcomes are endless. As injuries and bruises change quickly over time, capturing a photograph at the time of the injury and chronologically afterwards will more likely stand up to greater scrutiny in a court of law over someone's word. During the intake of the complaint information, the recipient should ask the complainant if they are in possession of any cellphone photos, voice recordings or text messages pertaining to their complaint.

When using photo documentation for physical injuries, the photographer should take two pictures of the person from every view and angle with an anatomical landmark. An anatomical landmark is part of the body that is easily recognizable and where the bone is at the surface, such as a shoulder or knee. This landmark can be used as a reference point and identifies the location of the wound. There should also be two pictures of each wound or other injury: one that identifies a landmark and one that provides a close-up (fills the film frame) of the wound.

The following guidelines should be considered when using digital photography in relation to its admissibility in court:

- The photographer should be present in the courtroom.
- The image should have a time and date stamp unless it obscures a meaningful part of the image.
- The image should be printed by a retailer or professional photographer.
- The date of the printing, a receipt of payment or other evidence to show that it was printed professionally.
- There should be a clear chain of custody indicating who took the image, where it was stored, how it was secured and who had access to the image while in storage.

For photographs to be admissible in court, they must be relevant to the case and represent the object or scene accurately as observed by the person who testifies to that fact. Organizations should have a written policy regarding the handling of the image and what evidence there is to show it was done properly. This may be requested if the situation goes to court.

A photo consent form is recommended for use in all cases where photographs are taken or shared. The form should state that the individual gives consent to the organization to take a photograph(s) of them for the sole purpose of an investigation or potentially a civil/ criminal court proceeding. This form should be signed, dated and witnessed, in addition to keeping a copy in the investigation file and providing the party with a copy.

In some situations, the individual being photographed cannot sign the consent form due to age or competency. In these cases, the power of attorney (designated family member, court-appointed party, etc.) may sign the form.

Once the complaint and supporting documentation have been received, the recipient should inform the complainant that the appropriate party, such as human resources, will follow up with the complainant within 48 hours of receiving the complaint. It should be clarified that this follow-up is for the purpose of informing the complainant of the next steps as opposed to the completion of the complaint process. Due to safety issues regarding retaliation, the recipient should ask the complainant how they would like the recipient to follow up, either by telephone (not to the complainant's home), email (to their organizational email), or in person (meetings should only be held on the organization's property). Once the follow-up process has been determined, the recipient should thank the complainant for coming forward with their concerns.

Following the complaint process, the recipient must then determine the next steps based on the issues presented. Although the complainant may use the word "harassment" or "bullying," it is important to note that legislative definitions need to be consulted and personal opinions, including what is subjectively believed by the recipient to be harassment or bullying, should not be considered. It is very important at this stage for the recipient to remain as unbiased as possible by disregarding the complainant and respondent personalities and only look at the individual issues presented. Additionally, the recipient should be very cautious not to impose their opinion on what has or has not been said during the complaint process.

To increase the chances of remaining unbiased, whenever possible, the recipient should review the complaint with a third party who is removed from the situation and department, leaving out names and positions of individuals involved. The third party should be requested to listen to the scenario and, based on legislative or applicable internal complaint definitions (i.e., discrimination, harassment, bullying), provide their input as to what the complaint appears to be.

Survival mode is supposed to be a phase that helps save your life.
It is not meant to be how you live.
~ Michele Rosenthal ~

Conflict Resolution

Conflict can be a good thing. I often hear people say, "I hate conflicts" or "I avoid conflicts at all costs." However, conflict can be positive. It can bring issues to the surface, allow ideas to flow and challenge our beliefs and traditional ways of doing things. On a basic level, an interpersonal conflict is a disagreement or difference of opinion between two or more parties. If the conflict is handled when it first surfaces in a productive and positive way, it can bring individuals, teams and even organizations to an increased level of productivity and efficiency. On the other hand, if the conflict is ignored, underestimated or left to the parties involved to solve when past attempts have failed, it can destroy trust, morale and relationships in a very short period. Moreover, if left unchecked it can lead to more serious issues or accusations, such as harassment and bullying.

In most of the harassment cases in which I have been involved, the issues began as a disagreement, collected people and emotions, caused a divide in the department and led to isolation, aggression and ultimately a formal complaint. However, if the conflict appears to be interpersonal and acted on immediately, there is a window of opportunity for conflict resolution. It should be noted that conflict resolution or mediation should not be attempted when an investigation is required by criminal or civil law.

Within some organizations, conflict resolution is the preferred and recommended method for dealing with a complaint prior to launching a formal investigation. An investigation should not be launched in cases where conflict resolution is a viable and potentially less invasive option.

I received a call from an employer who informed me that there was a potential bullying situation going on in one of his departments. As per the process, I received the documentation from the initial complaint, which was very limited, and then scheduled a meeting to interview the complainant. Upon speaking to the individual, although they claimed they were being harassed, harassment was not what they were experiencing.

The scenario that was presented was that there were 11 employees in one small office space. The staff were out most of the day but required to come into the office several times a week to complete paperwork on the computer, make client phone calls or attend meetings. There were only four desks and four telephones in the office in addition to one small meeting table that could accommodate six people. After obtaining more information about the staff's roles, responsibilities and workflow, I suggested a group conflict resolution session for the affected staff, which was successful and will be discussed later in the chapter.

When attempting to resolve a conflict, maintaining the relationship is important. However, if a serious incident has occurred; if it is suspected that one party will use the forum to escalate the dispute or is unwilling to listen or discuss the issues; or if determining the truth, fault or sanctions about the situation is a primary focus, then conflict resolution is not a viable option.

In one case of a perceived conflict, the situation was not assessed properly prior to starting the process. Unfortunately, one of the parties had ill-will intent that was not identified. After one party stated their concerns, the other party stated, "Yes, I agree with you. Some days I may not say hi or be somewhat challenging in my communication style, however at least my child did not commit suicide." Eighteen months prior, the other party's teenage child committed suicide. Immediately following the comment, the session was stopped but the damage was done. The party who lost their child left the session, went to their doctor and was put on a mental stress leave "indefinitely."

In retrospect, the depth of anger and resentment the one party had regarding the other individual over a past unresolved issue was apparent. The ongoing inappropriate behaviours, such as sarcastic remarks and ongoing gossip, should have had more weight on the decision to offer conflict resolution. This case illustrates that conflict resolution cannot substitute when an investigation is required as per legislation or an internal process.

It is important to note that if there are differences in power between the parties, conflict resolution may not be a feasible option. If an agreement is made to deal with the present conflict or tension between the parties, it may end up backfiring on the manager, particularly if future discipline against the reporting staff is warranted.

This was particularly apparent in a case involving a frontline staff member accusing a manager of harassment following a conflict resolution process. According to the complainant, a few weeks after the process, the manager started to make inappropriate comments and disclose confidential information said during the process in front of others. The frontline staff member felt that they were being targeted. The formal complaint came when the manager wrote the staff member up for continuously coming in late and not using the proper attendance system when calling in sick. According to the respondent, although admitting that inappropriate public comments were made, they felt that after the process, the complainant became very defiant when requested to do specific job duties in addition to suddenly not following a number of processes, including signing in at the beginning and end of a shift. Moreover, the manager felt that the conflict resolution process was now being used against them every time there was a disagreement or concern raised. They no longer felt the reporting relationship was respected.

Conflict resolution is a *voluntary* process, the purpose of which is to disclose issues and emotions in a productive and safe environment. As the process is non-disciplinary, in unionized environments representation is not required or desired. As a courtesy, the union may be made aware of the invitation for a member to participate, however, is not requested to attend, as the presence of any additional parties in the room interferes with the focus of the session. The ideal outcome is to determine a mutually acceptable solution to enable better future relations. The forum will also give all parties a clearer understanding of and compassion for the other party's point of view. The structure of the process should be formal with clearly defined roles and ground rules for all parties to follow.

The process will identify and discuss key issues relevant to workplace relations and address one point at a time based on a consensus. Ultimately, the desired outcomes include clarifying any misunderstanding, solving existing problems, meeting all parties' interests and improving future interactions.

Although the terms "mediator" and "facilitator" are often used interchangeably, a mediator is required when a conflict needs a resolution whereas a facilitator manages a process. Formal mediators are trained professionals mandated by a code of conduct and follow a specific process. For clarity, the term "facilitator" will be used as it cannot be assumed that those leaders involved in informal workplace conflict resolutions are formally trained.

The Anatomy of the Conflict Resolution Process

The following is an outline of the recommended five-part conflict resolution process:

The Opening

Facilitators welcome the parties and establish ground rules to create a respectful process. The parties are reminded that they are attending the session on a voluntary basis and informed of the facilitators' role. The process is explained in detail and all questions addressed prior to the session commencing.

Part One: Individual Issues and Concerns

Both parties are given an opportunity to individually and directly state their concerns or issues pertaining to the other party. While these statements are taking place, there is an expectation that the other party will refrain from interrupting the speaking party. This allows for all issues to be presented in a systematic way. The parties will take turns until all issues have been identified. All issues will be recorded on paper by the facilitators and used as the basis of the process discussion and, ultimately, creation of the conflict resolution agreement.

Part Two: Facilitated Discussion

The parties can react and ask questions about what was said in Part One by the opposite party. This discussion is guided by the facilitators who will ensure that ground rules are followed and a respectful dialogue occurs.

Part Three: Stating the Issues and Building the Agenda

The facilitators, in agreement with the parties, record the areas of concern on a flip chart. These issues will build the agenda for further discussion.

Part Four: Brainstorming Ideas

Participants brainstorm and identify solutions for each of the concerns identified. Each idea is to be respected and objectively analyzed for practicality to ensure a successful and realistic implementation plan.

Part Five: Writing and Signing the Agreement

The issues along with viable solutions are recorded in a conflict resolution agreement, which is to be thoroughly reviewed by the parties. Once agreed upon, all parties sign the agreement and receive a copy. The agreement will be the foundation for future interactions between the parties.

The Closing

This is an opportunity to wrap up any loose ends and thank the participants for their co-operation in working out a mutually acceptable agreement. Next steps, if any, are to be discussed and committed to at this time. At this point, the facilitators' job is complete, and a manager will be responsible for monitoring and altering the agreement accordingly.

Separate Meetings

Separate meetings are an important component of the process. They enable the facilitators to privately assist the parties to proceed when high emotions are negatively charging the session. Facilitators should take turns conducting these sessions and remain unbiased so as not to appear to be taking sides. If an individual requires more than one separate meeting, the facilitator should be different each time.

Facilitator Preparation

Prior to the conflict resolution process, each facilitator needs to be aware of the parameters around the parties' decision-making restrictions. The purpose of this is to ensure that the parties are not making suggestions or decisions in areas where they do not have approval or responsibility to do so. Commonly restricted areas include the budget, policies and procedures, hours of work and, if relevant, the collective agreement.

The assignment of the facilitator role should be determined on a case-by-case basis.

Direct manager or supervisor involvement is appropriate if a management decision is not warranted, parties are comfortable with supervisor/manager assignment or the issue presented is not of a job performance or disciplinary nature. However, the direct manager or supervisor of the parties involved may not be a viable option if the manager has a known bias regarding which party is "right" or "wrong" or the manager is experiencing a high level of frustration or anger towards either party involved in the conflict. This scenario should also be avoided if either party feels uncomfortable with the manager in that role or perceives the manager as being unfair or favouring one of the parties.

Prior to taking on the role of facilitator in a conflict resolution situation, the facilitator must answer the following questions honestly: Why was I asked to step in? Why do I want to step in? Would someone else be a better choice? Can I be impartial? Do I have a stake in the outcome? Are the parties comfortable with me in this role? If there is more than one facilitator involved, both parties must ask and answer the above questions honestly. If any of these questions poses an issue, then another facilitator should be sought out, ideally one that does not have a reporting or blood relationship with any of the parties. In some cases, based on the parties involved or biases present, an external facilitator or mediator should be considered.

The parties involved in the conflict need to be approached by their direct supervisor/manager to explore the possibility of the resolution process and it is the supervisor/manager's responsibility to ensure that the process is fully explained, understood and agreed upon by all parties. If possible, the facilitator(s) should be determined prior to the parties being approached about the conflict resolution process. This will increase the parties' comfort with the process and allow them to voice their level of acceptability with the person(s) being offered.

The following is an example of a script that supervisors/managers can use to explain the conflict resolution process to the parties involved in the conflict:

The goal of the conflict resolution process is to reach an agreement that all participants find reasonable and in their best interest. The primary purpose of the process is to discuss complaints and emotions in order to work out mutually acceptable solutions to improve future relations and gain confidence in handling future conflicts.

This is a voluntary process and the parties may choose whether to participate. Participants may leave the process at any time if they feel uncomfortable, unsafe or that the process is not meeting their needs.

This is a confidential session and all parties including the facilitator(s) will keep confidential everything that is said during the session.

The conflict resolution process will include the parties involved in the conflict and, depending on the situation, a facilitator(s) who may be your manager or two unbiased trained internal managers.

Conflict resolution is a non-disciplinary process that does not require union or legal representation. The process is based on resolution, not punishment.

The conflict resolution process is as follows: Each party will have an opportunity to discuss their concerns and the situation that brought them to the point of requiring assistance to resolve the conflict situation. During this time, there will be no interruptions. Following this, there will be an open discussion and the facilitator(s) will help you determine the important issues and concerns. If the parties reach an agreement on the common issues, they will be recorded and then the parties will discuss options for resolution. Once the parties have come to an agreement, a conflict resolution agreement will be created and signed by both parties. Only the aspects to which all parties have agreed will be included in the agreement. This session may take up to two hours and if more time is required, another session will be scheduled.

All parties must agree to participate in order to proceed. If all parties agree to participate in the process, they should sign a pre-conflict resolution agreement indicating that they are participating in the process voluntarily, with goodwill and agree that the facilitator(s) is neutral and unbiased. In the case where one party disagrees, the manager must explain to the other party that all parties must agree but at this point this is not the case. All parties should be reassured that if the situation remains the way it presently is, the option will be available in the future, however, if the situation worsens or bullying or harassing behaviours are exhibited then the next course of action may be discipline. This may be perceived on the surface to be a threat, but it is simply a reality of what may occur if the parties do not work together professionally in the future.

Once all parties have been oriented to the process and agree to it, the facilitator(s) needs to assess and book an appropriate place for the process. This would include a space that is psychologically and physically safe and away from the parties' work area and colleagues. If possible, the space should also include a secondary space for separate meetings or breaks if needed. It is recommended that the space be booked for a minimum of three hours. In addition, supplies should include paper, pens, a flip chart, markers, water, a box of tissues and a "do not disturb" sign for the door.

Seating arrangements should be determined on a case-by-case basis, taking into consideration the level of emotion involved in the conflict, familiarity of the parties and psychological issues of all parties. Seating arrangement options include a roundtable, which is ideal if minimizing status differences is important; or a square or rectangular table with the facilitator(s) between the parties, which is recommended if the parties feel intimated or threatened in some way by the other party. In some cases, there may not be a table at all to encourage parties to let down their guard. However, one downside of not having a table is not having a space for drinks or be able to take notes. In the case of a more formal situation, the setup could include a rectangular table where the facilitator(s) sits at the head of the table. This may be helpful in situations where there is anger or negative emotions on behalf of the parties. Moreover, this setup results in the parties speaking to the facilitator rather than each other, which may de-escalate an already tense situation. On the other hand, if using a square or rectangular table where the parties sit across from each other, this will inevitably encourage the parties to speak to each other.

If there are co-facilitators, prior to the process they need to discuss the following division of tasks: facilitating different session components, dealing with difficulties that may arise and notetaking.

Notetaking is a critical component of the process as the discussion that takes place between the parties will form the basis of the agreement. Therefore, it is important for the facilitators to decide who will take detailed notes and who will serve as facilitator to navigate the process and build a strong rapport with the parties. The role of notetaker and facilitator may be interchanged throughout the session if deemed necessary or desired by the facilitators.

The Facilitator Process

The Opening

The purpose of the opening of the conflict resolution process is to set a positive tone and encourage civil interactions and honesty.

The following is an example of a script that facilitators can use to kick off the conflict resolution process:

Welcome everyone and thank you for coming to today's conflict resolution session. I commend you for having the courage to try this process.

Before we get into the content of what brought you all here today, I would like to explain a few things about the purpose of the facilitator(s) and their role. This is a non-disciplinary process that focuses on resolution as opposed to punishment and at any time during the process if you do not wish to proceed for any reason, you will be free to terminate your involvement.

The role of the facilitator(s) is to encourage constructive conversation and help you find your own solutions to the issues. The facilitator(s) is not a judge, cannot determine facts about what has happened, and will not tell the parties to fix the situation or provide solutions.

If the facilitator(s) is not the manager of the parties involved, it should be noted here that the facilitator(s) has no conflict of interest, namely any reporting or blood relations with any of the parties, and has no vested interest in the outcome of the resolution.

This process honours confidentiality, and all parties, including the facilitator(s), are expected to keep confidential what happens in this room and the contents of the discussion. You should also be aware that a part of the process involves the facilitator(s) taking notes. The purpose of the notetaking is to ensure that the issues raised are captured. These notes will be a critical part of the process in that they will assist with the agreement that will be formulated at the end of the discussion. That said, all non-essential notes from this session taken by any of the parties involved, including the facilitator(s), will be destroyed.

If the facilitator(s) is not the manager of the parties involved, it should be noted that the referral source (the person who requested the conflict resolution) is only informed that the process was held and whether an agreement was reached. The referral source will not be given any details regarding the discussion.

It should be noted that although confidentiality is a primary focus of the process, exceptions to confidentiality are any issues that cannot be kept legally, professionally or morally confidential by the facilitator(s). Examples include any threat that is made, if a crime is disclosed or if it appears that either party is a danger to themselves or others.

The process will include the following components:

Part One allows each person to take a turn speaking of anything that they feel is relevant to them attending today's session. Each party will quietly listen without interruption while the other party is speaking. During this part of the process, we will take notes, which will be used later to create the agenda and brainstorm ideas.

Part Two is a facilitated discussion that will allow each party to respond to the other party's statement or ask for clarity. The discussion will stay within respectful and professional boundaries.

At any time during the process, any party may request a separate meeting with the facilitator(s), or the facilitator(s) may request to speak to one of the parties. This is a normal part of the conflict resolution process for the purpose of checking out concerns, confronting unhelpful behaviour or helping to think through options.

Part Three of the discussion shifts to the future and each of you must agree on an agenda of issues that need resolution. For this exercise, we will use the flip chart.

Part Four involves working through each issue on the agenda and generating ideas for each. During this process, we will be adjusting and weighing alternatives and ultimately begin to craft a workable mutually satisfactory agreement.

The final component is if a mutually satisfactory settlement occurs between all parties, we will then write an agreement containing the decisions that were made. Once this is complete, each of you will sign the agreement and take a copy for your reference. A copy of the final agreement will be given to your manager(s) for information and monitoring purposes. This agreement will not be part of your personnel file or be given to human resources (or the union, if applicable).

If a resolution cannot be accomplished using this process, the notes taken regarding the issues and concerns raised will be destroyed.

Lastly, as a reminder, you all signed an agreement prior to coming here today, which states that it is a voluntary process of a non-disciplinary nature, that there is goodwill to openly and honestly try to resolve the issues presented and that confidentiality will be honoured. Do you still agree with that statement?

If any of the parties do not agree with or challenge the parameters of the statement, the facilitator(s) should reiterate its importance. If they still do not agree, the process should be discontinued and, depending on the circumstances, be revisited at a later date.

If the agreement is signed, the facilitator may begin the process by asking, *Are there any questions before we proceed?*

Part One

Thank you for agreeing to proceed with this process. Before we start, as this is your process, I would like you to establish a few ground rules before we begin.

The participants need to take control of the process and set a framework for behaviour expectations. Oftentimes when asked to create ground rules, particularly when there have been past conflicts or a tense environment, the rules tend to be negatively stated. For example, rules may include the following: no interruptions, yelling, swearing, eyerolling or disrespect. These ground rules should be recorded on a flip chart for future reference. Once recorded, the facilitator(s) may assist the parties to frame the rules in a more positive light to start the process in a less confrontational or accusatory manner.

Examples of reframed ground rules may include:

- Keep the discussion focused on the workplace
- Mirror professional behaviour
- Be conscious of body language
- Keep to the issues at hand
- Speak to the issue, not the person

Once the rules are established and agreed upon, the next step is to select someone to start the uninterrupted discussion. This may be determined by the situation, however, the facilitator(s) may ask the parties to decide who will go first. The way this is handled by the parties may be a clear indicator of how things will proceed going forward. In a less than ideal situation, the facilitator(s) may choose who goes first based on the level of agitation. On the surface, this may appear to be rewarding negative or aggressive behaviour, however, it may actually allow Part One of the process to run more smoothly as the most agitated individual may be the one who is least likely to meet the behavioural expectation of refraining from interrupting the other party when speaking. Once it is decided who will start the process, the facilitator(s) may start the process by asking the party, *Can you tell us the concerns that brought you here today?*

The facilitator(s) must stay in control of this part of the process by being consistent and fair, reassuring the parties that there is equal time for each of them. The ground rules should be repeated when necessary and any party who is not honouring the process by continually interrupting or breaking the ground rules will be dealt with accordingly, including being asked to leave the session if necessary. At any point, the process may be terminated and may or may not be revisited as an option at a later date.

The rule of no interruption includes the facilitator(s) as they must model the behaviour requested of others. There may be a time, in private, when the facilitator (s) will need to assist with a reluctant party or remind them of information they presented previously. However, the facilitator(s) may interrupt if there is disrespectful or abusive behaviour, if one party is preventing the other party from fully participating in the process (verbal intimidation or aggressive body language), if there are hurtful accusations or personal attacks, or if one or more parties have stopped listening.

When parties are unable or incapable of following the process or allowing another party to speak, the facilitator(s) will need to redirect and take control of the situation. If the listening party is continually interrupting the speaking party, one technique that may be helpful (but is not ideal) is for the facilitator(s) to request that the speaker speak directly to them and not the other party. If that does not work, request a separate meeting with the interrupting party to assist the person to calm down or think through issues. To take control of the situation without alienating any of the parties or discouraging them from continuing in the process, the facilitator(s) must be clear and firm with the party in describing their behaviour, its effect on the process and other possible consequences, and then obtain a commitment for change.

At the end of each party's speaking time, inquire if there is anything else they wish to say and then thank each party for their input: *Thank you for your input and honesty. Unless you have anything additional to add, we will move to the next step in the process.*

It is appropriate for the facilitator(s) to acknowledge the party and what was articulated during their uninterrupted time. Most importantly, their story, feelings and interests need to be understood and validated.

Although it can be difficult, the facilitator(s) needs to control or limit the number of "turns" each party gets during this time. If it is apparent that an issue has been exhausted and the parties begin to repeat what was previously said, the facilitator(s) may say the following: *The issue that you are presenting is one in which you have brought up in a previous part of the process. I understand that it is a very important issue for you and I will ensure that it is included in the agenda to be discussed. Are there any other issues that you would like to present that have not already been presented?*

Once Part One has been completed, it is important that the parties are encouraged and supported to move on to the next step in the process: *Before we move on to the next step in the process, I would like to remind all of you of the positive steps and progress that you have made up until this point. From what I have observed, I think we are prepared to move on to part two of the process with the confidence that we will be able to resolve the matters at hand. If everyone is comfortable, I would like to move us to the next level and provide you both with an opportunity to respond to the other party's concerns and issues in a professional manner. Are there any questions before we proceed?*

Part Two

Once Part One has been completed, the facilitator(s) will indicate that the discussion is open to everyone, focus the conversation and ask basic questions to assist with bringing clarity to the issues presented.

The next step is an open discussion whereby the parties respond to each other's statements and explore information, perceptions and feelings. The role of the facilitator(s) is critical during Part Two of the process, including keeping parties' emotions in check, assisting in building rapport and, most importantly, helping the parties listen to each other. It should be noted that the facilitator(s) is in control of the process and the parties are the owners of the issues and their own solutions.

The following is an example of a script to assist with this part of the process:

The purpose of Part Two is to provide a vehicle for open discussion whereby the parties are given the opportunity to respond to each other's statements and explore information, perceptions and feelings. As with the rest of the process, this will be structured to allow the parties to speak openly, express beliefs and ask questions.

To make this part of the process as effective as possible, I would like to revisit our ground rules to ensure that respect and professional behaviour are at the forefront of our minds. (Review ground rules)

You now have an opportunity to respond to issues or concerns that were previously presented by the other party.

In order for us to have a structured conversation, I will ask that the first "listener" be given the opportunity to respond to what they heard in the uninterrupted time and ask for any clarity or further information. Would you ____________ like to start?

If a natural exchange does not occur, the facilitator(s) may, in some cases, assist by asking questions to obtain additional information or explore the parties' interests. This would be determined on a case-by-case basis and only if the facilitator(s) felt that there were unresolved issues between the parties that could hinder the process. It should be noted that the facilitator(s) needs to accept any emotions, but should not make the parties talk about feelings. If the facilitator(s) is getting the sense that the parties are tired, becoming emotional or frustrated with the process, the facilitator(s) needs to check in with the parties to ensure that they are coping well.

As noted previously, separate meetings are necessary if the conflict is turning negative and there appears to be a turning point in the process that may result in the process failing. Part Two of the process tends to be when the participants may be the most disruptive or difficult to manage. If the facilitator(s) needs to confront the parties about behaviours or disruptive tactics (in a separate meeting or as a group if both parties are exhibiting similar negative behaviours), they should describe the behaviour, its effect on the process and any possible consequences. In addition, the facilitator(s) should speak to the parties' interests and explain what is expected of them to continue the process. The party being addressed should verbally agree to change their behaviour.

The following is an example of a script to confront negative behaviour or disruptive tactics:

I brought you into a separate meeting today because I have some concerns about how the process is going. From my perspective, I am noticing that you are constantly interrupting the other party and appear to have hostile body language, including __________ and __________. I feel that your behaviour is negatively affecting the process and I do not want it to result in us having to terminate the process. I understand that this is extremely stressful for all parties involved, however, I also know that you have both committed to being here and creating a better working relationship. Is there anything that you wish to talk to me about so that you can feel better about being here and be more conscious of how your behaviours are affecting the process?

Before we go back into the session, can you promise me that you will continue to be open and respectful to the other party in order for this time spent to be productive and lead to a positive outcome?

Part Three

The purpose of Part Three is to reframe issues and concerns as a set of issues for problem-solving, organizing how issues will be discussed and creating common ground for negotiation. The basis for this stage in the process will be the notes that the facilitator(s) took. The facilitator(s) must review their notes with the parties as a group and select key issues that can be negotiated (note that fault-finding, truth-seeking, opinions and emotions cannot be negotiated). Key issues to focus on during the setting of the agenda are those that were mentioned frequently during the first two steps in the process, those that are emotionally charged and those that are potentially negotiable.

It is important to frame the agenda using positive and impartial language, rather than negative language that may have been presented. For example:

Presented Issue: *"You interfere with my work area"*
Reframing the Issue: *"Defining work area boundaries"*
Presented Issue: *"You think you are my boss and try to tell me what to do"*
Reframing the Issue: *"Honouring roles and job duty boundaries"*

The agenda must reflect each party's concerns and present problems as shared concerns. Before the facilitator(s) can move on to building the agreement, they must first ensure, and confirm with both parties, that the agenda is accurate and complete.

In addition, the parties must be aware of the guidelines/parameters for discussion (i.e., budget, policies and procedures, hours of work, collective agreement, etc.), determine how issues will be discussed (order and priority), and be aware of the criteria for acceptable decisions (mutually agreed upon).

The following is an example of a script on outlining the process for setting the agenda:

Thank you for participating in this continued process, I applaud you for getting through the first two steps as it can be challenging and stressful. Now that we have completed the exchange, we will proceed to the next step, which is building the agenda. The purposes of this process are to reframe your concerns as a set of issues for problem-solving, define and organize the issues to be discussed, and create a common ground for negotiations.

We are going to refer to the notes that we have taken thus far to assist us. As we go through the issues presented, I am going to record them on the flip chart. Once everyone agrees that all of the issues have been captured, we will determine which items on the list are priority issues and how we are going to come to a resolution and move forward.

The facilitator(s) will begin to record the items discussed on the flip chart using positive and neutral language. The items may be written as one list of "our" concerns to create an equal and respectable atmosphere. Separate lists may be generated and written on the flip chart only if absolutely necessary, no common ground could be established or if the parties seem to think that they are polarized in their issues. Once these are recorded, the facilitator(s) can cross-reference the lists to identify similar issues that are being presented by both parties (i.e., mutual respect, honouring job responsibilities, respecting job duties, etc.). This may assist the parties in realizing that they are not that different after all. Following this discussion, if there still is not a meeting of the minds or common understanding about the conflicting issues, those issues should be put aside and excluded from further discussions or the final agreement. Outstanding issues may be given to the appropriate party, such as a manager, once the process is complete and discussed in a potentially different venue or monitored for any future escalation or interference with the parties.

Now that all of the items that we captured during the process have been recorded, are there any other items of importance missing?

At this point, one of the parties may bring up an issue that was not presented during the first two parts of the session. If this occurs, the facilitator(s) must go back to uninterrupted time to ensure that the item is articulated and fully discussed before being recorded on the flip chart. Going back to Part One is a normal part of the process and may be done a few times.

Now that we have all of the items listed, do you all agree that there are no more items we need to discuss? (get full agreement from each party)

The facilitator(s) will list the restrictions based on what they know or have been given (i.e., budget, hours of work, collective agreement, policies and procedures, etc.). At this point, the list must be reviewed to ensure that all items can be negotiated and there are not any non-negotiable issues on the chart, including emotions, opinions or items that should be dealt with in a different forum, such as a team meeting. Once the parties have discussed this, items will be numbered on the flip chart indicating the order of discussion.

Now that all of the items have been identified and prioritized, we will move on to the next step of coming up with solutions to the issues presented and begin to build our agreement.

Part Four

To create the agreement, collectively the parties should select the issues from the agenda in the order that the parties listed as priorities and then elicit action items.

Are there any questions before we brainstorm ideas for the first item? Who has a suggestion for this option?

When opening the brainstorming session, the facilitator(s) should collect a number of suggestions from the parties before facilitating a discussion on their merits and exploring what each party may personally offer. It is important to challenge the parties to try unexpected or new approaches to deal with the issue. While gathering ideas, they should be recorded on a flip chart using the parties' own words. The facilitator(s) should listen, repeat and record the idea to ensure it is reflective of what the individual is saying. Once all ideas have been recorded, the facilitator(s) should reread the list and ask for any final additions.

During this part of the process, the facilitator(s) must ensure that the suggestions being evaluated are respected by all parties and discourage any negative or critical responses. If negative or unhelpful comments are made, the facilitator(s) must stop the process and review the original ground rules.

One of the most common issues that arises during a conflict resolution process is a lack of communication. It appears that this, in many cases, is the root cause of a number of other items that are noted. For example, a concern may be that there is a lack of clarity in respect to job duties or roles and responsibilities. This may be caused by the fact that job descriptions are not updated or job functions have not been clearly defined by the manager. In some cases, there is no proper or formal venue to facilitate communication within departments, between other departments or between shifts, causing misunderstandings and tension among employees.

During the brainstorming portion of the process, the following options may be suggested to improve communication:

- Establish informal check-ins or huddles at the beginning of each shift for updates or job duties to be assigned
- Create a logbook that all staff must complete at the end of their shift
- Develop an email or text message communication system or alert that includes all relevant parties to keep everyone abreast of any changes or relevant job-specific issues
- Launch regular formal department or intradepartmental meetings

During the conflict resolution process, previously detailed with the 11 employees, once their concerns were aired, the staff had a number of practical ideas that could be implemented to improve the work environment and decrease stress among the co-workers:

- Invest in additional telephones and desktop computers
- Provide the staff with laptops to allow them to work remotely
- Stagger the hours and limit the number of staff in the office at the same time
- Book meetings involving more than two people in another location

Assessing the Agreement

Once all of the ideas have been presented, the parties must be able to evaluate and refine their suggestions. The parties must consider the following questions for each option presented:

- *What are the advantages of this option?*
- *What are the disadvantages of this option?*
- *What are the possible consequences of this option?*
- *Does this option meet everyone's interests?*
- *Can this option be realistically carried out?*

For the action plans to have meaning, the following questions must be answered, agreed upon and recorded:

- *Who will be responsible for carrying out each suggestion?*
- *When will the suggestion be implemented? What are the specific timelines?*
- *Are there any other parties other than those of us in the room with whom we will need to communicate this action plan?*

Upon reviewing the options above and answering the questions for all suggestions identified, it was discovered that due to budget and funding constraints, the most practical solution was to design a schedule that allows no more than six people in the office at the same time. In addition, whenever possible, all meetings that did not involve all employees were to be held in the boardroom, which was in the same building. This way staff were still able to conduct their business without interrupting others and at the same time maintain a less chaotic atmosphere.

Part Five

Once the suggestions have been evaluated and agreed upon, the facilitator(s) must confirm the required details so that the agreement is tangible. These action items must be recorded on the flip chart in thorough detailed to ensure success.

The purpose of writing an agreement is to provide tangible evidence of the accomplishments of the conflict resolution process and outline the terms of the agreement. In addition, the agreement prevents future arguments and misunderstandings, and indicates a clear end point to the process.

The agreement should not include any details of the discussion that took place during the process. In addition, all notes and flip chart paper from the process should be destroyed. To demonstrate commitment to the process and ensure confidentiality, all notes may be gathered at the end of the meeting (once the agreement has been confirmed) and shredded in the presence of all parties. If any additional meetings are scheduled and all parties agree, the notes may be collected at the end of the session and given to the facilitator(s) for safekeeping.

The agreement is a standard document that includes the names of all persons present, including the facilitator(s), as well as the points of agreement and areas yet to be resolved. The agreement must be signed by all parties and each party given a copy. The designated manager(s) who is going to monitor the agreement should also receive a copy of the document.

Additional Conflict Resolution Meeting(s)

At any point in the process, it may be determined that the parties need to meet again to complete the process if the parties are tired, distracted or the agreement feels rushed or premature. If there is a need for the parties to meet again, the facilitator(s) must ensure that the following areas are covered prior to the primary meeting ending:

- The process to this point is thoroughly summarized
- All loose ends are tied up
- All parties are committed to attending a second session
- There is an agreement regarding how the parties should act between sessions
- There is a review of tasks assigned if any

A second date is to be confirmed *prior* to the parties leaving the session. The date should be as close to the initial session as possible to maintain a commitment to the process and disallow further conflict to occur between the parties prior to the confirmation of a final agreement.

Beginning a New Session

It is in the best interest of everyone involved that no new parties be included in the second session. The introduction of any new parties may break the momentum, cause confusion, require backtracking in the process and, ultimately, compromise all of the work completed in the first session.

Upon commencement of a second meeting, the facilitator(s) must review what was previously resolved, confirm the agenda and start with Part One for each party, focusing on any progress, new information or rethinking *what was not covered in the first session.*

It may become apparent during any part of the process that a resolution to the conflict will not be reached. Factors that may influence this include one party accusing the other of dishonesty, a poor attitude by one or more parties, or too many issues to handle.

Facilitator Debrief

Following the completion of the conflict resolution process, the facilitator(s) should review the session overall and answer the following questions:

- Was conflict resolution the best and most appropriate option for the situation presented? If yes, why? If no, why not?
- Did the process achieve the intended goal of a final agreement? If not, why?
- What part of the process was the most challenging? What were those challenges and were they overcome? If not, why?

- What, if anything, could the co-facilitators have done for the process to run smoother (i.e., enforced the ground rules more consistently, requested separate meetings sooner)?
- Was the room setup and seating arrangements appropriate for the situation? If not, why?

  From an individual's point of view, each facilitator should self-reflect on their own role in the process and determine:
- What was my greatest strength?
- What was my biggest challenge?
- What would I have done differently if I were to facilitate this session again?

Lastly, the facilitators should discuss and determine if they were a positive match as co-facilitators, which would include a compatible skill set, communication style and teamwork philosophy. If the co-facilitation was deemed as incompatible or out of sync, the facilitators should learn from the experience in order to be more comfortable working together in the future. If one or both parties did not feel comfortable or supported during the process and believe that those differences or stresses could not be rectified, future co-facilitation is not recommended. Although the resolution outcome is the responsibility of the parties involved, the facilitators' ability to work harmoniously will directly or indirectly affect the process.

The greatest challenge of community life is to create synthesis, embracing diversity in a unified whole, resolving differences with the healing spirit of love and dedication to the good of the whole.

~ Corinne McLaughlin ~

Investigation Best Practices

In most jurisdictions, there is specific legislation regarding employer duties pertaining to the expectations of receiving and handling workplace violence or harassment complaints. Workplaces are required to have specific procedures for employees on how to report an incident, including the process to follow if the alleged harasser is the supervisor or employer. Occupational Health and Safety Acts mandate protection for all employees from workplace harassment, including requiring employers to conduct a thorough investigation into all incidents or complaints received. In addition, employers are obligated to notify the complainant in writing of the investigation's outcome, including any corrective action.

A complaint is generally a result of a series of incidents that have occurred over a period of time and then disclosed at the complainant's discretion. In my experience, most people will withstand the harassment or bullying for approximately six to 18 months before they take any action, such as filing a complaint, quitting their job or taking a leave of absence due to stress.

According to the *Cambridge Dictionary*, an allegation is "a statement that someone has done something wrong or illegal, but which has not been proved to be true." This may include an allegation of impropriety, such as a behaviour that is dishonest, socially unacceptable or unsuitable for a particular situation, i.e., a manager having a sexual relationship with a subordinate. Complaints and allegations must be separated into individual grievances for assessment purposes. Ideally, all internal and external complaints received should be briefly assessed by the recipient and forwarded to the proper authorities, such as a manager or the human resources department. The next steps will be determined based on the issues presented.

The complaint assessment must be as unbiased as possible. A necessary way to accomplish this is for the assessor to disregard the personalities of the complainant and respondent, thereby only assessing the individual complaint or issue. For example, if an allegation was that X threw a file at Y, then the investigation should focus on the question, "Did X throw a file at Y?" When the complainant or respondent is known to the assessor, the focus tends to be on the question, "Is X capable of throwing a file at Y?" The assessor tends to psychoanalyze the situation and make comments such as, "I have known X for years and they have never been aggressive, Y must have done something to make them mad," or "I know that X and Y had an issue years ago where Y got X in trouble. I'm sure that X is just trying to get them back and is now making a story up about them." With this kind of dialogue, the severity of the incident is diminished and it is unlikely to result in a mandated investigation.

A complainant must be informed that the following three things cannot be investigated:

1) Emotion: "I am afraid of person X."

   When this statement is made, the complainant must be asked to describe the incident(s) that has occurred with person X that has made them afraid. If the response is that person X said, "I'm going to kill you," then it can be investigated. However, if the response to the question is that there was no specific incident and the complainant is "just afraid" of person X, then no investigation can be conducted. Genuine feelings and emotions are real, but they are also intangible and cannot be investigated.

2) Perception: "I think person X is out to get me."

   As with an emotional statement, when a statement based on a perception is made, the complainant should be able to describe the incident(s) that has occurred that led them to the perception that person X is out to get them. If the response is that person X said, "I'm going to get you fired from this place as soon as possible," then it can be investigated. However, if the response to the question is that there was no specific event and the complainant just thinks person X is out to get them, then that perception cannot be investigated.

3) Opinion: "Person X is a bully."

   As with emotions and perceptions, if an opinion statement is made, the complainant must be able to explain in detail the incident(s) that led them to the opinion that person X is a bully. If the complainant cites several concrete, tangible examples of inappropriate behaviour, then those incidents can be investigated. However, if the response to the question is that there was no specific incident or examples and the complainant just thinks person X is a bully, then that opinion cannot be investigated.

Upon receiving a complaint or allegation of workplace violence, it may be immediately determined that a criminal offence has occurred, such as an assault, vandalism or theft. In these cases, the police must be contacted immediately. It should also be noted that police involvement may not be deemed necessary initially, however, may be required as the case progresses and new information is revealed. If the police are contacted, the investigation team should not interview any of the parties, including the complainant, respondent or witnesses, or continue the internal investigation until given official permission by the police. The police are responsible for deciding whether there are grounds to commence a criminal investigation in a reported case of a breach of the law and then conducting the criminal investigation. Police authority to handle the criminal aspects is drawn from the jurisdiction's Criminal Code, which sets out all criminal offences, penalties and procedures for dealing with people accused of committing a crime.

At this stage, the assessor should not review either party's personnel file, including any background information such as any past discipline. This information may influence the investigators and create a biased investigation. Personnel issues or a history of behaviours should only be reviewed by the appropriate parties once the investigation is complete and sanctions or next steps are being determined.

Investigation Team

The purpose of an internal investigation team is to provide a structured system to effectively respond in a timely manner to allegations of violence in the workplace, including discrimination, harassment and bullying. The team should be mandated to provide an unbiased investigation and make conclusions based on a balance of probabilities (50 percent + 1). There should always be a minimum of two investigators on the team, each with a distinct role of either the interviewer or notetaker. Only highly skilled and professionally trained individuals should conduct investigations independently. In addition, two investigators should be present during all interviews to preserve the integrity of the investigation and omit any possibility of false accusations against the investigator. The investigation team should remain consistent throughout the investigation process and the team members' assigned positions should not change unless absolutely necessary. In the case where a team member is unable to attend an interview or complete the investigation, the remaining member should maintain or assume the position of interviewer as it is easier to replace the notetaker who, unlike the interviewer, does not need to know the intimate details of the case to take notes.

When conducting a formal investigation, the employer should ensure that the following Supreme Court of Canada principles of natural justice are followed:

1. **The right to be heard.** The respondent has the right to be informed of the complaint prior to the investigation commencing. The notice should be sufficiently detailed and timely to ensure that the right of the respondent to respond is meaningful and informed by the facts.
2. **The right to adjudicators free from bias.** The respondent has the right to have the investigation conducted by an investigator or investigation team who is unbiased and will treat them fairly and without prejudice. The investigator should not have any blood relation or reporting link to any of the parties. Therefore, it is imperative that a manager does not investigate their own staff.
3. **The right to reasons for decisions.** According to the Supreme Court of Canada, a fair hearing includes the respondent receiving the rationale and detailed evidence for the case decision.

With few exceptions, once it is determined that an investigation is warranted, the respondent should be put on an immediate paid leave of absence. This recommendation is often the most difficult decision for employers because it is an uncommon practice in organizations. On the other hand, employers must be extremely cautious not to jump to a conclusion of guilt when an allegation is made or make the accused party believe they have been already judged. Unfortunately, in recent years there have been a number of high-profile cases whereby the respondent has been terminated immediately after the complaint was filed without having the opportunity to fairly defend themselves.

Several factors should be considered when the employer is determining whether to place the respondent on a leave of absence:

- Was the nature of the conduct physical violence or a breach of health and safety legislation? Any physical altercation that occurs on the employer's property should result in the respondent being sent home and reporting the incident to the police.

- During the investigation, can the parties be safely separated considering the office location and layout, including hallways and common areas? Can the respondent limit their time at work or work remotely to have limited day-to-day interactions with the complainant and/or witnesses? Is there an option for the person to work at another location?
- What is the risk of intimidation or reprisal by the respondent to the complainant or any of the witnesses involved? If the situation involves a complainant who is a frontline staff member and a respondent who is a manager, the actual or perceived intimidation or reprisal that may occur during and after the investigation can be quite powerful.

Moreover, allowing both parties to remain in the workplace may cause extreme tension, resulting in a toxic work environment not only for the two parties, but for everyone else working in that office space or location.

The Right to Be Heard

When the respondent is put on notice as a result of the complaint, it should be made verbally and in writing. Prior to the meeting with the respondent, if applicable, the union should be informed of the employer's duty to investigate and a representative should be present during the notice meeting. If a union representative is also a witness to any of the allegations, due to a conflict of interest, they should not be the individual to represent the respondent. The primary role of the union representative in the meeting should be to provide support to the member, clarify any of the expectations presented and, most importantly, act as a resource once the meeting is completed. In addition, if the respondent is placed on a paid administrative leave, the union representative may help the member gather up their belongings and escort them off the property. On the other hand, if it is deemed more appropriate for management to facilitate the respondent's exit, then they should take control, particularly if the respondent has an aggressive or threatening response to the meeting. For health and safety reasons, security may be more suitable to take on that role. If the respondent has an aggressive verbal or physical reaction to the information presented, the police should be notified and utilized as appropriate.

A formal letter placing the respondent on notice should include the following information:

- The general allegation (i.e., discrimination, harassment, bullying, code of conduct breach) should be clearly cited, including an internal policy or external legislation that was allegedly breached. To preserve the investigation's integrity and safety of the parties concerned, complaint specifics should be kept confidential, including the complainant's name, until the respondent is present during their investigation interview.
- If applicable, the decision to place the respondent on a paid leave of absence during the course of the investigation.
- The fact that the respondent will be invited to an interview and given the opportunity to respond to all allegations. The respondent has the right to an opportunity to respond to the complaint. Although this may be obvious, there have been cases where the employer has interviewed alleged witnesses about an event and, as a result of their testimony, decided to terminate the respondent without speaking to them first. As noted in the letter, the respondent will have an opportunity to meet with the investigators in due course to hear the exact allegations against them and tell their version of events.
- Direction to the respondent to refrain from entering organizational property without prior permission from a designated person. This includes attending any previously scheduled work-related or paid events on or off site, such as a volunteer recognition event, pre-paid conference or fundraiser. There should be no exception to this rule regardless of the individual's position

or their role in the scheduled affair, unless it is a private engagement, such as a party to which a co-worker on leave receives an invitation.

- The importance of and exceptions regarding confidentiality along with the sanctions for breaching confidentiality.
- The expectation of no retaliation, including clearly stating the sanctions for any such acts.
- The existence and offering of external support systems, such as an employee assistance program (EAP), if available.

Copies of the letter should be given to the respondent and, if applicable, the union. A signed copy should also be kept on file. If the respondent chooses not to sign the respondent letter, the manager should write on copies the person's full name and where a signature is required "Declined to sign" and give them a copy of the statement. Do not write "Refused to sign" as that holds a negative connotation and may appear judgmental. The manager should also stress that although the individual(s) may decline to sign the form, the conditions still apply.

Following this, the same letter should be sent to the respondent by registered mail. This way the respondent is informed of the expectations in verbal and written form in person, and a final copy sent to their home. This will prevent the respondent from later claiming that they did not fully understand the conditions and expectations of being sent home and directed not to contact anyone through any forum (including social media) with the exception of those listed in the letter. I have had clients who run round-the-clock businesses where respondents have appeared on site in the middle of the night claiming they were not aware that they could not visit their friends at work while on their leave.

The Right to Adjudicators Free from Bias

When a manager or leader is the named respondent in a formal complaint, it can become extremely complicated for an internal party or the human resources department. It is highly recommended that a third-party external investigator conducts the investigation for any formal complaints regarding workplace discrimination, harassment or bullying whereby the named respondent is a manager. An actual or perceived conflict of interest or biased investigator will discount even the soundest investigation and unbiased outcome. Frontline staff tend to believe that human resources or leadership will by default stand on the manager's side and therefore do not have faith that the investigation can be justly conducted.

According to Michael McDonald, a former professor at The University of British Columbia Faculty of Medicine at The W. Maurice Young Centre for Applied Ethics, a conflict of interest is defined as "a situation in which a person, such as a public official, an employee, or a professional, has a private or personal interest sufficient to appear to influence the objective exercise of his or her official duties." The conflict becomes an issue when a person is in an "official" capacity, such as a direct manager, that requires decisions and actions to take place. Such competing interests can make it difficult to fulfil the member's duties impartially. Even if there is no evidence of improper actions, a conflict of interest can create an appearance of impropriety that can undermine confidence in the ability of that person to act properly in their position. An actual or perceived conflict is equally as important.

On a few occasions, I have had a party to the complaint state that my investigation findings as the external investigator will be in favour of the organization that hired me. I have been challenged on the fact that the employer is paying my bill. I am very clear in informing all parties that I am not on any side or favouring anyone.

In one case, a perceived bias caused me to decline a request to investigate. On my website, I have a list of clients to demonstrate my credibility and serve as a reference for my work. A repeat client, who requested that I conduct an investigation involving one of the supervisors regarding a harassment claim filed by a frontline employee, called to inform me that when the complainant had been told that I was the external investigator, they had looked at my website and saw that their employer was listed as a client. The complainant's immediate reaction was that they would lose their case assuming I would side with the respondent since they were "management." Knowing this, I told my client I could not take the case. The client was adamant that they would not allow the complainant to dictate the process regardless of the complainant's perception. I respectfully declined the request and explained that if the case findings did not result in favour of the complainant, using me as the investigator could ultimately be used against the employer. I was confident that my investigation would be unbiased, however, in my opinion, the fact that the complainant had claimed I had a bias prior to the investigation even commencing excluded me from the process.

In another case, I completed an investigation and the harassment complaint was substantiated. As dictated by the employer, the sanction for the respondent was to have several one-to-one self-reflection sessions with an external coach. My client asked if I could conduct these sessions. I indicated that I could fulfil this requirement, although they needed to ensure that the respondent was comfortable with me in that role. I wanted to ensure that the individual did not perceive me, the complaint investigator, to have a bias against them. The respondent perceived no issues with me being the external coach and actually preferred I take on that role since I knew the case details.

It is recommended that all members of the investigation team be asked to declare if they have a conflict of interest regarding the assigned case. If no conflict is disclosed, each member should sign a conflicts of interest and ethics statement release.

If a conflict of interest is present, depending on the conflict, the team member may be excused from the case. For example, if one of the parties involved was the investigator's blood relative, they would need to excuse themselves from the case. However, if the investigator attended the same high school as the complainant, there may or may not be a conflict depending on their present relationship status. Each situation should be handled on a case-by-case basis.

In one case, I was conducting an investigation and as part of their internal investigation training, the employer wanted one of their managers to be coached by me during the investigation and be part of the interviews. During the interview preparation, the manager noticed that their cousin was a witness in the case. After reviewing the cousin's role in the complaint, it was determined that there was no actual conflict of interest. Their relationship was documented in the interview notes. Having a potential conflict of interest may not be a problem, however, failing to disclose a past or present personal or professional relationship could later appear deceitful.

Although not necessarily deemed as a conflict of interest, some cases are more challenging for the investigator. Each person who takes on the investigation role either internally based on their job description or professionally based on their chosen career can be guaranteed that the human side of things may come to light when least expected.

I received a call from someone who was being bullied at work. Ethically, and due to the boundaries of my liability insurance, I have to be extremely careful not to give advice when I don't have a formal contract and am not privy to all of the case details. That said, I would give general advice as to resources and options that are available to the individual to set them in the right direction. The person, who wished to remain anonymous, described to me a situation of alleged bullying that was taking place with a co-worker. While considering whether to make a formal complaint, they had shared their concerns with a few peers requesting input into the decision-making process.

Following this, one night as the individual was approaching their car in a shopping mall, high beams from another vehicle were turned directly on them. When the lights came on three individuals were standing in front of the other car's lights and could not be identified. Based on the body shapes and sizes, they assumed it was two males and one female. In a loud voice, the female voice said, "I know where your kids go to school." The lights were then turned off, the individuals got in the car and drove off. The individual was so afraid that they could not drive their car for nearly an hour.

The person was calling me to ask me what to do. They knew it was the bully that made the threat. I provided a number of options, including the obvious one to call the police and report the threat. The caller then said to me, "Really? Call the police, is that what you are telling me to do?" I stated that I was not "telling" them what to do, but rather providing them with that as an option. They then said to me in a quiet voice, "Can I ask you a question? Are you a parent?" I hesitated and then said yes. Then they said, "Picture you are the person on my end of the phone and you are calling me, and I was telling you to call the police after all the extreme incidents you have endured at the hands of this bully. Would you call the police if someone in the dead of night told you they knew where your child went to school?" When the question was posed, my 12-year-old son flashed in front of my face. I never did directly answer the question, however when taking off my professional hat and just being a mom, my answer would have been no.

Confidentiality

It may be a fair assumption that internal investigators would keep case issues confidential, however, I have had experiences to the contrary. Generally, investigators are in a leadership position and they have regular meetings with management to discuss the ongoing issues. During these meetings, the investigation and its status are discussed with the whole management team. Briefly updating the management team is acceptable, but the investigator should not disclose the case details. Doing so may lead to numerous issues, including the investigation parties refusing to openly and honestly share their knowledge of the case details. Therefore, in addition to addressing a conflict of interest, the investigator ethics statement must also cover confidentiality. This statement should be signed prior to disclosing the case information.

Sanctions for investigators breaching confidentiality should be in accordance with the organization's confidentiality policy. However, they may also be more specific and detailed in either the statement itself or a separate policy. These documents should be signed, dated and kept in the investigation file for any future internal or external challenge.

Roles of Investigation Team

Upon signing the statement, the investigation team will discuss the case details, which are usually outlined in a formal written complaint and/or the notes of the complaint recipient. At this point, the roles of interviewer and notetaker should be determined based on team members' skill levels and competency.

Interviews are an investigator's means of obtaining information from persons connected with an incident. The role of the interviewer is to help the interviewee provide, in their own words, their account of the matter being investigated, review their account of the incident to be clear on key points, and ask questions so that the interviewee clearly explains matters not previously covered, depending on the elements of the incident under investigation.

Notes are the most readily available record of an incident. The objective should always be to make notes that will remain meaningful months or even years after the event. It is common to rely on the memory of associated events to give full meaning to cryptic notes or single words, however, this is not an acceptable practice during the investigation process. Notetakers must write their notes bearing in mind that if they no longer worked for the organization, anyone could pick up their notes and know exactly what transpired during the interview process. Notes should begin with the assignment of the case and continue through to its completion. What is heard, said and done during the investigation needs to be recorded. Notes should be taken as events occur or at the first available opportunity as a delay in notetaking may raise questions of reliability later on.

The position of the notetaker is critical to any investigation. The purpose of this position is to accurately and efficiently record all pertinent facts collected during the interview process. This team member must be highly skilled in the area of active listening and extremely meticulous in taking notes. Having perfect penmanship is not a requirement for the position as notes may be typed later as long as the originals are retained in case they are ever requested during a formal hearing. Notes should never be rewritten or divert from the original notes taken but can be typed out following the best practice that they will be transcribed exactly as taken. The original notes should be kept for verification of originality and to ensure they were not tampered with or changed following the original interview.

Without the interview properly transcribed, the whole investigation could be in jeopardy. I have found that executive-assistant-level employees who are not in the union and bound by the rules of strict confidentiality make excellent notetakers. This individual would sign the confidentiality and ethics document and be bound by the same conditions as the other investigator(s).

Allegations

Based on the case information presented, the team will determine the individual allegations to be investigated. Although the complaint may fall under the umbrella of harassment, individual incidents and/or allegations must be separated out.

The following is an example of an alleged harassment complaint received that required an internal investigation:

To Whom It May Concern,

At this time, I would like to bring forward some concerns I have regarding my interactions with my current supervisor A.B. I believe that I am being targeted and bullied, resulting in the deterioration of both my physical and mental health.

I am very intimidated by my supervisor and afraid that they will become very reactive if they find out about my complaint and, as a result, will increasingly try to find reasons to attack my work performance.

The targeting is usually done quietly except for several interactions when I was alone with A.B. There have been many events during the last 24 months, I will provide some of the more recent ones.

A few months ago, A.B., in front of the other staff, stated to me, "You have issues you need to deal with." I was shocked by the comment and I pressed them for examples to support their statement, which they declined to provide. This challenge clearly made A.B. angry and they asked the other staff to leave the room.

Then alone with A.B. I again asked for concrete examples. A.B. stated that I knew exactly what they were referring to and until I admitted what I was doing, there was no more room for discussion.

Later that day in the hallway, A.B. told me that "someone" has concerns about my communication. Again, when pressed for the name of the individual and specifics, the comment was deflected. Two days later, A.B. told me that I could not assist with completing the order forms because there had been a complaint. I asked who made the complaint and to see those forms but A.B. would not tell me who complained, produce the forms and say in which way I had made an error.

A.B. said that I "should reflect" what I conveyed through my body language. A.B. deliberately kept me to the point where I was going to be at least 20 minutes late for my shift. When I finally got to the line, I had difficulty keeping it together.

During a weekend shift, there was informal discussion among the staff concerning department coverage. It was decided that if there was to be coverage, it was my turn to provide it. When I returned to work on Wednesday, a co-worker warned me that A.B. was angry with me for working the weekend shift. My co-worker informed me that A.B. had sent an email before the weekend that said, "No one is authorized to work the line this weekend." The email was sent to all staff but me.

A few days later after a meeting, A.B. called me into their office and chastised me for having worked the weekend. A.B. appeared angry, their tone condescending as though I was an idiot and they completely refused to accept any responsibility for their failure to communicate, blaming the issue on "technology."

In the second more recent event, in front of others A.B. announced for the second time that I was going to have to do something about the 122 vacation hours I had currently banked. I was somewhat surprised that A.B. seemed to have no awareness that this was "private" information and that they did not have a right to share this with other staff.

A.B. told us there were communication issues among the line and that I had better start to put on a better face and sit with the line people on my breaks and not go to my car. We had no idea what A.B. was talking about.

A.B. also stated while looking directly at me that they "expected their directions to be followed" and then falsely accused me specifically for directly speaking to the union president recently about confidential information. I started to explain that I was not complaining but rather talking about a family issue, but A.B. cut me off before I could finish. I stopped trying to explain as I have learned when to keep my mouth closed or A.B. will become even angrier with me.

Later that week, A.B informed everyone that after seven years I would no longer be in charge of the children's holiday toy drive and that a co-worker would be put in charge. This was a direct retaliation against me for speaking to the union president.

As a further example, after eight staff (including me) worked very hard on a company fundraising event, A.B. came into the department and exuberantly praised everyone individually except for me. I was totally iced out of the conversation.

Other events in the past were less subtle. A.B. allowed a co-worker to wear earphones and play music and then refused to give me the same option.

When I first started in the department, my hours were 7 a.m. to 3 p.m. Yesterday, A.B. informed me without explanation that beginning the following week, I would be working from 10 a.m. to 6 p.m. I knew this was again was to punish me for speaking to the president. When I questioned A.B., they refused to provide any explanation other than they could because they "were the boss."

In summary, I believe that an argument can be made that I have been bullied since being supervised by A.B. It is with the deepest regret that I proceed with this complaint.

In order to streamline the investigation and prepare for interviews, specific allegations need to be extracted from the complainant's statement verbatim to maintain the integrity of the complaint and remove any unnecessary information. In addition, this process tends to remove any opinions or emotions, which allows the investigation team to focus on the appropriate areas without being swayed in any direction.

Allegation 1:
In front of the other staff, A.B. stated, "You have issues you need to deal with," and offered no concrete examples.

Allegation 2:
A.B. said that "someone" had concerns about my communication. Again, when pressed for the name of the individual and specifics, the comment was deflected.

Allegation 3:
A.B. told me that I could not assist with completing the order forms and that there had been a complaint. No additional information was offered.

Allegation 4:
A.B. said that I "should reflect" what I conveyed through my body language.

Allegation 5:
A.B. deliberately kept me to the point where I was going to be at least 20 minutes late for my shift.

Allegation 6:
A.B. was angry with me for working the weekend shift. My co-worker informed me that A.B. had sent an email before the weekend which said, "No one is authorized to work the line this weekend." The email was sent to all staff but me.

Allegation 7:
A.B. called me into their office and chastised me for having worked the weekend. A.B. appeared angry, their tone was condescending as though I was an idiot and they refused to accept any responsibility for their failure to communicate, blaming the issue on "technology."

Allegation 8:
In front of others, A.B. announced for the second time that I was going to have to do something about the 122 vacation hours I had currently banked.

Allegation 9:
A.B told us there were communication issues among the line and that I had better start to put on a better face and sit with my line on breaks and not go to my car.

Allegation 10:
A.B. stated, while looking directly at me, that they "expected their directions to be followed."

Allegation 11:
A.B. falsely accused me specifically for directly speaking to the union president recently about confidential information.

Allegation 12:
In retaliation for speaking to the union president, A.B. informed everyone that I would no longer be working on the children's holiday toy drive.

Allegation 13:
After eight staff members [including complainant] worked very hard on a fundraising event, A.B. came into the department and exuberantly praised everyone individually except me.

Allegation 14:
A.B. allowed a co-worker to wear earphones and listen to music but refused to give me the same option.

Allegation 15:
As a form of punishment, A.B informed me without explanation that beginning the following week, I would be working from 10 a.m. to 6 p.m.

Investigation Strategic Plan

Once all of the allegations are clearly separated, an investigative strategic plan is developed and implemented. All strategies should begin with thoroughly reviewing all information related to the complaint, including all statements received or documents produced. It is important that unless relevant to the case, the investigation team should not review any past performance issues or complaints in the complainant's or respondent's personnel files. To remain unbiased and avoid falling into the trap of confirmation bias, the team must only review case-specific documents. Any past disciplinary situations or complaints, particularly regarding the respondent, should have no direct bearing on the present case. The investigator or investigation team are investigating an act, not a person. If personnel files were reviewed prior to the investigation and the accused did not have any past complaints, one may conclude that they are "innocent." On the other hand, if an employee had a past record of a similar act, one may automatically assume that the claim is only true as the result of an apparent pattern.

There have only been a handful of cases in which I requested the respondent's personnel file following the individual's interview. One allegation presented during a case was that the respondent had a communication style and way of interacting with peers and superiors that caused others to feel uncomfortable or on edge. During their interview, the respondent challenged me to review their performance appraisal over the past five years to see if there were any negative remarks or behavioural concerns. Upon reviewing their personnel file, it was noted that the respondent had many areas indicating a need for improvement, including interpersonal skills, listening and accepting feedback. As much as the respondent wanted to prove their case to me, their personnel file resulted in the opposite effect by shedding light on the respondent's interpersonal weaknesses.

The fact that someone does not have a prior record either at work, criminally or civilly does not necessarily mean it is their first *offence*; it could be that they have never been caught in the act before.

Confirmation bias is an important concept to consider when conducting an investigation. According to *Psychology Today,* confirmation bias is as follows: "Once we have formed a view, we embrace information that confirms that view while ignoring, or rejecting, contrary information that casts doubt on it. ... We pick out those bits of data that make us feel good because they confirm our prejudices. Thus, we may become prisoners of our assumptions."

One clear-cut example of confirmation bias is seen quite often on talk shows that provide guests with DNA results. When photos of an infant or child are displayed on a screen beside a photo of the alleged parent, the individuals involved will spend a tremendous amount of time comparing face shape, eye colour, position of the ears, skin colour and hairline to either prove or disprove their theory of a biological connection. Both parties are absolutely convinced that they are right. Inevitably, one party is incorrect except their deep desire to be "right" caused them to misinterpret physical evidence and convince themselves that the infant and adult are blood-related.

Generally, when people think of conducting an investigation, they think solely of interviewing witnesses. Oftentimes this is done without proper planning and evidence collecting. Keywords to remember at this stage of an investigation are observation and recording rather than action. The investigation team needs to plan a thorough strategy that includes timelines and steps to be taken. Deciding in which order the "evidence" will be collected is key to a successful investigation.

Case documentation will be determined on a case-by-case basis. The following documents and records, if relevant and available, should be collected and reviewed *prior* to any interviews: relevant organizational policies, procedures, standards, guidelines or codes of conduct; job descriptions; staff schedules; incident report forms (internal and external); occupational health/medical reports; initial and interim investigation reports; safety representative reports; minutes of any meetings where the incident(s) was considered; pre-incident and post-incident documentation; risk assessments and permits to work; employee health and safety training records and course syllabus; records of repair, maintenance, inspections and testing; manufacturer's literature relating to personal protective equipment supplied to employee; housekeeping and general inspection records; and hazard warning signs or notice.

Additionally, any relevant electronic documentation should be considered, such as emails or text messages; company phone records; recorded telephone calls such as customer service calls; key fobs and swipe cards; and video surveillance, with or without voice recording. In addition, with consent, personal cellphone records may also be accessed.

Sketches or drawings may also be helpful tools in assisting with the planning of the investigation as they may provide clarity and simplify explanations. They may be particularly helpful when used to assist a party in describing an incident that occurred in a specific location. When using sketches, it is important to include a detailed location of the scene (i.e., NE corner) along with the date and time that the sketch was made. The artist should include all essential elements of the scene but not unnecessary details that may confuse the sketch's intent. Standard symbols such as a stick person may be used to simplify the sketch. Avoid cluttering the sketch by identifying objects with a number or letter and then describe them in the notes or legend.

Lastly, if measurements are relevant, take accurate measurements and sketch the scene to scale, however, if this is not possible, draw the scene with approximate proportions. In several cases I found sketches to be invaluable for the fact that they simplify explanations or events and make it easier for the notetaker to follow the interview questions and responses.

In one case, an incident took place in a staff lounge with a number of players and other events occurring simultaneously. Prior to the interviews commencing, a diagram was drawn where the incident occurred and copies were made. When witnesses were interviewed, they were given the diagram. They were asked, according to their recollection, if the diagram was accurate. If so, they were asked to add objects and individuals present during the incident in question. Once the sketch was completed, it was dated and signed by the individual and kept with the investigation file. If requested, the individual could obtain a copy of the sketch for their records and future reference. I have also found blueprints of architectural drawings and floor plans to be helpful, not only with investigations but also when conducting a threat assessment in order to access and secure a physical site.

Interview Preparation

Once all allegations and relevant documentation have been reviewed, the interviewees need to be determined and interviews should be coordinated so that the schedule allows for sufficient time for the interview, post-interview discussion and completion of notes. Although internal investigations are not civil or criminal investigations, best practices for internal investigations, whenever possible, should incorporate the same legal principles. When selecting individuals who may be potential witnesses in a case, several factors should be considered in determining whether their statement would be admissible. Witness evidence is admissible if it is germane or relevant to the case/accusation and proves or disproves at least one fact in the case. For example, the witness saw the complainant and respondent enter a room together. Although the witness does not have extensive knowledge of the situation or the conversation that transpired, their statement can at least confirm that the complainant and respondent were in the same room at the time of the alleged incident.

Primary witnesses are those who have been named in a case and known to have at least one piece of information relevant to the case. Secondary witnesses are those who have not been named in the case but may have relevant information pertaining to the case, such as a contractor or visitor in the building at the time of the incident. Confidentiality issues must be considered if there are potentially external people on the witness list.

Prior to scheduling interviews, the investigation team should determine which primary witnesses to interview along with any secondary witnesses who may be called upon. Once primary witnesses are interviewed, secondary witnesses may be confirmed as primary witnesses or eliminated altogether.

A witness is only allowed to give evidence as to what they observed or perceived through one of the five senses: sight, sound, taste, touch or smell. Evidence that is not generally accepted includes hearsay, which is evidence based not on a witness's own knowledge but on a statement that the witness has heard from another source. There tends to be a lot of hearsay evidence in workplaces that unfortunately makes its way into the investigation forum. Unfortunately, work environments can be breeding grounds for rumours and gossip, which can confuse the facts of the case and the minds of the investigators. Investigators must be tuned into what witnesses actually know firsthand versus what they have been told by others or heard through the grapevine.

Once the interviewees have been identified, they need to be formally informed of their interview time. At this stage, it is critical that they are requested to sign a confidentiality statement. If this part of the process has been completed, such as when the respondent was put on notice, there is no need other than to verbally remind them of the conditions. All statements should be signed *prior* to the interviews commencing.

External Experts

Like hearsay evidence, opinion evidence or evidence that goes beyond a statement of fact to present an opinion or conclusion is also not generally accepted in a court of law. Therefore, it is not recommended that investigators ask witnesses the question "why" as it pertains to a witness's theory as to why a situation may have occurred. For example, if someone witnessed someone pushing another person, the interviewer may ask the witness, "Why do you think X pushed Y?" As the question is posed, the witness may feel obligated to answer and say, "Well I heard that last year they had dated the same person" or "I think they applied for the same position and Y got it instead of X." Although these may sound like feasible explanations, what they actually do is cloud the mind of the investigator. The only person who could answer that question accurately is the individual who committed the act.

Exceptions to opinion evidence include opinions of professionals with specific skills, such as medical doctors or forensic specialists such as accountants or document examiners. I have used experts to assist in some of my cases in the past and one particular expert was extremely helpful. There was a case of an undisclosed injury to a vulnerable individual. This person was non-communicative and there were no witnesses at the time the injury took place. I secured the expertise of a board-certified plastic, reconstructive and craniofacial surgeon. The physician reviewed the medical documentation and circumstances surrounding the injury and presented an expert opinion on the potential cause of the injury. In addition, they were able to discount the theories of the injury's origin that were posed by potential respondents. This medical opinion was filed as a supportive document with my final report.

According to the Canadian Society of Forensic Science, document examiners are not handwriting analysts: "Examination is not limited to handwriting and signatures, it encompasses many others including the physical materials used to produce the documents: paper, printers, stamps, writing instruments, binding devices, inks, and the interaction between the aforementioned. The document examiner relies on a combination of optical and analytical instrumentation for observations. These observations must then be carefully interpreted to determine if the evidence provides more support for one proposition (hypothesis) compared to another (competing) proposition."

Types of documents that can be examined may include but are not limited to:

- Threats including extortion, threatening or anonymous letters, and harassment
- Accident investigations, including certificates of compliance
- Regulatory compliance, such as workplace safety audits, fire safety maintenance logs and manufacturing compliance standards
- Identity documents, such as employee identity cards, education records and certifications
- Financial documents, including securities and investments, banking and money transactions
- Financial transactions of goods and/or services, such as offers to purchase and commercial or residential real estate

In one case, threatening anonymous letters were being sent to the complainant from an internal source. There were five letters in total sent and more than 300 employees who could potentially have sent them. Using a forensic document examiner and additional technology, we were able to shortlist the number of suspects to eight and eventually able to determine who sent the letters. Although there was a cost to the client for the service, there would have been no other feasible way to discover the culprit.

Employers need to look beyond their own internal resources when conducting an investigation. A few years ago, I was contacted by a client to investigate a case of wrongdoing. After a thorough investigation, I concluded that there was no evidence to substantiate the accusation and in reality, the evidence pointed to the complainant and a malicious report. The original respondent who was falsely accused of a major policy breach was brought back to the organization after being on a paid leave and the individual who made the original accusation was put on a paid leave of absence pending the malicious report conclusion. During the second investigation, a supervisor received an anonymous call stating that the individual who was back in the workplace was participating in an illegal act. The caller did not identify themselves. My client informed me that the individual at home accused of making a malicious report had left an accusatory voicemail. I asked my client how they knew it was this individual and they said that all of the managers listened to the voicemail and were certain that it was left by that individual. I respectfully stated that although they may be correct, none of the managers were trained in voice patterning or could be considered an expert in this case regardless of the fact that they worked with this employee for years. The only way to prove the identity of the caller was to seek the opinion of a voice-patterning expert.

A voice-patterning expert is a trained professional who specializes in voice and speech recognition and voice patterning. Among other specialties, their expertise may be in one of the following areas: spoken dialog systems, speech recognition, multimodal systems, voice processing, speech processing, speech standards, English syntax and grammar, natural language processing, web technologies, assistive technologies and voice technology.

My client was open to this recommendation and contracted the examiner to come to the workplace to conduct the examination. The respondent was called at home and informed that an anonymous message was left on voicemail and that some people think they were the one who left it. They were further informed that in order to clear their name, a voice-pattern analyst had been hired and all the individual had to do was come in for 10 minutes and read out the message. The analyst would then be able to eliminate them as a suspect. In this case, the union was informed of the strategy to clear the member's name. After many conversations, the respondent declined to participate in the voice analysis. As a result, the employer fired the individual. It was deemed that no arbitrator would support the notion of an innocent person being offered an opportunity to prove their innocence and turning it down.

Although still considered somewhat controversial, another service that may be utilized in an investigation is that of a polygraph, often referred to as a lie detector test. According to the American Psychological Association:

"The instrument typically used to conduct polygraph tests consists of a physiological recorder that assesses three indicators of autonomic arousal: heart rate/blood pressure, respiration, and skin conductivity. Most examiners today use computerized recording systems. Rate and depth of respiration are measured by pneumographs wrapped around a subject's chest. Cardiovascular activity is assessed by a blood pressure cuff. Skin conductivity (called the galvanic skin or electrodermal response) is measured through electrodes attached to a subject's fingertips.

The recording instrument and questioning techniques are only used during a part of the polygraph examination. A typical examination includes a pretest phase during which the technique is explained and each test question reviewed. The pretest interview is designed to ensure that subjects understand the questions and to induce a subject's concern about being deceptive. Polygraph examinations often include a procedure called a 'stimulation test,' which is "a demonstration of the instrument's accuracy in detecting deception."

In several cases, I have had mainly respondents and, on occasion, the complainant request a lie detector test. It seems that their request is sometimes due to the stress they are under or desperation to prove their innocence. Without client consent, I would not offer such a service to any of the parties, however, if it is requested during an interview, I will inform the employer and they will ultimately decide if that is a direction they wish to take.

It is important to be aware that there are individuals who claim to be experts when in fact they are not. Anyone seeking external support should check within their own jurisdiction to determine the credentials one needs to qualify as an expert.

The order of the interviews should be as follows: complainant, primary witnesses and then the respondent. One exception to this practice is when it relates to a client, patient or resident involved in the case. Due to a number of circumstances, such as unavailability or physical or mental health, they may not be able to participate in the interview process in accordance with the schedule. I have worked on several cases of resident abuse in long-term care facilities where the resident's memory may be compromised at certain times of the day or their retention of current events is short. It is important in those cases to interview that individual first to gain the most information possible. In addition, it may be recommended to tape the interview so that if the resident is unable to testify as the case unfolds, there is a clear record of their statement. Videotaping requires the permission of the resident and/or power of attorney (POA)/substitute decision-maker. Employers should check their jurisdiction to determine the laws pertaining to videotaping and audio-recording an interview.

Ideally all parties, specifically the complainant and the respondent, involved in the case should be interviewed a minimum of two times. This will assist in determining consistency and truthfulness in the testimony presented. Only having the parties explain their version of events once without an opportunity to question them a second or third time will end up in the forbidden "they said versus they said" and nothing will get resolved. In most of these cases, the complaint is deemed unsubstantiated. Although there may be two or more distinctly different versions of events, it does not discredit the claim. A more accurate and fair finding would be that the case is inclusive, meaning not proven or disproven. In one case, I interviewed the respondent eight times. Although most of those interviews were approximately 20–30 minutes in length, they were necessary. In that case and a number of others, my clients told me that the union filed a separate grievance alleging the member had been harassed during the investigation process due to the number of interviews. In the end, if the internal or external investigator has a valid reason for each interview, there is no harassment. On the other hand, if there is no rationale for the request then a harassment complaint could potentially be substantiated.

In cases where either the complainant or respondent is on a medical leave during the investigation process, I recommend that medical clearance to be interviewed is given by their attending physician. This clearance note should include the date of the interview, purpose of the interview (investigation) and a statement that the party is physically and emotionally fit to attend the interview. There have been employers who did not request clearance when the party agreed to attend the interview only then for it to be used against them at a later date. This scenario generally occurs when the complainant was off work and the investigation findings were not in their favour. The argument was that not only did the employer allow the original harassment to take place, but in addition they caused further stress and anxiety when directing them to be interviewed while on a medical leave.

It is important that the interview schedule follows a systematic approach and not simply to accommodate a person when they are at work. Whenever possible, witnesses with the most information should be interviewed first and witnesses with the least information interviewed last. In some cases, interviewees need to be paid to come in on their day off to accommodate the interview schedule.

In situations whereby any of the parties are a union member, they have the right to have the union present during the interview. Generally, employers have the employee make those arrangements if they wish. In a non-unionized environment or when a manager is named as the respondent, the organization should have a policy indicating whether they are permitted to have an internal support person present during the interview. This person should be a peer and not in any position above or below the respondent, and it cannot be anyone who is a witness to any of the allegations.

As a rule, I do not recommend that any external party such as a friend, family member or domestic partner be allowed to attend the interview. Those situations prove to be very difficult to manage given the emotions at play and, more importantly, the employer has no power to enforce confidentiality. There is no deterrent or consequence that can be implemented to prevent an external party from speaking about the case to other employees, people on the street or the media.

In one case, an external party was allowed in a complainant interview. This was a sexual harassment case whereby the complainant would not attend if her sister was not present. After consulting with the employer and legal counsel, the requested was granted. Prior to the interview, the sister was informed that her role was solely supportive and she should refrain from answering any questions asked to the complainant or coach her in any way. She was also made aware of the importance of confidentiality.

The sister was respectful of the boundaries. The interview was short and the complainant did not disclose much detail regarding her complaint. The term "sexual harassment" was repeatedly stated, although concrete examples were extremely limited. When the interview was complete and the parties were preparing to leave, I heard the sister say to the complainant, "You should have told her about the text messages." As we were still in the formal setting, I asked the parties to sit back down and I directly asked about any messages that she may have received from the respondent. For the next 2.5 hours, with permission, I reviewed and took screenshots of hundreds of text messages, images and inappropriate emojis that were sent over a three-month period. In addition, there were several social media posts and conversations using a media app that had been secretly recorded. In the end, as a direct result of the inclusion of the external party in the interview, the respondent was not only terminated, but the police were also contacted to follow up on some threats and extortion.

Individuals who are mandated to attend an interview may ask to bring a lawyer. Although generally at this stage legal counsel may not be necessary, the individual has a right to bring one. In that situation, I will only conduct the interview if my client invites their lawyer to the interview. I make it very clear that the lawyers play no active role in the interview process and if they attempt to do so I will end the interview. From my perspective, it is not a courtroom, arbitration or trial, and their role is simply to be an observer. An unavoidable outcome of this scenario is that the client must pay for the lawyer in addition to the external investigator.

Interview Question Preparation

Some organizations have templates for investigations. In my experience, this practice is not ideal as it will not necessarily elicit the case-specific information that is required to render a decision. However, there are standardized questions that may be asked in the preliminary stage of the interview to provide the investigator with some background, context to the complaint and previous relationships and interactions between the parties.

Standard Questions for Complainant X and Respondent Y:

- Describe your work history.
- Describe the history of your relationship with (X or Y). How often and in what capacity do you work with (X or Y)?

- How would you describe the quality of your work relationship with (X or Y) from the beginning until the complaint was filed?
- Do you have any community ties to (X or Y)?

Witnesses play a unique role in an investigation and although questions posed should be directly related to their knowledge about a specific event or incident, contextual and relationship insights can be equally as valuable.

Standard Questions for Primary Witnesses:

- Describe your work history.
- Describe the history of your relationship with X.
- How often and in what capacity do you work with X?
- How would you describe the quality of your work relationship with X?
- Do you have any community ties to X?
- Describe the history of your relationship with Y.
- How often and in what capacity do you work with Y?
- How would you describe the quality of your work relationship with Y?
- Do you have any community ties to Y?
- Have you ever had the opportunity to work with X and Y at the same time? If so, can you describe the quality of their work relationship?

Case-Specific Interview Guides

An interview guide is a carefully structured outline of topics and subtopics to be covered in an interview based on the complaint received. Each complaint or allegation is a separate part of the interview guide. The guide will help the interviewer develop specific areas of inquiry rather than a list of questions. The degree of structure of the interview guide will ensure that all important areas are covered. The interviewer should use language that effectively communicates to the least sophisticated interviewees without oversimplifying. Interviewees may not see the relevance of a question, however, it is the interviewer's responsibility to explain the question's relevance in relation to the interview's purpose and motivate the interviewee to respond freely and accurately. Moreover, if the interviewer cannot determine the relevance for asking the question, then the question should not be asked.

Interview questions need to be customized to each interviewee. The questions should focus exclusively on information the interviewee has regarding the specific case, rather than generalized questions. If the questions asked appear to be beyond the interviewee's information, this may cause embarrassment, resentment or insult. Moreover, questions should be clear and simple. Avoid acronyms unless common to the workplace or within a specific industry and the interviewer is confident that the interviewee understands the acronym.

The interviewer must also keep in mind that due to a variety of personal, religious or cultural reasons, some question areas may be uncomfortable for interviewees to answer. Examples of a difficult question area may be sexual harassment or assault. All questions asked that appear to cause the interviewee discomfort need to be dealt with in a sensitive manner.

In one of my cases, I was investigating a complaint pertaining to the sexual harassment of a woman who openly disclosed her religious background. She was extremely uncomfortable answering questions related to some of the respondent's comments directed at her. Rather than further embarrass her by verbalizing her responses in the interview, we decided that she would write out her responses instead. After I asked the question, she documented her answers, passed me the piece of paper with her response and I would transcribe it into my interview notes. With her permission, I kept her written responses in case it was questioned later.

Handling Individuals with Difficult Behaviours

Due to the nature of the investigation process, it can be charged with emotion and sometimes evoke unprofessional behaviour. It is important for the investigation team to brainstorm strategies for a variety of potential reactions they may receive from the parties in addition to tangible responses, such as calling security. Investigators need to allow individuals to express their views and emotions to a certain degree. The interviewer must be comfortable with others expressing strong opinions and behaviours so that they may guide and manage the process successfully.

The following is a selection of behaviours that may be presented during the process and strategies to implement in response.

Extreme Anger

- *Behaviour:* One party is releasing a flood of pent-up genuine emotion. Is there something important this person desperately wants everyone to understand?
- *Strategy:* Restate the party's concerns or ride it out, then take a break.
- *Behaviour:* One party is deliberately trying to disrupt the process.
- *Strategy:* A break, separate meeting or termination of the process may be necessary.
- *Behaviour:* One party is verbally attacking the other party.
- *Strategy:* This is unacceptable under any circumstances. A termination of the process may be necessary.
- *Behaviour:* One party is exhibiting potentially violent behaviours.
- *Strategy:* Terminate the process immediately and call security or the police, if necessary.

Anguish/Crying

- Take it in stride.
- Quietly offer a tissue or a glass of water.
- Only acknowledge the situation if the emotion becomes unmanageable or disruptive to the process.
- Sympathize in a general way.
- Say very little.
- Take a break if requested.
- Terminate the process if emotions cannot be contained or questions are not being answered.

Silence

- Acknowledge feelings of fear or discomfort.
- Give the person space by taking a break.
- Request clarification and encourage the person to contribute.
- Terminate the process if the person continues to refuse to answer questions.

It should be noted that although emotions are real, they may also be used as a tactic to terminate the interview. Regardless of the reason for the termination, the interview must be rescheduled to obtain the information that is required to complete the investigation.

The Setting

Interviews should be held in a setting that is free from interruptions or distractions, away from the parties' workspace and/or immediate colleagues. Depending on the type and size of the organization, for larger spaces it is feasible to have the interview room in a remote low traffic area of the building. Some of these locations also have several entrances and exits to the building, which allow interviewees to enter and exit the building without having to go through a reception or lobby area or walk among other employees. This is especially important for the respondent who, in many instances, may have been off work on a paid leave of absence pending the investigation and is more likely to create a higher level of discussion and scrutiny if they are seen in the building. The interview room should not have a window in the door and if it does it should be covered during the interview. In addition, if the window faces a parking lot or a high-foot-traffic area, the window should be covered for privacy and to limit distractions.

Smaller organizations with a less discrete layout may consider conducting interviews after regular office hours, if possible, or in an external space. Most communities either have space for rent, such as a hotel or office building, and some may have free access to buildings like a library or community centre.

Regardless of the space obtained for the interviews, the safety of all parties, including the investigation team, is of paramount importance. If possible, rooms should have exit doors and if not, the investigation team should be seated closest to the door. The room should be prearranged whereby the investigation team directs the other parties where to sit and the interview should not start unless all parties are present in the room. If proper resources are available, interviewees should be checked in by reception or a designated person and escorted to the room once the remaining person(s) in their party arrives, such as a union representative. The table in the interview room should be rectangular and the investigators and other parties should sit at opposite ends. This allows for more personal space for everyone and if any party becomes upset or aggressive, there is enough physical space between them to prevent any physical harm or be given the chance to exit the room in a timely fashion.

In some cases, depending on the seriousness of the allegation—namely that of physical violence or the temperament of the interviewee—I have arranged for my client to have on-site security in the building should the interview present any danger. Although not ideal as it may cause behaviours to escalate, if deemed necessary, security personnel may be located inside the interview room. Depending on the circumstances and the intended message, security officers may be in uniform or street clothing.

It is also important for the investigation team members to have a sign or code word they can use if they feel that the situation is getting out of hand and the interview needs to be terminated early. This, along with an escape strategy, should be determined prior to the beginning of the first interview. Although it tends to be assumed that these steps are only necessary when interviewing the respondent, it is important to recognize that everyone has the potential to become violent regardless of their position in the investigation. Also, the table should have water (supply plastic glasses, not glass) and tissues and be cleared of any items that could potentially be used as a weapon, such as a stapler or scissors. The best defences against violence are due diligence and proper safety preparation.

The investigation team should also consider that a complainant, respondent or witness may not speak English or English is not their first language. All individuals whose first language is not English should be offered a qualified interpreter. The offer of an interpreter and the individual's response should be documented as it may be challenged later. If an interpreter is required, the employer needs to contract an externally qualified interpreter and not rely on the person's family member or an internal staff member. I have witnessed more than one case where an interpreter was translating a medical procedure, misunderstood the words being spoken by the clinician and translated completely opposite directions of what was actually being prescribed.

One of my cases involved an elderly man whose first language was not English. Through his daughter, he alleged that a health-care provider had struck him during a daily routine. The daughter reported the incident and the employer of the health-care provider contracted me to conduct an investigation. For this case, I worked with a staff member who was going to take on the role of notetaker. This individual also spoke the same language as the senior, however, was not there in the capacity of interpreter. The man's daughter demanded to be in the interview, and not only would she be seeking answers, but would also act as her father's interpreter. As expected, the interview was tense, however, I was able to obtain the information I needed to determine the next steps.

After debriefing with my client, the staff member who served as the notetaker asked to speak to me in private. She informed me that during the interview, the daughter was not interpreting what the father had been saying, but instead something completely different. Apparently, the father had said he felt that the staff member did not mean to strike him and that it was an accident. He further stated that he liked the staff member and did not want to get her into trouble as he was not hurt. After hearing her father's statement, the daughter reported to me that the staff was always mean to him, that her father had stated that he was afraid of the staff member and did not want that person working there anymore. The notetaker also told me that the father was very upset with his daughter who was arguing back and forth with him about what needed to be said so that he is treated better. After receiving this information, I was no further ahead in my interview than I was when I arrived earlier that day. What was said by the resident and transcribed in the notes was simply inaccurate.

In another case, a customer alleged that a staff member had been rude and potentially racist to them. The customer did not speak English, however, through a family member had raised the concerns on the organization's website, which had a complaint and feedback area. When the family member was called for the customer to come in for an interview, the family member could not attend and therefore could not be there to interpret. The employer contacted a staff member in another department who spoke the same language as the customer and requested them to assist the complainant in the investigation process. Upon completion of the investigation, the respondent was sanctioned for breaching the organizational code of conduct. One month later, the staff member who served as the interrupter resigned. As a longtime employee, this turn of events was completely unexpected. When the situation was further explored, the resigning staff member disclosed that after the interview, they had been severely bullied by the respondent's co-workers. They were called a "rat" and an "ass kisser," and a rumour had been started that they were having an affair with the manager of their department. Due to the extreme pressure the staff member had faced, their mental and physical health was compromised to the point of seeing resignation as their only option. The employer quickly discovered that the interpretation request had been a catalyst for the bullying and the loss of a dedicated employee.

The Opening of the Interview

The opening of an interview may be the most important part as it sets the tone. Interviews should be presented in a non-accusatory format and not conducted like an interrogation. What is said and done during the opening will influence how the interviewee perceives the interviewer and the situation, and may determine if the interview will continue at all. It is important that the tone set at the beginning of the interview is one that is intentional and appropriate to the investigation process. The opening has two purposes: (1) to build a rapport with the interviewee and (2) to orient the interviewee to the process.

At the opening of the interview, the interviewer should introduce themselves and the notetaker as the investigation team (internal or external) and explain the role of each for the interview process. For example, the interviewer's job is to ask questions and elicit responses. The notetaker's job is to document the interview and ask clarifying questions when warranted. Following this, the interviewer should make a general statement about the case that is under investigation without giving away all of the case facts known to date. For example, the interviewer may say, "The purpose of this interview is to gain relevant information as part of a workplace harassment complaint."

By describing the purpose of the investigation as gaining information regarding a complaint, the interviewee has a clear picture of how the interview will proceed. In addition, follow-up at the end of the interview should be discussed, such as requesting a written statement from the party and the potential for the request of further information at a later date.

If there is a lawyer or union involved, they need to be reminded of their position in the interview. They should only ask process questions and not any specific allegation questions. The party should refrain from answering for the interviewee. In one of my investigations, the union representative was extremely aggressive and requested several items that were unrealistic, including a copy of my questions and access to my notes. After several attempts with the human resources adviser to rectify the situation, I left the interview 90 minutes later with virtually no questions asked or responses recorded. When the union representative became verbally abusive and aggressive towards me, I walked away from the conversation. This debate between the union, human resources and myself also occurred in front of the complainant. In retrospect, the discussion regarding expectations and boundaries should have been conducted without the complainant present. In the end, I terminated my contract with the client, stating that the union crossed boundaries and therefore the success of a second interview was impossible.

When interviewing a witness, it is crucial to remind them of the importance of being truthful and forthcoming in the interview and inform them that they are not the focus or the respondent in the case. From my experience, witnesses are often the most nervous. Many have told me that they do not "want to get involved." Reassuring the interviewees of their roles and requesting their assistance seems to go far in the moment. The fact that they have information to assist with determining the allegations and bringing the case to a close makes the process a little less stressful. It is recommended to give the individual an estimate of how long the process will take and request a commitment to that specific amount of time. Interview times should be scheduled longer than anticipated since ideally the interview should be completed in one session rather than asking the interviewee to come back at another time to complete the interview, which may cause additional anxiety for the interviewee.

After the opening has been completed, all information explained and any clarity provided, and confidentiality is re-enforced, the interview can commence.

Notetaking and Free Recall

People think faster than they can speak. Effective listening requires energy to compensate for the differences in thinking and speaking. People forget 50 percent of what they hear immediately and two months later another 25 percent. The average person speaks approximately 125–140 words per minute and the average notetaker writes at a rate of about 25 words per minute. If the preliminary work to prepare for the interview has been done properly and methodically and the individual possesses the core competencies, the notetaker should not have difficulty keeping up with the interview. On the other hand, when interviews are imprecise or the interviewer discusses issues or concerns that are irrelevant to the case, the notetaker may be thrown off course.

Best practices for notetaking include:

- Case numbers assigned to each case and references in all notes relating to the case.
- Record notes in a numbered, coil-bound notebook.
- Ensure names, positions, addresses, telephone numbers and any other relevant information are correct. If any information is unclear, indicate this.
- Restrict the use of notes to investigate materials of a professional nature and do not include any personal opinions of the interviewer or notetaker on any aspect of the case.

I worked on a case with an accredited professional involving a sexual harassment allegation. Through the investigation, the complaint was substantiated and it ended up in a legal arena. All of the case notes were requested and provided. When we arrived to the lawyer's office, the respondent lawyer handed the complainant a piece of paper from the stack of documents before them. On the paper was the investigator's written notes and in the margin a picture drawn of an outline of a female's body, including a few details pertaining to their private areas. This diagram had no relevance to the case details. The investigator was mortified and had no rational explanation as to what possessed him to draw the picture. Unfortunately, despite his high-quality investigation skills, he lost all creditability.

If a detail is recalled later that should have been included in the original notes, make a fresh notation in the investigation notebook and cross-reference it with the original note. Original notes in memos and reports can be expanded, however, these do not replace original notes, which should always be preserved.

The designated department must maintain secure storage of notes to ensure that the investigation notes are kept confidential. Notes may be disclosed to a legal adviser, law enforcement officers or any other individual as directed by human resources or a legal adviser.

The interviewer and notetaker should listen carefully to what is being said and pay attention to qualifying words like *sometimes*, *rarely* or *usually*. In addition, the parties need to be aware of signals that a change of direction in the person's statement is coming with words like *but*, *however* or *on the other hand*. The speaker is making an important point if they pause before or after an idea, use repetition to emphasize a point or use introductory phrases to precede an important idea. The notetaker needs to be an "assertive listener" and ask for clarification if they do not understand what the interviewee has said.

The term "free recall" is permitting the interviewee to answer questions without unnecessary interruptions. Since the parties being interviewed have had no pre-interview preparation, they tend to just answer questions, be it in a relevant format, with or without lengthy preambles or in a rambling manner. Regardless of how they respond or their communication style, unless the interviewee is completely off track and not at all on subject, the interviewer needs to refrain from interrupting the interviewee and let them express themselves. It is important to allow the information presented to flow from the person's memory the way it is stored. It is essential to complete the free recall process before the interviewer seeks further information or clarification. On the other hand, if there is confusion as to whom the individual is speaking of or the flow of the response, a member of the team may gently stop the individual to seek clarity. Moreover, if the interviewee is jumping back and forth between allegations, the interviewer must respectfully halt the conversation and redirect the person to the allegation being discussed. It is imperative for the interviewer to understand the importance of the chronological order of pre-planned questions and areas of inquiry in order to make the interview a smooth process.

To obtain the most value, a witness should start the free recall at a point preceding the incident that is being investigated. The type of recall that has the richest source of information is that which is scarce or has an abundance of details. Once the interviewee has completed their version of events, the interviewer can ask more pertinent questions to obtain the relevant answers. A clue as to when a person has finished talking, although their mouth is still moving, is when they start to repeat the same thing. This may also be an indication that the point or incident repeated is very important to them.

The Body of the Interview

Once the opening is completed, the interviewer may ask the standard questions previously stated. The purpose of these questions is for the team to obtain a contextual framework to the background relationships and observations of the parties. Asking both the complainant and respondent to describe their perception of the history of their relationship with the other party can be very telling. In some cases, the parties will have a similar perception, including the catalyst that put the relationship into a downward spiral. However, in other situations, the parties describe two distinct incidents that caused an issue between them. I have had cases where the respondent has walked into the interview with a blank look on their face after being sent home on a paid leave of absence to declare to me that they have no idea what they are being accused of and they actually considered the complainant "a good friend." Regardless of the answer to this question, it gives the investigation team a clear understanding of where each party is coming from.

The question regarding whether the parties have any social ties is also very important for the witnesses. In the dozens of cases I have worked on, I have had former spouses, family members and high-school sweethearts as part of the interview process. This relationship may or may not constitute a conflict of interest, however, it is information that may play an important role later in the investigation.

Upon completion of the standard areas, the interviewer may guide the conversation towards the individual's knowledge of the case using the prepared interview guide. The establishment of background facts or conditions present will help put a statement into its proper context. The purpose of reinstatement context is to cast the witness's mind back to the day of the incident. Example statements may include: *Before you tell me everything you remember about X, I would like you to cast your mind back to that day. Were you working? Was it your day off? What assignment were you doing? What activities did you engage in before you went to work?* and/or *Now walk me through the date in question, when you first got to work.*

Although there are 15 allegations in the case example explored earlier, only the complainant and respondent will be asked to provide a response to all allegations presented. As for the witnesses, they will only be asked those of which they are known to have knowledge. For example, in a few allegations the complainant stated that the respondent exhibited some of the alleged comments and behaviours in meetings in front of others, whereas other allegations were made in private. The witnesses to the public events will be asked about those allegations only as they would not have knowledge of the other non-witnessed allegations.

The following are types of interview questions and examples:

Open Questions

These are open-ended questions, which only specify a topic. This allows the person considerable freedom in determining the amount and kind of information to give, such as, *Tell me about your employment history.*

Moderately Open Questions

These questions contain some restrictions but still allow for considerable leeway, such as, *What do you know about the relationship between the complainant and the respondent?*

Closed Questions

This type of question is restrictive in nature and may supply answer options, such as, *Did you work on May 7, 2019 or May 8, 2019?*

Moderately Closed Questions

This type of question asks for a specific piece of information, such as, *How long have you worked with the respondent?*

Primary Questions

These questions introduce topics or new areas within a topic that can stand alone even when taken out of context. For example, *Tell me the agenda items for the staff meeting you attended last week.*

Secondary Questions (also called Probing or Follow-Up Questions)

Secondary questions are an attempt to elicit further information following a primary question or another secondary question. These questions may be an open or closed format. They are essential when a respondent does not answer a question or their answers are incomplete, superficial, vague, irrelevant or inaccurate. For example, *You mentioned that at the meeting for agenda item number four, you discussed the staff schedule. Describe that conversation.*

Silent Probes

Silent probes are used when an answer is incomplete or the respondent seems hesitant to continue. If a witness does not reply to a question right away, the interviewer should remain silent for a few moments. Using appropriate non-verbal signals like eye contact, a head nod, or sitting back in the seat rather than repeating the question right away can be effective. If an individual honestly does not know the answer to a question, they will remain silent, despite the "awkward silence." Generally, if a party is withholding information, silence tends to make them uncomfortable. If the silence drags on too long, that individual will tend to fill the silence with words and continue talking despite their initial hesitation.

Nudging Probes

If a silent probe fails, oftentimes a nudging probe will be helpful. This technique "nudges" the interviewee to reply or continue with an answer. Usually the probe is simple and brief. For example, *I see. And? Go on. So? And then? Please continue. Yes?*

Informational Probes

Informational probes are tools to extract additional information or explanations from the interviewee. These types of questions may be used if the answer seems superficial. Example statements include:

Tell me more about X. What happened after X? How did you react to X? or *Explain further.*

If the answers still seem vague, questions or statements such as, *I am not sure I understand your response* or *What did you have in mind when you said X?* can be helpful and elicit additional information.

Some answers seem to suggest feelings or attitudes in addition to factual material. A witness may state, "When they said that, I couldn't believe my ears. I was totally shocked." In that case, the interviewee may be probed further by asking, *Why do you feel that way?* or *How strongly do you feel about that?*

If the interviewer believes that the interviewee is not being forthcoming or has previous information that contradicts their response, the interviewer should direct the person to recount the incident in a different order than initially told. This technique can reveal information that may otherwise be hidden or missed. It should also be noted that dishonest interviewees find it difficult to recall incidents or stories when they are requested to do so in a different order than what was previously rehearsed.

Clearinghouse Probes

Clearinghouse probes are essential when the interviewer is unsure whether all important information has been elicited and/or there are no further questions in mind. At the end of each interview question area, prior to moving to the next area, the interviewer needs to "clear the house." Example questions include: *What have I not asked that might be important? Have I missed anything that you can think of?* or *Before we move on to another issue, is there anything we have not covered?*

The Interview Closing

When all questions have been covered, the interviewer will check in with the notetaker to ensure there are no outstanding questions or concerns that have not been addressed. If anything is determined to be outstanding, the interviewer will continue questioning the interviewee until all questions have been addressed. If it is determined that there are no outstanding issues, the interviewer will proceed with the closing.

Careful handling of an interviewee during the closing moments may elicit facts that were not presented earlier. A reluctant complainant, respondent or witness may let their guard down after *formal* questioning is finished. Sometimes a person who held back important facts during an interview may mention them immediately after they think the *official* interview is complete. If immediately following the *official* closing of an interview the interviewee continues offering information or adds new information, the interviewer should formally reopen the interview process to gather and record the new information presented. It is important to mention at the beginning of the interview that nothing said or done during the complaint process is ever "off the record" or "just between you and me."

In my frontline days working with seniors in the community, I became very familiar with the concept of getting the most information at the end of a meeting or interview. When I would visit senior clients, I would spend 45 minutes to an hour with them. Most of the seniors lived in apartments and whenever I was about to leave, after they told me everything was fine and they have no issues requiring assistance, they would come to the apartment door or elevator with me and just as the door was closing they would disclose something.

I have a vivid memory of the door closing in an elevator when one of my clients in her late 70s told me that her neighbour was doing some grocery shopping for her at the time and she had to go have a "wash" before he returned. I asked her what she meant by that and she said, "Oh because I can't possibly pay him to help me out so he gets sex in return." After a moment of shock, I escorted her back to her apartment so that she could explain to me what she was talking about. After hearing her story and learning that she was not actually interested in having sex with her neighbour, I arranged a shopping service and contacted the proper authorities.

Written Statements

Written statements are permanent records and may be used in a formal setting, such as a court or an arbitration, as evidence or to refresh the memory later. Written statements should be requested after every interview and stated in the interview opening. If the person is interviewed three times, a separate statement for each interview will be requested. Statements are important for several reasons. When individuals are stressed and anxious during the interview, their memory can be unclear when asked about specific incidents. By providing a statement after the interview, the individual can answer the questions in a less stressful environment, check dates and times, and look up supporting documentation. In addition, the more statements received, the more fact comparisons and consistency can be determined. I suggest that statements be in a narrative format as opposed to a form to ensure accessibility for the interviewee. In the narrative format, the person relays the information in their own words in the first person as opposed to trying to fit information in little boxes or only answer the questions that are posed.

A general practice that I have adopted is following the interview, I will send an email to the interviewee with the questions from the interview. These include the general questions in addition to the allegation-specific questions. If the individual is a union member, I will inform them that I can include the union in the email if they wish. No email should be sent, regardless of its content, to a personal email account because confidentiality cannot be guaranteed. In the case of an employee who does not have a business email, it could be sent to a designated individual, such as the union or their lawyer, and then that person may forward it a personal account. Only if the interviewee is comfortable, the investigation questions could also be sent to a manager who would forward it to the appropriate person. Once an agreed-upon date of return is determined, the document is sent. The written response is sent directly to me and not the third party.

It is also important to remember that although we live in a world filled with technology, there are still some people who do not possess or know how to use email. In those cases, the individual should be given a paper copy of the questions. Their statement may be typed or handwritten and forwarded to the investigator directly or by the employer.

At the end of the interview, it is important to reiterate to the interviewee that they may be requested to attend additional interviews depending on the investigation process. Lastly, the investigation team should remind them of confidentiality and thank the attendees for their co-operation.

Evaluating Information: Credibility Testing

In 1951 in British Columbia, there was a case, *Faryna v. Chorny*, in which Justice C.H. O'Halloran stated the following regarding witness credibility:

Opportunities for knowledge, powers of observation, judgment and memory, ability to describe clearly what he has seen and heard, as well as other factors, combine to produce what is called credibility. . . . A witness by his manner may create a very unfavourable impression of his truthfulness upon the trial Judge, and yet the surrounding circumstances in the case may point decisively to the conclusion that he is actually telling the truth. I am not referring to the comparatively infrequent cases in which a witness is caught in a clumsy lie.

The credibility of interested witness, particularly in cases of conflict of evidence, cannot be gauged solely by the test of whether the personal demeanour of the particular witness carried conviction of the truth. The test must reasonably subject his story to an examination of its consistency with the probabilities that surround the currently existing conditions. In short, the real test of the truth of the story of a witness in such a case must be its harmony with the preponderance of the probabilities which a practical and informed person would readily recognize as reasonable in that place and in those conditions.

Potentially once all evidence has been collected, the interviews have been completed and the written statements have been received, the evidence that has been gathered from the various sources should be compiled to give the team a clear picture of the case as it has progressed to this point. Facts that conflict with information gathered from other sources must be resolved through further interviews, further document review or obtaining an expert opinion. Evidence should also be checked for completeness, however, some gaps, uncertainties and conflicting information may need to be accepted due to the lack of information.

There are several excellent resources available focusing on neurolinguistics, which is the study of how language is represented in the brain in addition to how and where our brains store our knowledge to speak, understand, read and write. Neurolinguistics can be used to determine truthfulness and when an individual could be constructing a story or being dishonest. Moreover, micro-expressions, which are involuntary facial expressions present for less than one second, can be more revealing than true emotions. In order to rely on these tools, investigators should be thoroughly trained and qualified as they may be challenged on their credentials later.

The following are questions that should be asked pertaining to the creditability of each party interviewed or produced in a written statement:

- **Plausibility:** Does the testimony appear to be believable and make sense? This question relies on the concept of rationality or reasonability. Does the statement or version of events make sense?
- **Demeanour:** Did the person seem to be telling the truth or lying? During the credibility assessment, it is natural for the team to want to interpret or psychoanalyze an interviewee's verbal and non-verbal behaviour, however, the interviewer must be conscious of pitfalls in the process of this evaluation. There are many individual, cultural and environmental circum-

> stances that may cause a person to change their behaviour. These changes may have nothing to do with deception on the part of the individual. Some people can lie without showing any nervousness or outward signs of lying. Some people may show extreme nervousness when they talk to anyone in authority.

I have conducted investigation case reviews where the investigator has documented "Appears to be lying" in their formal notes without any evidence contrary to the witness statement. On the surface, this statement is judgmental and may be used to discredit the findings as it may appear that the investigator is biased. Without any formal education or expertise in reading body language, in a formal setting the investigator would have to actively defend the statement made with evidence.

Motive to Falsify

A motive, i.e., the reason behind an individual's action, is not always apparent. Someone may have a deep-rooted issue with another individual that, unless explored, never makes its way to the surface. As previously stated, the foundation questions for all parties that explore work relationships and community ties can be key to revealing the existence or lack of a motive.

Corroboration

Generally, statements or testimony can be either substantiated or unsubstantiated through eyewitnesses or individuals who saw the person shortly after the alleged incident, in addition to documentation. Although the latter did not directly see the interaction, they may be able to describe the individual's demeanour or repeat the initial version of events they were told. It can be assumed that if someone in the workplace was threatened or mistreated by anyone in isolation, the first thing they would do is seek out a support person. There have been many cases whereby someone had a bullying incident occur and, as a result, their colleague covered for them or switched job duties to protect that person from further incidents. Although this may appear to be considered hearsay evidence, it is simply an observation, a repeating of information or a stated reaction to an alleged event.

A challenge faced during investigations could be if there are alleged eyewitnesses who were present during an alleged occurrence of harassment who have a difference version of events or perception. Perception is the interpretation of sensory information that allows an individual to understand their environment. Conflicting perceptions may occur when asking witnesses to describe an interaction or the parties' demeanour.

Imagine the following scenario: several allegations of bullying, incivility or disrespect are cited during a meeting or at a public event. Oftentimes, when asking perception questions regarding tone of voice, level of respect witnessed or interpretation of professional behaviour, I will get a range of responses. Some witnesses will say that nothing out of the ordinary was observed, others will say that one particular party was aggressive and some others will say the opposite. Again, these answers can oftentimes be referred to the beginning of the interview when contextual and relationship questions are answered. Friendships, work relationships and perceived enemies can influence individual responses to events and their perceptions.

In many cases, emails or text messages are available and may be reviewed at any time during an investigation. It is important for the investigator to consider that individuals will generally submit only the documents or messages that support their side of the case. Cut and paste is a very effective tool when attempting to present a specific picture or fabricate a situation. Case documentation is not helpful until the investigator has received the complete information trail from both parties. Although employers may be uncomfortable doing so, they have a legal right to review employees' organizational emails and phone records. In the presence of a manager or IT professional, I have reviewed thousands of emails, phone records and documents as part of the investigation process. Although a cumbersome and in some cases expensive process, one email can make the difference between an unsubstantiated and substantiated finding. In addition, it can also be an important factor when assessing credibility.

Malicious Complaints

Although organizations have goodwill, laws, policies and procedures, there are certain individuals who will use tools developed to create a safety net for employees for their own physical, emotional or professional gain. Over the years, I have encountered complaints that, when thoroughly investigated, are not true incidents of workplace discrimination or harassment or client abuse; instead they are malicious reports intended to hurt someone's personal or professional reputation. Although excluded from my formal investigation reports, I often tell my client when there are findings of malice to advise the respondent to take a personal stand and file a complaint of defamation of character on the individual who falsely accused them. However, I think many individuals do not take that route for fear of further retaliation or simply being exhausted from the investigation process. Another unfortunate reality is in cases whereby the bullying or harassment occurs on a social media platform and their bullying words, pictures or videos forever remain on the internet. The bottom line is that sanctions for a malicious report should be made clear and enforced.

Findings

Each allegation must be thoroughly examined and result in a separate finding based on the balance of probabilities. A preponderance of the evidence means that one side has more evidence than the other, even by the smallest degree (50 percent + 1). An allegation finding can be one of the following:

- **Substantiated**: To establish proof or competent evidence (>50 percent).

- **Partially Substantiated:** Part of the allegation can be proven.
- **Unsubstantiated:** The allegation cannot be proven (<50 percent).
- **Inconclusive:** An allegation can neither be proven nor disproven.

A substantiated allegation means that it is likely that the allegation is true or the incident occurred as stated by the complainant. Like the justice scales, the truth tips the scale even by only one degree. Obviously the more evidence the truth side has, the more difficult the finding will be to challenge in a post-complaint forum.

A partially substantiated finding can be unclear for some. To provide some clarity, consider the following scenario: An employee files a complaint of workplace violence. The complainant states that they were in the boardroom preparing for a meeting when the respondent entered the room. Upon their arrival, the complainant allegedly said, "Wow, that's different, you are early for a change." The respondent immediately came within inches of the complainant's face and in a loud, angry voice stated, "Who the hell do you think you are? You're not my boss. All you are is a little ass-kisser that no one likes. If I had it my way, I would kick your ass from here all the way to the parking lot, but a loser like you is not worth me losing my job over." At that point the complainant immediately left the boardroom. When the complainant opened the door, two custodians were standing there with a look of shock on their faces. On their way to the human resources department, several people tried to stop the complainant and wondered why there were tears streaming down their face. The complainant did not provide an explanation but stated, "That is the last time they are going to get in my face and threaten me. I have had it. This time I will win the fight."

Later that day, they file a complaint that includes the incident from earlier that day and other minor allegations. As part of the investigation, the team interviewed several parties regarding the alleged incident in the boardroom. Although neither of the primary witnesses heard the exact words spoken by the respondent, one of the custodians heard one muffled loud, angry voice inside the room and witnessed the look of panic on the complainant's face when they left the room. The other staff interviewed who spoke to the complainant in the hallway did not witness what had transpired in the room, however, they could confirm the emotional state of the complainant in addition to their words, "That is the last time they are going to get in my face and threaten me." At the end of the investigation, the finding for that specific allegation was partially substantiated as it could be established that the two parties were in the room together, the respondent raised their voice and the complainant immediately left the room in a negative emotional state. No part of the alleged statement from the respondent could be verified (the respondent denied making the alleged comments) including, "I would kick your ass from here all the way to the parking lot."

An unsubstantiated finding means that it is unlikely that the allegation is true as stated by the complainant or, in some cases, did not occur at all. I have had case findings where an incident was alleged and the complainant provided names of witnesses who were present. When I interviewed those individuals, it turned out that one witness was on vacation and two others were working at the opposite end of the building at the time of the alleged incident. The lack of proof to support an allegation may often be the result of the investigator not digging deep enough into the evidence or failing to persistently interview the parties until the truth is revealed. An investigation with a thorough and relentless process will rarely end in a conclusion of "they said versus they said."

An inconclusive finding can be confusing and frustrating for the employer and the complainant. It may be the result of an allegation where there were no witnesses present during or immediately after the alleged incident. I have been involved in cases where two employees were working together when an incident occurred but when it came time to interview the witness, they were no longer employed at the organization. Moreover, when the respondent was placed on a paid leave of absence, they then resigned from their job and were no longer accessible to be interviewed. In some cases, complainants take a medical leave prior to or after filing a complaint and never return to work.

Report Writing

The investigation report is a complete record of the investigation, including physical evidence, written statements, interviews and any other relevant documentation. The report reflects the facts of the investigation and forms the basis for decision-making and recommendations pertaining to an investigation. In addition, a report is an assurance that the investigation was conducted and a demonstration of the investigation team member's accountability. The report is used by the employer to determine the responsibility of the respondent and next steps or sanctions, if any. In the end, the report is a record that may be used in arbitration, legal proceedings, coroners' inquests or disciplinary hearings.

The following format is suggested for the report:

Executive Summary:

- Investigation's scope of accountability, including roles and responsibilities
- Names of complainant, respondent, witnesses and investigation team members
- A brief complaint summary, including the alleged policy or legislation breached
- Specific allegations
- Individual allegation findings (substantiated, partially substantiated, unsubstantiated or inconclusive), including a brief explanation of the evidence or lack of evidence considered
- Complete list of evidence reviewed
- Investigator's signature and date of report conclusion

Appendix:

- Interview notes
- Written statements
- Full documentation/evidence reviewed

It is important to note that the report should not address or recommend any sanctions as this should not be part of the investigator's scope of accountability.

When I was first conducting investigation work, I would provide the client with my report and all documents listed above. After a few years following this practice, I was informed by a lawyer that it was best for my client that I only provide the report and keep all other evidence in my possession. The rationale presented was that I was hired in good faith by the organization to conduct the investigation and once the work was completed, the report should stand on its own. It was stated that the employer could get lost in all of the paperwork and therefore lose sight of the findings, and, more importantly, have access to some information recorded during the interviews that may put the interviewee in a vulnerable position should they have provided any negative commentary about the employer. Therefore, in order to maintain confidentiality and decrease the possibility of the employer or a manager retaliating against a party, the specific statements should be protected and only disclosed when legally required. Additionally, it was stated that if any party was disciplined in the future even in a completely different set of circumstances, they could make the assumption or claim that the discipline was retaliation for being part of the investigation, specifically what they said during an interview, particularly if the respondent was a manager.

Taking this advice into consideration, now when filing my report, I give my client the option of receiving the executive summary only or the full package. In all cases, only the summary has been requested and only in an arbitration or court hearing has all information been released.

Investigation Outcomes

The investigation team may be asked to provide the employer with general recommendations based on what was uncovered during the investigation.

Examples of recommendations may include:

- Developing and/or reviewing risk assessments, policies, guidance or systems
- Redesigning jobs, activities or areas
- Introducing and/or revising training courses
- Using more appropriate equipment
- Introducing and/or revising instructions
- Enhancing communication on specific safety issues
- Selecting procedures for staff and/or contractors
- Adjusting environmental controls
- Enhancing personal safety measures

These recommendations should be provided in a separate document and excluded from the investigation report.

Sanctions

When a complaint of workplace discrimination, harassment or bullying has been substantiated, many sanctions may be applied. The decision regarding the sanctions does not lie with the investigation team but rather the appropriate organizational leadership personnel. Oftentimes when the term "zero tolerance" is used in relation to workplace violence and harassment, employees think it means automatic dismissal. Sanctions may include one or more of the following: a formal apology, educational sessions, counselling of the employee about their behaviour, a verbal warning, a written warning placed in the employee's personnel file, transfer of the individual, suspension or loss of privileges, suspension or discharge of the employee, concerns addressed by the Human Rights Commission, legal/police intervention, or concerns addressed by professional colleges.

When I interview complainants, at the end of the interview I will ask them what they are hoping will be the end result of the complaint. Most people assume the response will be that they want the respondent fired but I rarely hear that response. The complainant will often say that they don't think they can work with the respondent again but that has nothing to do with anyone being terminated. They will often say, "I never wanted it to get to this point. I know they have a family and I don't want to see anyone lose their job. I just want to come to work, do my job and be left alone." How simple would the workplace be if that request was honoured?

Condemnation without investigation is the height of ignorance.

~ Albert Einstein ~

The Triumphs

As I read my book from cover to cover, 25 years passed before me in a flash. Writing about my cases was like watching a movie in slow motion. I realized that making a true commitment to empower and assist people with negotiating the complexities of legal, social and familial systems is not for the faint of heart.

In our personal lives, we can choose the people with whom we interact. In the workforce, however, that choice is somewhat limited. At some point, we will be involved in work situations that include interacting with individuals with whom we will share a strong professional and/or personal bond and others whom we will not. In our work lives, we are intertwined with peers, subordinates, supervisors and clients, limiting our freedom, autonomy and independence. A high level of emotional intelligence is critical to the success of those interactions. Being in touch with ourselves will help us to understand the potential impact we have on others and how others influence us. How we choose to respond to each interaction is an individual choice.

We all must take accountability for our actions and realize that in a workplace of any size—whether it has four or 4,000 employees—we all contribute to the health, safety and well-being of each other. Establishing codes of conduct and ground rules builds trust, allowing employees to feel safe. Even if the rules are not openly discussed, simply having them shifts the paradigm of the relationship. When those rules are broken, there is a violation of trust, a sense of betrayal and a feeling of attack against our individuality. When there is an imbalance in a relationship and trust is eroded, the outcome can be devastating and create feelings of self-doubt.

For years I internally punished myself for calling the police and having charges laid against the physician who sexually assaulted me. The guilt I felt for the pain I put my husband and family through for two years (not counting the years of recovery) was immeasurable. The only thing that kept me grounded was the fact that I did nothing wrong that day. All I did was visit an accredited health-care clinic.

Disturbingly, the game isn't always played fair. On the surface it appears that the individuals who do not possess a moral compass are those who rise to the next corporate level, inevitably rewarding the respondent with a substantial pay increase while leaving the complainant a weakened soul. Over my career, I have watched technology replace simple conversations with lengthy emails that include others who have no real vested interest in the issue. Cyber-bullying is now the way to befriend someone with the intent and ability to terrorize them.

Although sometimes it is difficult to accept, one thing that has kept me doing this work and pushed me to do more is the belief in the greater good in people. There is power in reconciliation. In situations where the respondent genuinely takes responsibility for their actions, there is great potential for healing. Some individuals, particularly those who have been bullied, do not believe that a bully has the capacity to own their behaviour, let alone change it. Over the years, I have had individuals approach me after a training session or call me and say, "Denise, I think I am a bully and I don't want to be." Unfortunately, in some situations their negative way of interacting is a learned behaviour. Other times the individual was initially a target and then when they were not supported by anyone (including peers, superiors or management), they felt that they had no other recourse than to bully back. The saying, "If you can't beat them, join them" is too often stated. Although no excuse warrants bad behaviour, sometimes survival of the fittest becomes one's reality.

Trying to understand the core reason for a bully's behaviour or the cause of a toxic work environment is essential. As renowned addiction expert Dr. Gabor Maté says, "No society can understand itself without looking at its shadow side."

Regular health and safety inspections are required in all legitimate workplaces. However, these formal reviews only take into consideration the bricks and mortar of a building or workspace. What is lacking is a mechanism to adequately assess the emotional health and safety of employees. The fact that an employee's mental health can be destroyed by relentless bullying cannot be ignored. A broken spirit will occur far more frequently than a broken water pipe. We need to secure the psychological health of our workplaces for future generations.

Employers and managers must take the time to schedule monthly mental health audits with their staff. Managers need to walk the hallways of their workplace at different times of the day to get a sense of what is normal so that they notice when things are off or toxicity begins to seep into the workplace and intervene before it is too late.

Employers and managers cannot be the only parties to proactively protect the workplace; peers and labour leaders also need to look out for each other as well as for management. In other words, everyone needs to be everyone's keeper. According to the Koster survey, more than half of the bullies in the workplace either named by the complainant or witnessed by others were peers of the target. In workplaces with an "us versus them" mentality between labour and management, the tension and toxicity is palpable. I have not seen that mentality ever lift an organization from a toxic level to a healthy workplace.

Management should utilize the time in staff meetings to focus on relationships and check in with their employees, rather than recite basic department updates or report findings that could be communicated in writing, such as an email. Appreciation from management is important for staff to hear, however, without an understanding of the workplace culture, it will not be received as genuine. It is critical for management to address the workplace challenges in addition to committing to take meaningful action.

Rules are meant to be upheld and respected, not broken and maliciously challenged. The philosophy of managing "up or out" is critical. Everyone deserves a chance to learn and grow. Although, if an employee is consistently not meeting that bar, it should not be tolerated. Expectations of civility should be the same for all employees regardless of their position, credentials or salary.

It may seem to some that the days of joking and laughing at work are gone and a fearful atmosphere of being accused of a wrongdoing has been created. Thankfully, some words, actions and behaviours that were accepted years ago have been banished from the workplace. Having a light and fun workplace must be balanced with celebrating each other's differences and extinguishing isolation. We should be refocusing on the greater good and re-enforcing a well-defined way of working with others, such as Robert's Rules of Order. Is there any way that some of the traditional ways of interacting in the workplace can be utilized and taken off social networking platforms?

Horrific cases such as those at Ontario's OC Transpo, Sears Canada and Hotel-Dieu Grace have resulted in an improved employment system whereby employers are held accountable for protecting employees from external as well as internal threats.

In 2013, Eric Donovan, a 47-year-old from Prince Edward Island, had a cardiac arrest. The Workers Compensation Board of PEI found that there was a direct correlation between the bullying he experienced at his workplace by his supervisor and his death, and awarded survivor benefits to his widow. For six years, Mr. Donovan's widow fought for legislation to include bullying as unacceptable. On July 1, 2020, the Eric Donovan Act will take effect. The act requires employers to define harassment in the workplace and proactively identify and eliminate sources of harassment, including bullying behaviour, by setting policies and conducting investigations.

As I recall every face and story I have been told, I recognize the immense amount of courage from the complainants in coming forward. Although some of them may not have formally won their case, they put the respondent on the radar of a formal accountability system, whether it was human resources, a professional college, a government official or police services.

In closing, I would like to share one final story that summarizes the triumph and courage of all targets of bullying. A woman approached me after a public workplace bullying session, with attendees from different organizations and sectors. She informed me that she did not represent a company and came to the session after hearing about my work. She had recently resigned from her place of employment as a result of being bullied by her direct supervisor. She stated that the behaviour consisted of fault finding, verbal attacks about her work and personal life, disrespect towards her education and work ethic, and false accusations. The situation was made worse by the fact that the behaviours and interactions were always behind closed doors without any witnesses. Several times she went to her supervisor's boss and told him of her most recent encounters. The manager, although somewhat supportive, kept saying that he needed "proof" in order to take any action.

Since she didn't have any proof to show to others, she continued to work in this toxic environment for over two years. She explained that recently she reached a turning point. As she was getting ready for work one day, she stepped out of the shower and looked in the mirror. She was shocked to see the eyes of her mother and a weathered face. She opened the medicine cabinet and looked at the prescription bottles for high blood pressure, anxiety and sleep, all of which had been prescribed in the past year. As she was dressing, she realized that her clothes were hanging off her body as a result of unintentionally losing 25 pounds. She made her bed on only one side, as her husband of 20 years no longer slept in the same bed. On her way out, she gathered her medication and took a picture frame of her and her husband off the dresser.

When she arrived at work, she knocked on the manager's door. As she entered the room, in a loud voice she said, "I have the proof you have been asking for." She emptied the bag of drugs and placed the picture of her and her husband on the desk. The manager was perplexed by her actions. She said, "Now the proof is right in front of you. Look at the picture of me taken two years ago when I cared about what I looked like and took pride in my marriage. Look at my husband who I no longer sleep with. Look at the drugs I now take on a daily basis to survive and make a living. Look at the shadow of the woman who stands before you. No witnesses, recorded conversations or confessions could document my suffering any more than what you have in front of you. Today I am walking out of this office for the last time. I quit and whatever my fate is from this day forward cannot be worse than what I have endured working here."

She explained to me that as she walked out of the building that day, it was like the weight of the world had been lifted off her shoulders. She went directly to her doctor, booked individual and marital counselling, and promised herself that no matter what, she would never allow anyone to treat her with anything less than complete respect.

Like this brave woman, we all need to love ourselves enough to know how we deserve to be treated.

Please, refuse to accept the unacceptable.

Sympathy's easy. You have sympathy for starving children swatting at flies on the late-night commercials. Sympathy is easy because it comes from a position of power.

Empathy is getting down on your knees and looking somebody else in the eye and realizing you could be them, and all that separates you is luck.

~ Dennis Lehane ~

Reader Discussion Questions

The following questions can be contemplated individually or as a group. The purpose of these questions is not to determine if someone is right or wrong, but rather to stimulate productive and meaningful conversations.

I would be very interested in receiving your responses or discussion points. Please log in to my website at kosterconsultingassociates.com or email me at koster@istar.ca.

Workplace Violence

1. How can an employer ensure there is a balance between employee safety and a positive and welcoming client/customer experience?
2. How can workplace violence be monitored on a consistent basis without relying on employees filling out incident reports?
3. How can an employer support employees who are in a domestic violence situation while respecting confidentiality and their personal relationship?
4. If an employer is indirectly made aware of a domestic violence situation that has not been openly disclosed by the employee, do they have an obligation to address the issue to ensure that both the individual and all other employees are safe?
5. How can an employer rebuild trust and safety in the workplace following a physically violent incident?

Workplace Discrimination and Harassment

1. What is the difference between a microaggression and humour?
2. What is the difference between flirting and sexual harassment?
3. Should there be a mandatory retirement age? If so, how should that age be determined? If not, could an employee work indefinitely?

4. How can religious freedom and health and safety be equally honoured? Does safety supersede religion or does religion overrule health and safety?
5. If traditional gender-specific attire such as ties and dresses are allowed in the workplace, does that only pertain to staff members who self-identify as a specific gender?
6. In a recent case, a female employee was directed to wear a bra as it was a "family" business. When a staff member is wearing appropriate business attire or a company-issued uniform, under what circumstances, if any, does the employer have the right to tell them which undergarments to wear?
7. What, if any, limit should be put on the amount of bereavement leave an employee can take while still honouring an employee's individual family structure?
8. If an employer is indirectly aware of an employee's disability, which the employee has not openly disclosed, are they still obligated to accommodate that employee?
9. If an employee openly discloses their sexual orientation, does the employer or other employees have a right to inform others?
10. Should employers be able to ask a job candidate if they smoke cigarettes? Why or why not?
11. If an employee has a general tattoo or piercing on a visible part of their body and another employee has a commemorative tattoo on a visible part of their body, can the employer request that one, both or neither be covered up while in the workplace?
12. Should the consequences for code and non-code harassment be equal? If not, why not?

Workplace Bullying

1. Do bullies really know that they are bullies?
2. If an employee is respectful to a target in the workplace but publicly bullies them online or through personal text messag-

es outside of work hours and off company property, is the employer obligated to intervene?

3. If a bully and target are blood-related, is the employer under the same obligation to intervene? If so, would there be any strategies that may be different if there was not a personal relationship?
4. When, if ever, should an employer be made personally liable for an employee harming themselves as a result of being bullied in the workplace? What if they harmed another employee?
5. When, if ever, should a manager be made personally liable for an employee harming themselves as a result of being bullied in the workplace? What if they harmed another employee?
6. When, if ever, should a peer or co-worker be made personally liable for an employee harming themselves as a result of being bullied in the workplace? What if they harmed another employee?
7. How can an employer make a bully accountable for inappropriate behaviour while supporting them to change?
8. In a case where bullying is substantiated, should the target, bully, neither or both be transferred to another area?
9. After an investigation is conducted and bullying allegations are substantiated, and the bully and target must continue to work together, what steps can be implemented to keep both parties safe and limit the chance of retaliation?
10. What steps should an employer take to address a toxic workplace and create a healthy work environment?

Taking and Assessing a Complaint

1. What can an employer do to ensure that employees feel safe reporting incidents of workplace violence, discrimination, harassment and bullying?
2. (If applicable) What can unions do to ensure that employees feel safe reporting these incidents?

Conflict Resolution

1. Under what circumstances can a direct manager facilitate a conflict resolution process between two direct reports?
2. Under what circumstances should an external facilitator or mediator be contracted to provide conflict resolution or mediation services?
3. If a conflict resolution process between two or more parties is not successful (i.e., does not result in an agreement), under what circumstances should the process be offered a second time? Under what circumstances should it not be offered again?

Workplace Investigations

1. How can an employer enforce confidentiality if employees are related or live in the same house?
2. Can the consequences for a breach of confidentiality be enforced when employees who are related by blood or a partnership share confidential information? Should employees who have a domestic partner who works for a different employer face the same consequences when they go home from work and disclose confidential company information?
3. Can an employee complainant, respondent or witness refuse to come in for an investigation interview? If so, under what circumstances would this be acceptable?
4. Can an employee complainant, respondent or witness refuse to answer questions in an investigation interview? If so, under what circumstances would this be acceptable? If not, what are the consequences for not responding?
5. Can an employee complainant, respondent or witness refuse to provide a written statement as part of the investigation process? If so, under what circumstances would this be acceptable?
6. In incidents of workplace bullying, are witnesses considered bystanders or are bystanders viewed as witnesses?

7. Is there any circumstance where an employer should not ethically or legally be able to review an employee's workplace phone records, emails or written correspondents? If so, under what circumstances?
8. When does the use of an individual's personal social media account become an employer's business?
9. Should audiotaping interviews be permissible during an investigation? If so, on what device should it be recorded? Should any party be allowed to tape an interview on a personal device?
10. Under what circumstances should an employee be terminated for a malicious report? Under what circumstances should an employee NOT be terminated for a malicious report?

Note from the Artist

Alfred G. Villeneuve

The message carried by the title of my poem is philosophically at the core of my work and life. In my painting, I exert a discipline to find what I call "equilibrium" in the composition, which has little to do with style, colour or line.

It is the psychological balance between what was, is and could be in relation to what I am compelled to put down on canvas.

In "The Tea Lake Graces," I created a purposefulness to force the viewers eye up, to look beyond what is before them, allowing the three Red Pines to guide their gaze into the azure skies above, where the Threes Graces have always resided.

This relates to me, in darkest times, when we look to and perhaps beseeching something or someone that is beyond our realm for aid or security. In doing so, the head and heart are uplifted with expectation.

Beauty, Charm and Grace exist eternally in Nature. It is there one can reflect and revive that which makes one whole again.

It is where I continue to go to find that regeneration of the body and spirit, and it is my hope that others will be inspired to go too.

The last element binding all of these thoughts together is the revelation through the pattern of pine needles cascading down the face of the large grandfather stone, which materialized, unbeknownst to my brush, into an impression of a large bird in flight passing over. In my culture, I had been taught by an elder and medicine man about the awesome presence and power of the Thunder Birds. This revelation seems to anchor the rise and triumph of the Human Spirit, to overcome what was, and be delivered to a place of peace, harmony and life.

Printed in Dunstable, United Kingdom

71753798R00167